A Place in the Woods

The Fesler-Lampert *Minnesota Heritage Book* Series

This series is published with the generous assistance of the John K. and Elsie Lampert Fesler Fund and David R. and Elizabeth P. Fesler. Its mission is to republish significant out-of-print books that contribute to our understanding and appreciation of Minnesota and the Upper Midwest.

Portage into the Past: By Canoe along the Minnesota-Ontario Boundary Waters by J. Arnold Bolz

The Gift of the Deer by Helen Hoover

The Long-Shadowed Forest by Helen Hoover

A Place in the Woods by Helen Hoover

The Years of the Forest by Helen Hoover

North Star Country by Meridel Le Sueur

Listening Point by Sigurd F. Olson

The Lonely Land by Sigurd F. Olson

Of Time and Place by Sigurd F. Olson

Open Horizons by Sigurd F. Olson

Reflections from the North Country by Sigurd F. Olson

Runes of the North by Sigurd F. Olson

The Singing Wilderness by Sigurd F. Olson

Voyageur Country: The Story of Minnesota's National Park by Robert Treuer

HELEN HOOVER

A Place in the Woods

ILLUSTRATED BY ADRIAN HOOVER

University of Minnesota Press
MINNEAPOLIS

First printed in hardcover by Alfred A. Knopf, Inc., 1969
First University of Minnesota Press edition, 1999
Reprinted by arrangement with Alfred A. Knopf, Inc.

Published by the University of Minnesota Press
111 Third Avenue South, Suite 290
Minneapolis, MN 55401-2520
http://www.upress.umn.edu

Printed in the United States of America on acid-free paper

Library of Congress Cataloging-in-Publication Data
Hoover, Helen.
A place in the woods / Helen Hoover ; illustrated by Adrian Hoover.
p.   cm. — (The Fesler-Lampert Minnesota heritage book series)
Originally published: 1st ed. New York : Knopf, 1969.
ISBN 0-8166-3129-8
1. Natural History—Minnesota.   I. Title.   II. Series.
QH105.M55H62   1999
508.776—dc21   98-51141

The University of Minnesota is an equal-opportunity
educator and employer.

11 10 09 08 07 06 05 04 03 02 01 00 99   10 9 8 7 6 5 4 3 2 1

To all the people

who asked the questions

I have tried to answer here.

Foreword

The writing of this book takes me back through quite a number of years and I see our early days here with the broadened vision that distance brings. I know now that what happened to my husband and me here could have happened in many other locations in the North Woods of Minnesota, or in any other place where such boreal forest stands. I realize that many people influenced our lives in one way or another, far too many to bring into this narrative. I am quite sure that a blow-by-blow account of our experiences would bore the reader beyond hope after a few pages.

So I am writing of a Village and a Trail and a Lake and a Lodge, which may bring us just a little closer to people who have other villages and trails and lakes and lodges of their own. I am using Hilda and Sven, Jacques and John—very real people although these are not their names—to stand in the place of many who did so much for us. And I am telescoping events that weary even me when I recall their ambling and disconnected sequence.

The series of misadventures that beset Ade and me during our first month here came with such regularity that they now hold an aura of the ridiculous. The obstacles that we struggled to overcome have dwindled to minor incidents against the forest background. I now see that our lack of communications—and funds—brought us deep awareness of the strength and courage to be drawn from the steady renewal of the forest, and gave us the many hours we spent enjoying and learning to understand, within our human limitations, the living creatures who shared the land with us.

Those limitations are very real because there is as yet no way to communicate more than superficially with other species, or to understand their mental processes. Thus we cannot *know* how an animal thinks or why he behaves as he does. We can only believe, and such beliefs range all the way from the conviction that animals are capable of abstract thought to that which sees them as mere puppets, jerking about on the strings of instinct. I cannot accept either of these ideas, again within my limitations of human thinking: the first because abstractions are almost always thought about in words or mathematical symbols, which animals do not use; the second from my own observations during the past dozen years.

I believe that animals are acted upon both by instinct and by thought *of their own kind*, the proportions of these varying with species, individuals, and the circumstances of their environment.

Two bugaboos related to these beliefs haunt authors who write nonscientifically about animals. I should like to explain my thoughts on them, in the hope that this may lead to a better understanding of both my wild friends and me.

First, there is anthropomorphism, whose complex definitions can be boiled down to attributing human characteristics to animals. This always seems backwards to me because the animals came first and we might better be concerned with how much like animals people are, rather than the other way around. Aside from that, attempts to show that human observers cannot be certain of the meaning of animal actions may produce a piece of writing overloaded with "apparently," "as if," and similar terms, which are often superfluous. "Apparently," for instance, is ambiguous, because it may mean either "certainly" or "seemingly," but even when used to mean "seemingly" it is usually unnecessary because everything seen by anyone is "apparent" to him. For example: "A man gave me a friendly smile." This means only that his smile looked friendly to me. Actually, it might have been the pre-election smile of a weary politician or the professional smile of a confidence man. Again, we use "apparently" with really astonishing contradiction. People who study birds know that their feathers do not contain blue pigment but that the blue color seen by the normal eye is an illusion produced by light reflecting from brownish-gray pigment. However, they do not say "the apparently blue jay . . ." although this would be correct. On the other hand, I have read, "The bobcat apparently yawned." It is hard to imagine how anyone who saw any cat yawn could be in doubt about what the animal was doing, and yawning is not a function reserved to humans, anyway.

So, if I say, "The fawns played happily together," or "The hare, terrified, leaped away from the step when I opened the door," I mean that is how it looked to me—and in these cases I may well be right. But if I say, "The hen glanced apologetically at me," I am deliberately amusing myself with the idea of an apologetic hen. I doubt very much that anyone would take this seriously, whether he does or does not know some chickens personally, and to carefully explain that the hen really wasn't apologizing verges on an insult to the reader's intelligence.

The second trap is teleology, the ascription of purpose to nature. Here again contradiction lifts its head. A great many people believe that there is purpose in the creation as a whole, but become indignant at the idea that any animal but man may have purpose. Purpose, which carries the feeling of determination, may be too strong a word as not even many human actions carry purpose. Intention seems a better word. In any case, the evidence of my eyes tells me that wild creatures, aside from or in combination with instinctive behavior, do have to make choices, especially when strange elements, such as people, enter their world. They often move in patterns, but they develop special patterns in special situations. Let us consider Old Harry, the begging woodpecker.

In the spring, when bears begin to amble through our yard, we bring in our suet feeders, both to save them from being clawed to bits or carried away, and to discourage the bears from hanging around our buildings. One particular male hairy woodpecker refused to be thus mulcted of his suet. Every morning he settled on a cedar branch that overhangs the cabin door and set up a din of squawks and squeaks. If Ade went out with a feeder, Old Harry flew ahead of him to the proper tree, waited behind the trunk until the feeder was hung on its nail, and then had breakfast. If Ade opened the door and went back in or walked to the tree without the feeder, the bird flew to our kitchen window and proceeded to thump and bang and take the sill apart fiber by fiber until the suet was supplied. (And there were no insects in that dried and painted windowsill.) Try as I may, I cannot believe that Old Harry did not intend to get his suet.

Now and then, no matter how wary I am, I find myself tangled up in both teleology and anthropomorphism. In *The Gift of the Deer* I described how the book's hero, our buck Peter Whitetail, pounded into the clearing and stopped by the house, showing signs of terror. In trying to find out what had frightened him, I smelled smoke coming from the west, the direction from which he had come. I walked that way to discover and put out a fire left dangerously close to a small empty cabin, and I wrote that I wondered "why Peter had come to tell' me of the fire." I think now that I made a poor choice of words because a reviewer interpreted this to mean that I thought Peter had come to tell me to put out the fire. At least, that is what I decided after I read his statement that such a conclusion was "scientifically reckless." I'd go even further and say it would be scientifically silly.

The details of the incident may make this clearer. After I smelled the smoke I walked through the woods and saw Peter's tracks on a fresh light snowfall, those going away from our cabin his usual ambling footmarks. At a point where the fire could be seen he had stopped and moved about a little, then turned and bolted back along the way he had come. There were no other tracks except those of some fishermen who had built the fire and who, when I saw them, were settled half a mile away on the lake ice. I could be sure that the fire had frightened Peter, whether he knew anything about fire, perhaps from a blazing forest, or not, because deer are very cautious about anything new in a familiar place. This fire was not only new but it moved, a combination guaranteed to alarm quite a few members of the animal kingdom. That the fire might have burned the cabin had no place in any mind but my own, and I still do not *know* why Peter, and a number of other wild animals since his time, have come to our cabin or to Ade or me when they were frightened.

In opposition to this incident, if a stray dog should bark near a burning building and it was saved because someone heard the dog barking, the dog would very likely be rewarded with a good home for the rest of his life, and few people would question the dog's intention. Well . . . I said it was contradictory.

This leads indirectly to emotion and sentiment, with their offspring sentimentality. A strong man is not above weeping when his dog is hit by a car and killed, but when our old doe, Mama, was killed in this way on our side road, I should have been thought overemotional if I had grieved openly for her. I see only one difference in the relations between a man and his dog and between myself and Mama: A dog—or any other domesticated animal—is expected to give and does give a large return for the care and affection spent on him. A deer— or any other wild animal—takes food or protection or what little man can offer if he will, and is not expected to return anything.

Sentiment covers any thought that rises from or in connection with any feeling whatsoever and a person who truly appreciates wild creatures can hardly fail to have some feelings about them. Sentimentality has come to mean maudlin sentimentality, once applied to the foolish tears of the very drunk, and there is no reasonable place for it in human reactions to the wild world. It is not easy to look on the body of a fawn killed by wolves with pity for the pain and terror of its end and not flounder into a morass of sentimentality, where the wolf is cruel and evil because he feeds himself as he must and the fawn is a heart-wrenching symbol of youth and gentleness, wrongfully destroyed. This sort of thing is true anthropomorphism and complete piffle.

Once one sees the difference between this natural killing and that of a man who shoots, say, herring gulls for the pleasure of destroying, he can feel compassion for all wild creatures and sorrow at the loss of some special animal, and no longer needs the protection of thinking as coldly as a computer. I made this adjustment during my early years in the forest. There were fewer people and more wild hunters then, so that I had ample opportunity to observe the working of natural balance and to learn to look at all the wilderness denizens without prejudice.

Then, too, in those early days before the power line, lights went out and boats came in early, so that summer nights belonged to the murmur of wind in the pines, the patter of rain, or the booming of thunder, the lonely, lovely voices of the loons. Before mechanized snow vehicles made woods travel both noisy and easy, winter days and nights were as still as they were white, with only the whisper of falling snow, the zinging crack of ice on the lake, and—rarely—the heart-shaking song of wolves to contrast with the stillness. Before the blacktop came, the twisty old road beckoned only to those who loved the land and, out of that love, cherished it and left it as fair and clean as before they came.

Those were precious years, and this is how our part of their story began.

Acknowledgments

My thanks to *Nature Magazine,* no longer
published I am sorry to say, to *Audubon
Magazine,* and to *Defenders of Wildlife News*
for material that first appeared in their pages;
to the many people who assisted us in those
early days; to my editor and agent for their
encouragement and advice; and to my husband
for constructive criticism and the many
hours patiently spent on the illustrations.

H.H.

CONTENTS

A PLACE IN THE WOODS

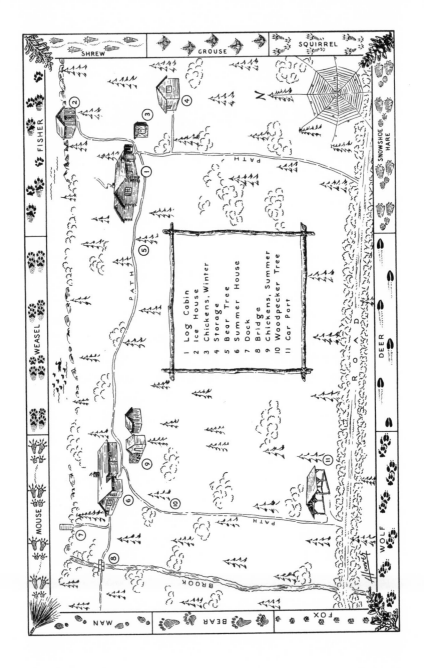

SHREW

GROUSE

SQUIRREL

FISHER

SNOWSHOE
HARE

N

WEASEL

DEER

1 Log Cabin
2 Ice House
3 Chickens, Winter
4 Storage
5 Bear Tree
6 Summer House
7 Dock
8 Bridge
9 Chickens, Summer
10 Woodpecker Tree
11 Car Port

PATH

PATH

PATH

ROAD

BROOK

MOUSE

WOLF

MAN

BEAR

FOX

1 The Place

The calendar above the sink in the tourist cabin said April 26, and this was Monday and the third morning of our vacation. On Friday afternoon my husband had left the premises of the textbook publisher where he was promotional art director and picked up me and my bag at the laboratory where I was a research metallurgist. Both jobs were exacting and wearing, so we had driven slowly from Chicago, over quiet, unfrequented roads, letting ourselves unwind as we drifted along, to finally reach the Village on the North Shore of Lake Superior.

Now I felt wonderful and I also liked the cabin. The oilcloth on the table was green-and-white checked, the blue paper on the shelves had scalloped edges, and the spotless white curtains sported crisp yellow ruffles. There were two rockers, one probably walnut under its green paint, the other carefully repaired wicker—from a set once the pride of someone's front porch? There was an oil lamp, too—"We turn the light plant off at nine." The cabin had atmosphere and comfort, which is more than one can say about many of the sanitized motel units that have taken its place.

From the window I looked east, past the rocky shore to the great lake, sparkling green and blue and purple as a peacock's tail. Stretching inland was Minnesota's vast North Woods, where we thought we might find a vacation cabin of our own. There was a blast from our car horn. Ade was back from the office of the U.S. Forest Service, bringing, I hoped, some helpful information. I gave the cabin door the extra little push that made the lock catch and hurried to slide into my half of the front seat.

"Well?" I asked.

"He doesn't know of any place for sale except a lodge, and almost all the big timber's in the national forest, but there are government lots to lease quite a way up the Trail. He says the country's pretty wild in there and we might like it—but maybe not when we see the road."

"Bother the road! We've been over some of the worst roads in the country."

Ade agreed and we turned onto the Trail, which proved to be a two-lane blacktop. True, there were potholes, but one would expect them at the end of this area's bitter winter. I was wondering what the fuss was about when we suddenly bumped onto gravel.

The road narrowed to little more than a single lane and began to wind and dip and rise. Its surface was mostly mud with pools of water, some slick with ice at the bottom. Along the edges boulders lurked behind clumps of brush and red flags drooped above washouts. There were sharp, blind hills, beyond which the road turned in whatever direction the rugged land had offered least resistance to first, the animals, next, the Indians, and last, the roadbuilders. Ade murmured to himself and drove. I hung onto the edge of the seat and was thankful that I was not afflicted with motion sickness. I was also scared stiff.

To keep my mind off what might happen if we met somebody at one of the blind spots I tried to watch the scenery, but the behavior of the road was too distracting. I was aware only that, although there had been some green in the Village, it was colder inland and the road was lined with silent ranks of bare birch and aspen and occasional evergreens, all small, second-growth trees. Then the Trail rose gently toward a hilltop, beyond which only misty blue sky was visible and where giant white pines, ancient and weather-scarred, stood along the verges like colossal guardians at a gateway. This was a virgin stand, small, but to us promising.

In the days of the Great Depression we had cheered ourselves with dreams of a hideaway cabin of our own and had started looking for the place on the first vacation after our marriage, more than a dozen years before this one. Somewhere along our way we had come to feel that our cabin should stand in forest that had reached maturity in its own way, but we had found that accessible virgin timber not government- or corporation-owned was rare indeed. We had grown, not discouraged, but less hopeful as the years and the miles passed. Now I thought of the pines just behind us, saw the lofty crowns of others in the forest we were passing through. Perhaps we *could* find our place and spend a little time there.

"The country's getting wilder," Ade said. "Makes me think of Daniel Boone."

"It's too late for Daniel Boones now," I said, sighing. "Not enough room."

"*We* don't need very much," he said practically.

There were patches of snow along the road edges now and the sky had clouded over so that lakes we saw through the trees were milky gray. A few white flakes drifted down. Although the road had narrowed even more and sometimes its surface was water-slick bedrock, it no longer frightened me. But it did seem endless and I was thinking of the many miles we had covered in all our searching when Ade swung right onto a side road. We found the sign pointing to the government lots, but their trees were young, slim birch and aspen. I was depressed.

"If we don't find anything this trip, I'm going to give up."

"From one point of view you may be right," Ade said. "We're 652 miles from home, which is on the edge of too far, considering our two-week vacations. But here's a lodge. Food will do wonders."

We followed a driveway and pulled up before a log building nestled in small evergreens.

"I *am* hungry," I said, and paused, my eyes moving from the silent buildings to the rows of boats and canoes overturned on the dock to the CLOSED sign over the main lodge entrance.

"We can get out and stretch, anyway," Ade said, and I followed him to the dock.

An expanse of ice, a mile across and several miles long, mottled in grays from off-white to leaden, covered the lake.

"It's hard to believe it's still frozen," I said. "None of the ones we passed were."

"It's deeper and takes longer to warm up," said a voice from behind us.

We turned to see a tall, broad man in his forties, with graying fair hair, and a wind-reddened face smiling at us above a red-and-black plaid shirt.

"The ice is rotten and cracked all over. You can't see it from here in this light, but if a wind comes up it'll go out in hours," he explained, then hesitated. "I'm sorry, but we won't be open till the middle of May—spring fishing season."

Abruptly I was almost overcome with hunger. "We were hoping to get something to eat," I said, probably in a quavering voice.

"Come on in. My wife won't let you starve. I'm Sven Peterson, by the way."

We introduced ourselves as we walked across an open space to the main building, where a woman, perhaps ten years younger than Sven and wearing shirt and jeans like his, opened the door to us.

"Hilda, Ade and Helen Hoover from Chicago. They didn't know everything was still closed up here . . ."

"And you're hungry, of course—and by the time you'd get back to town . . . Goodness! Come in and I'll fix you something."

She chattered brightly as we followed her through a lobby with Indian rugs on the floor and snowshoes crossed on the walls. In her warm, spice-scented kitchen she waved us to chairs near the largest iron cook stove I ever saw and said, "Now, tell me . . ."

And proceeded, while she made sandwiches, to extract by some fascinating and wonderful process our Chicago address, a description of our apartment and of the lilacs that had been blooming outside the building when we left, and the whole story of our search for a vacation spot.

Sven went to sit beside her while we ate. Her hair showed no white, but otherwise they were much alike—tall, with the clear skins and shining blue eyes and flaxen hair of Scandinavia, straight of back, with strong shoulders. And you could tell they were like that inside, too—clear and shining, straight and strong.

When we had reached the coffee stage, Sven looked inquiringly at Hilda and she nodded.

"A fellow's got a place for sale two miles down the road," he said. "It's a sound cabin—he lives in it year-round."

"It isn't fancy," Hilda said to me. "He's a log builder and never has time for the place, like the shoemaker who didn't make shoes for his children."

"It has your big timber," Sven went on. "There hasn't even been a fire there for a couple of hundred years. Some of the trees are that old. His name's Carl Johnson. Why don't you go see him?"

So, expectant, but not too much so just in case, we thanked the Petersons, who waved payment aside, and drove on down the little back road. A mile beyond the Lodge the forest changed so abruptly we might have gone back in time, and we entered Johnson's steep access drive in the shadow of great pines like those we had seen on the Trail.

Dusk had come early here in the shadow of the big trees and light poured from the uncurtained windows of a small log house that seemed to be resting at the feet of hundred-foot evergreens. We interrupted Carl Johnson's dinner but he was delighted when he learned why we had come. Pulling a battered flying jacket around his heavy shoulders and a sweat-stained brown woodsman's peaked cap over his dark hair, he took Ade outside to see the property while there was still some light. I wandered around inside.

The three-room cabin was far from fancy. The raw-log walls and beamed Celotex ceilings were smoke- and water-stained. The hanging electric bulbs in kitchen and living room were shaded by yellowish, soup-plate reflectors like those in old-time factories. The furniture in the living room was dark and so large and heavy it crowded the smallish room, whose floor was made of rough boards, their knotholes covered by nailed-down circles cut from cans. One still read "Hills Bro . . ." There was no light fixture in the bedroom, and the windows wouldn't let in much light anywhere at any time. There was no plumbing, not even piped-in water. But there *was* electricity, and the kitchen had a good inlaid linoleum and built-in cabinets and cupboards. I tripped over the edge of a grill in the living-room floor and felt warm air rising from it, carrying voices from below. There must be a basement and some kind of furnace.

I was waiting in the kitchen when the men returned.

"We'll have to talk it over," Ade said. "How can we reach you?"

Carl said to ask the phone operator in the Village (Bell

System) to call the Lodge on the Trail line (maintained by the USFS). Sven would then pass on the message by the bush-line (maintained by those along the shore of the Lake who used it). And he hoped we'd decide in a hurry, because he wanted to go west within a week. He knew of a good job there.

We promised to let him know in the morning and left.

Stuffed with lake trout, Ade and I rocked by the stove in our tourist cabin.

"It doesn't have to be elaborate, just something like this place," I said. "A little paint and elbow grease . . ."

"It'd be a lot more work than you think. It'd take all our vacation time for quite a few years."

"Would you mind?" I asked. He shook his head. "I wouldn't either. What's included in the sale?"

"Cabin and furnishings, small extra cabin and ice house, two hundred feet of lake shore, and an eighteen-foot boat—a dandy. The far shore of the Lake is Canada, by the way."

"How much does he want?"

Ade named a figure. I measured it against our savings and felt my uncertainty increase. "It's too much for us, don't you think?"

"Maybe, and probably too much for the property, too. But we've looked a long time for a piece of land that was secluded and hadn't been 'improved' to death, and the handwriting's on the wall up here. The Trail is certainly one of the most beautiful wilderness roads on earth, as you'll see once you get used to it. But while you were prettying up for dinner, the fellow who owns these cabins told me there're plans to have it widened and straightened and blacktopped someday. He also said that Big Steel is about to build a Taconite sintering plant on the Superior shore, and that people here are trying to get REA to run power up the Trail, and carry Bell Telephone with it." He grinned as I started to speak, and went on. "Yeah, I know. If he'd told us earlier we wouldn't even have looked, but as long as we did . . . If we grab Johnson's place now, we'll go back a hundred years and have some privacy—for a while, anyway. We can fix the cabin and leave the land alone. We may not get another chance. I say let's buy it."

2

Three afternoons later, with money transferred and the title to the property checked, we met Carl Johnson in the Village State Bank and closed the deal. Then, the back seat full of groceries, we turned our faces toward the woods.

A warm south wind had been busy since our previous trip up the Trail. The ice and snow had melted and the tiniest of unfurling leaves decorated the raspberry canes. The birch tops were purpling with buds under a sapphire sky. A road crew, filling potholes, waved as we passed them. When we reached the side road I was enchanted to see that it had a sprouting centerline of grass. Then we rolled down our driveway, backed into a graveled turn-around, and got out to really see our place in the woods for the first time.

The land sloped sharply down from the road on the south to the lake shore that formed its northern boundary. The driveway was midway between the east and west boundaries and the turn-around lay south of the log cabin, which stood halfway between road and lake. Its buff-painted walls and red roof contrasted well with the evergreens behind it. East of the driveway was an area that had been used for cutting wood, and beyond this a small cabin built of unfinished rough lumber. A path, merely a dirt track kept clear by the pressure of many steps, led from the main cabin to the shore and ice-house, whose logs were weathered to silver-gray.

The area between the log house and the road was covered mostly with maple brush and I glimpsed a red squirrel, investigating the stems for sap. A stately spruce, taller than a ten-story building, stood apart, its roots spreading in the maple, with a single white-trunked aspen in attendance at each side. The tall pine and spruce at the entrance to the driveway made a backdrop against the sky and fine old white cedars sheltered the house. Big woods formed a wall at east and west, and that on the west was ours. The sky was clouding over as we crossed the tiny clearing and went past a towering pine and through a narrow thicket of maple and mountain ash into a dim and timeless place.

Broad trunks of pine and spruce rose to a dozen times the height of a man before their lower branches interlaced to form a roof. Ancient birches stood firm, their bark tattered, their topmost white branches often dead, but their lower branches still bravely budding. Most of the earth was in shadow and clear of brush, and we walked over a soft, springing carpet of brown needles. In scattered open spots, seeds from balsam firs had sprouted into little Christmas trees and clumps of red-twigged maple lifted fat brown buds. There were long, low mounds that marked the slowly rotting trunks of trees fallen long ago, their resting places blanketed with moss and decorated with the scarlet spore caps of fuzzy gray lichens. And there were other trees on the way to oblivion, half-uprooted, split by lightning or snapped by wind, leaning heavily on the limbs of their neighbors. But, wherever there was light and space enough, saplings lifted straight and tall, ready to fill the places of their dying parents. Birds twittered and chirped in the vaulted ceiling. A squirrel scolded us from a woody bracket growing on a stump. The breeze sighed through myriad needles to bring us the fresh, clear scent of resin.

We stood in silence, watching an early spider weave her circle of web. When rain began to patter on the needles high above us we hurried to the cabin. There was much for us to do there, but in the forest nothing but to enjoy its shelter, watch its life, and learn from its patient regeneration. This we could do at leisure.

Ade took the padlock from its hasp and closed the door behind us. It was dim in the kitchen and smelled of used lard.

"Let's get some air in here," I said, pulling gently, then tugging at a French window behind the table. "Must be stuck." Ade was flipping the light switch on and off, on and off. "No lights?"

"There's a wind generator that charges batteries in the

basement. He must have disconnected them for safety."

I picked up a note from the table and read: "I forgot to tell you that the window panels lift out after you remove the nails. Good luck."

Ade inspected the windows, dashed to the car through the increasing rain, and returned with pliers and a box of groceries. We got the panels out after a struggle, occasioned by the frames having warped, and laid them on the table.

"I'll have to sand their edges down or we'll not get them back," Ade said. "I'll have to get hinges, too."

"What good will *they* do?" I asked. "There isn't room to swing the windows in past the table top."

"Mmm—yes. We can forget the hinges and lean the panels against the wall behind the table."

"But then we'll have to put the nails back every time . . ."

"No. I'll buy some turn latches—or make some wooden ones. Right now I'd better get the batteries connected before dark."

I stared at him. "I always knew you were a man of many talents but all this efficiency is staggering."

He leaned against the table and grinned. "Never had a chance to show off before. I built my own wagon when I was ten—turned in pop bottles for money to buy the wheels from a junk man. You could always find bottles where people dumped trash. Being a Navy electrician hasn't done me any harm, either, and . . ."—he looked up at the filthy ceiling—". . . the time I worked with a painter is going to pay off now. General maintenance man, that's me. Anyway, I like to fix things."

"Yessir," I said meekly. "Hurry with the batteries. I'm going to get something to eat."

I pawed through the cans and parcels in the box and decided that chili and crackers and coffee would have to do. There was a big wood range with an open-front woodbox beside it—filled, I was glad to see—and a three-burner kerosene stove on top of the woodbox. Its small glass tank was partly full, and I remembered such stoves from my childhood. Fine. I found a can opener and a saucepan and a percolator amid a tangle of utensils in one of the big drawers under the kitchen counter and was about to light the stove when Ade came in, carrying a wood rasp and an oil lamp, and looking grim.

"You'll have to use the wood stove," he said. "The batteries are dead—until there's enough wind to turn the generator—and the kerosene can down below is empty. This lamp was on the bench but it'll need all the kerosene in the stove tank if we're to have light for a few nights. I'd rather not drive to town tomorrow for some." He filled the lamp and touched a match to the wick—and the soft light changed the whole atmosphere and took me back to farmhouses where I had gone with my parents, in a buggy behind a gray mare, over roads not much different from the Trail.

"We can go to bed early and get up early and use the daylight," I said, unconsciously and perhaps from the memory of the farmhouses, making my first adjustment to life in the woods, where one makes the most of what nature provides. "Have we any water?"

Ade pointed to a galvanized pail—full—on the counter,

with an enameled dipper, once white but now chipped and iron-stained, hanging on the wall above it. I filled the percolator, then paused. "Uh—do you know how to build a fire in a cook stove?"

"I spent two years on a homestead with an aunt and uncle, you may recall," he said, and favored me with amused glances while he laid birchbark shreds and selected wood from the box.

The lamp glow was restful and soothing after our exciting day and we began to yawn before we finished eating. I stacked the dishes and carried the lamp into the bedroom while Ade brought in the other box of groceries and our bags from the car. I was drooping at the kitchen table when he returned.

"The bed is single," I announced, "and it doesn't just sag—it practically drops you to the floor. And there is no bedding whatsoever. And it's getting chilly . . . and we can't fit the windows back . . ."

"Well," Ade said, "we've got our coats. And the old picnic blankets are in the trunk. And there's a sofa and a fold-out daven bed in the living room. Which one do you want?"

I woke with the notion that I was sleeping on the floor, not too unreasonable an idea as the daven bed seemed to be made of boards with a thin layer of cloth over them. Ade was still asleep on the sofa, head on one arm, feet on the other. I slid into shirt, jeans, and moccasins and stepped outside.

The sky was a deep violet-blue and evaporating water droplets flashed and glittered everywhere in the sun. The air

was scented with balsam and wet earth and—I sniffed again
—something like anise. I searched for the source of this unexpected odor and found that it came from a decaying log.
Moss, as softly haired as the pile of an elfin carpet, was
growing on the log's top and under a curled-back flap of bark
three infant snails were creeping along, wearing their eighth-
inch pearly shells. I looked through the trees to the lake. It
was ultramarine, a much deeper blue than the sky, and its
surface was gold-spangled by the light. I ran to the shore, saw
that there was no trace of ice, and realized that it had been
gone when we arrived the day before! How could I have
missed this? I sat on a boulder, charmed by the swirling ring
where a fish jumped, the swooping and crying of a gull, the
patterns made by the restless water as it touched the rocks of
the shore. We were surrounded by wonders and I'd have to
learn to look beyond the end of my nose or I should miss
many of them. But now I'd better do something about breakfast.

The smell of frying bacon brought Ade out, rubbing his
neck. Considering the hard daven bed, I don't think I made
too bad a deal when I agreed to sleep alternate nights on the
short sofa.

After we finished a whole pot of coffee, Ade found a second pail under the sink and filled that as well as the one on
the counter from the lake. Then he took the kitchen window
panels outside to cut them down while I looked into the dish-
washing facilities. There was a good sink with two basins—a
hole instead of a faucet, of course. The cupboard underneath
held a scrubbing brush, an empty detergent box, an almost-

empty can of Old Dutch cleanser, and a five-gallon tar can to catch water from the open drainpipe. I had a choice of Old Dutch or my Roger & Gallet soap for the dishes. I chose Old Dutch and started a shopping list with "detergent."

I scalded the dishes and set the kettle back on the range, feeling smug about having successfully built my first fire in it. Then I looked around the kitchen, wondering why Carl had added to the general impression of cavelike gloom by covering every stick of furniture with the darkest of mahogany stains. The white linoleum with its small green blocks would help, once it was scrubbed, but I had a feeling it wouldn't stay white long. Well, if I was going to make this dingy cabin into something like the one in the Village, now was the time to start.

I stowed our groceries in the empty icebox that stood to the right of the kitchen table and its three chairs, which were directly in front of the north window. The triangular corner cabinet at left of the table contained the remains of three sets of dishes—all cups handleless, inexpensive tableware, and some green paper napkins, slightly crumpled. Next to it, in the west wall, was the open doorway to the living room, then the woodbox and kerosene stove, with the big wood range at right angles to the wall. The open doorway to the bedroom separated the range from the sink. There were high cabinets above both. I managed to reach across the hot stove and pull open the cabinet doors to find an assortment of glasses. Carl must have lived on cheese spreads. Since the only way for me to reach the glasses was to climb on the stove, I turned to the cabinets on the other side of the doorway. To reach these, one only had to climb on the sink, which I did and found sealed jars of beans, corn meal, cement, and an unlabeled something that looked like flour. The counter, with a narrow window behind it, reached along the east wall from the sink to the outside door, its heavy drawers jammed with pots, pans, kitchen tools, and an occasional wrench, screwdriver, or ball of string. From the holey pans and cracked dishes, Carl had never thrown out anything.

I was kneeling on the floor separating sheep from goats when Ade came in to fit the window panels.

He looked at the piles spread around me. "There's a barrel in the icehouse. You can use it for discards and I'll add some rusty junk from the basement. It'll keep things together until I can get rid of the lot. There'll be a dump somewhere."

I wasn't too happy about having a barrel taking up space, but gave in when Ade said he'd roll it out of the way in the bedroom.

The living room was simpler. Centered in the north wall was a window. A home-built kneehole desk stood in front of it with a fourth kitchen chair pushed partway into the kneehole. I tried to push it farther out of the way but something blocked it. I looked under the desk and found a nail keg, half full of trash. Wastebasket, of course. Low bookshelves stretched from the desk to and around the room corners on both sides. The sofa was against the west wall under a large window. Two overstuffed chairs and a standing ashtray, very shaky and with flaking enamel, took up the south end of the room. A doorway to the bedroom had been cut at that end of the east wall and the daven bed took up the wall space between this door and the one to the kitchen. I wondered why the doorways had no doors, and also why a frayed rope had been stretched diagonally across the room. Maybe it was a clothesline. I took it down, coiled it, and added it and the ashtray to the heap awaiting the barrel. Then I gathered an armload of books from the shelves and settled on the sofa to look them over. I was chuckling when Ade came in saying, "I found some latches. That takes care of one window, at least." He paused. Then: "What did you find?"

"Novels, from 1880 to 1930. Some of them'll be fun. Did you bring the barrel?"

"I'll go after it now."

As he opened the door, air flowed through the kitchen and into the living room and I knew that the inside doorways had no doors so that air—and heat—could circulate. So many things were new, different here.

I went into the bedroom, which had two windows, the south one cut off by the bed, the east by a heavy chest of drawers. I saw now that the bedroom and kitchen were really one long room, divided in half by the stove, sink, kitchen cabinets, and two bedroom cupboards. The one behind the sink was a long box, entirely enclosed except for a narrow opening in center front. I got Ade's flashlight and looked inside. There was a high rod from end to end and a pair of battered men's galoshes in a corner. The clothes closet!

Its really startling feature made itself known when I began to hang things. The rod was a sapling trunk with the bark still on, just large enough and rough enough to make it impossible to slide a hanger after one had managed to jam it in place.

Crawling inside to reach the ends was so difficult that I hung everything in the middle. Telling myself that it really didn't sag very much, I made sandwiches for lunch.

We ate on the sofa, Ade exclaiming over the fine pen-and-ink drawings in a 1900 edition of *David Harum*, while I buried my nose in *Graustark*, which I had read and loved when I was in junior high.

He had just taken our plates to the sink, we having decided to wash dishes once a day to save hauling water, and I was gathering up the extra books, when three young mice of the jumping variety crawled familiarly through an uncovered knothole in the floor under the kneehole of the desk. They were grayish, with white feet, large delicate ears, and long tails, which swept the floor gracefully as they hopped to the empty lowest shelf of the corner unit of the bookshelves. There they chased each other round and round as though on a miniature carousel, then took a fast hop-hop around the room before disappearing down their knothole. They seemed very much at home. Perhaps this was their regular play or exercise. If so, I could watch them . . . but Ade had a thing about mice. He liked animals in general but a mouse was a mouse, no matter what kind, and up to no good. After trying vainly to think of a way to persuade him that these mouse triplets were special, I went to the bedroom and considered the cupboard behind the cook stove. It surrounded the lower part of the chimney, took up a lot of space, was dark, smelly, impossible to clean, and didn't seem to serve any useful purpose. I looked into the kitchen where Ade was whistling to himself as he picked at the logs with pliers.

"What on earth . . ."

"Nails." He held out a partially filled stewpan. "The walls are whiskered with 'em, inside and out. Maybe they were handy to hang things on."

"Fine," I said vaguely. "What good's this cupboard thing?"

"It's over the trapdoor to the basement."

I saw the trapdoor then and reached down to catch its edge—no handle—and was almost precipitated into the depths below when one of the leather hinges gave way, a rotten board split, and the door canted in my hand. Ade caught me just in time.

"Thanks," I muttered, more shaken than I wanted to admit.

"I'm going to nail that shut," he said. "We can go in the basement through the outside door."

While he hammered I sat on the bed and looked at the stained shabbiness of walls and ceilings, floors and furniture. I was suddenly tired, and Ade looked well worn, too. Maybe I was just disturbed by what could have been a nasty fall, but maybe not. More likely I was having misgivings about the job ahead of us. But no matter what, we had it to do. I wondered how many summers, how many hours of labor—and they would grow harder as the novelty wore off—it would take to get the house the way we wanted it. And when we would have the leisure to walk together in the forest we had found after so long. Then Ade straightened abruptly, set hammer and nails on top of the clothes closet, and said as if he had been reading my mind, "What d'you say we forget the whole thing and go down and look at the lake?"

We were stepping out the door when the clothes rod fell with a crash. Neither one of us even looked back.

Next morning, while the shadows stretched long and the dawn wind still blew, I went out to look at the low, early-spring growth. Along the east wall of the cabin was a barren stretch, kept dry by the big eaves, but just beyond it the round leaves of wood violets, the trefoils of wild strawberries, and the clustered ribbons of sweet Williams hid their green under the buff tangle of last year's grasses, whose tender new shoots pushed toward the light. Farther east and north between the cabin and the lake, a rusty carpet of fallen cedar leaves covered the shadowed ground. Only a few unfamiliar bits of green showed here.

Nothing had pushed through the deep layer of chips in the wood-chopping area but along its edges were lovely bronze leaves in fours and sixes, with pale-green shoots rising from their creeping stems. In scattered patches, small brown funnels opened upward, each a swirl of leaves. My flower book wouldn't help me with these until they bloomed, if they did, and we wouldn't be here that long.

The car parked just outside the south window spoiled the view, and the turn-around promised a lot of dust for the cabin. Near this graveled space and in the clearing west of the house, I saw the fiddleheads of ferns, just beginning to uncurl. There were bright-green miniatures, brown ones of a kind you see in almost every woods, and beautiful pale-green ones as thick as my fingers and covered with spun-silver hairs. I love ferns, and wondered if they would spread into the turn-around if left alone. Maybe Ade could park where Carl had chopped his wood. The little we'd need could be split anywhere.

Between the cabin and the forest on the west were raspberry canes, lots of them and already well-leaved. They weren't in the way and if we came up at the right time some year . . . I was remembering the taste of wild berries picked beside country roads when a chipmunk appeared from the dead grasses almost at my feet, squeaked, and vanished. Correction: we might eat some berries if we beat the chipmunks to them—and, after all, who had a better right to them than the chippies?

I walked around the corner of the cabin and along the north wall to a shallow, slant-sided excavation that led to the semi-underground basement entrance. The door was under a rough dormer and the whole looked like the top of a mine shaft. Ade came out, carrying jagged pieces of blue roofing paper, which he added to a pile of the same.

"Carl reroofed a couple of years ago," he said. "He was keeping this in case he might find a use for it someday, I guess. Want to come in?"

The basement floor was dirt. The air had the damp smell of old-fashioned cellars, only more so. Enough light came through three high, long windows, open for air, for me to follow boards that gave easier footing. At my right were tables with cluttered tops, more of the roofing in a heap, and a rusty something that must be the furnace. In front of me was a washing machine—"Gasoline engine," Ade said—and a tarnished copper wash boiler. Along the wall at my left, set on heavy planks, a bench held the big glass batteries for the lights. Curious, I walked toward it, missed my footing, and fell forward. I landed with my hands on one of the planks supporting the bench and started to laugh at myself. Then I felt the plank and my hands sinking into mud and looked up to see the bench with its jars of sulfuric acid tilting slowly above me. There was a sickening, frozen moment, until Ade had braced the bench with one hand and yanked me back with the other.

"Get out of here," he yelled. "Beat it. And stay out until I get those damn things moved.".

I didn't argue. I simply tottered back to the kitchen, lit a cigarette and sat, until both my shivers and the profane comments from below stopped and there was a shout for me to "come back down."

The batteries were on the floor in a corner, along with a jumbled heap of boards that had been the bench. Where it had stood, a pile of fallen stones and broken concrete lay beneath a hole in the wall, with mud and water oozing from it. I poked at the ooze. "It's almost liquid. I don't see how that little rain yesterday . . ."

"It didn't, only indirectly. There's an underground spring. I suppose Carl thought the wall would hold." I must have looked very worried because he went on quickly. "It's nothing to get upset about. I can brace the wall."

The mud was slowly rising above the board I stood on, or the board was sinking. I couldn't tell which.

"What good will the basement be if the whole floor turns into a mudhole?" I asked. "We'll have to drain it, won't we?"

Ade walked to a far corner, came back with two shovels,

and handed me one. An hour later a small stream was flowing briskly from the base of the broken wall, out the door, and down the excavation to disappear in the cedar duff. I was amused in spite of the incipient blisters on my hands. "A brook in the basement. Who else has one?"

Ade grinned and dug a small, deep hole near the door. I watched, fascinated, as it filled and cleared. He picked up an aluminum measuring cup from one of the tables, rinsed it carefully, filled it from the pool, and presented it to me with a flourish.

"I won't have to carry any more water from the lake this year, at least."

3

The easy solution of The Problem of the Brook in the Basement encouraged us.

Ade moved the batteries, with their potentially dangerous acid, to the ice house, rewired them, and said he would cover them with rags and the sawdust in the ice house so that they wouldn't freeze during the coming winter. While he was bracing the weakened wall, I started to collect trash outside but stepped on a nail that stuck up from a rotting board. Fortunately the nail was so dulled by corrosion that it only lacerated the bottom of my foot, but Ade told me firmly to work inside till he, wearing heavy-soled shoes, could get such junk out of the yard.

So I scrubbed the kitchen linoleum, polished the windows

and measured them for curtains, found jars in the basement for the mouse- and water-proof storage of nonperishable leftovers, and made my own long list of things to do. I enjoyed it, but underneath was always a longing for the peace and rest the forest could give.

In the evenings we sat on the shore, tired and happy, and planned for the next day, while the clear sunset sky frosted with mother-of-pearl and the rose in the east faded to mauve and then to gray, the lemon above the hills across the lake deepened to chartreuse and to green, and the western gold flamed and dulled and went out.

On the Wednesday morning of our second vacation week Ade went to town to get some supplies that he needed for the two days left to us before we would start back to Chicago. While the sound of the car faded, I stood in the sun and looked up at the trees. The green-furred, shelf-branched white pines; the pointed-topped balsams; the stubby-branched, thickly needled white spruces; the white cedars, not so tall but richly green with scaly leaves shaped like flattened ornamental shrubs. They all had strength and age, and the dignity of age, to balance my little human fretting. I sighed with contentment, and the sigh seemed strangely loud.

There was a great quietness around me. No leaf rustled. No wave lapped the shore. Not even an insect hummed in the cool but heavy air. I wondered where the birds were, the animals. True, they avoided the cabin, but usually squirrel invective or crow alarms burst out when we left the house. It was too quiet.

I went in and began to sweep with exaggerated energy at the living-room floor. You could only sweep at it because rough boards supply fresh dirt from their cracks as soon as you have removed a dustpanful. I wondered how long Ade would be gone: three or four hours on the road, time to shop, to eat—six or seven hours probably. With a start I realized that I was standing still and moving the broom, going through the motions so that I wouldn't think about the fact that, for the first time in my life, I was quite alone.

The Petersons were only two miles away, but that seemed very far. I looked at the Army field phone above the bookshelves. It was hooked to the bushline that reached the Lodge and some summer cabins, empty now. You rang two long, one short, for the Lodge, spinning the crank as one did on the phone in the house where I grew up. But Ade had disconnected it, pending the installation of lightning arresters, which he said it should have but didn't. Anyway, I shouldn't want Hilda and Sven to think me the kind of ninny who would call up for reassurance just because Ade had gone to town! Still, there was something daunting in the thought that for the rest of the day I was wholly dependent on myself. Rumbling came from the west. Thunder. I'd go to the shore and break up this silly mood by watching the storm clouds.

The water was quiet as ice, the western end of the lake leaden in the shadow of the thunderhead, the eastern still a tranquil blue. Then the big cloud was racing toward me and swaying veils of rain began to swallow the lake. Whitecaps flashed ahead of the rain, a moaning filled the air, and at my feet the water rose and sank in the long swells that preceded the squall. A pair of ducks—mergansers, I thought—lifted and sped homeward, skimming the heaving surface. Then wind roared across the swells, turned them sawtoothed and frothing, and the first big drops splattered down. I ran for the cabin, pushed by a wind that flung debris from the trees past my head.

I ducked inside, grabbed a towel from the kitchen rack, and was sitting by the west window drying my hair when the rain came down as though from a waterfall. I was puzzled by the roaring overhead until I realized that I had never before heard rain on a roof because I had always lived in houses with crawl space above the top-floor ceilings or apartments with other stories above me. This was another of the many things that were different here. Suddenly I wondered how sound the roof was. Well, if it stood up to this without leaking, we could scratch "Check roof" from the list of things to do.

I felt a jar, then another, as if something had bumped against the basement wall. I looked outside. The rain was falling in such torrents that I could just make out the big pine twenty feet away, and the frothing muddy water that covered the ground. The jarring came again, and a heavy crunch. Then I felt the floor sag and saw a crack between the floorboards and the bottom log of the north wall under the desk. I stretched across the desk and looked sideways through the window. A fan of water was spraying from the wall near the corner. Whatever had happened, it wasn't good, and I couldn't do anything about it—even if I knew what to do. I felt helpless and frightened. When I reached for a cigarette and saw my hand shaking, I sat down and tried to think calmly.

The basement walls, which were also the cabin foundation,

were below ground on the south and east sides of the building, leaving only enough room above ground for the narrow basement windows. On the west side, because of the sharp slope, the wall was more and more exposed from south to north until at the northwest corner it was seven feet high, matching the seven-foot wall across the north side of the basement. Now water was pouring in the open basement windows and finding its way out where it could, and in so doing it had split the north wall near the corner. Listening to the water as it washed and tugged and pressed at the broken wall, I looked at the logs and heavy roof beams around me. With ice at the pit of my stomach I drew myself a horrifying picture of drowning in a mudhole under a pile of timbers.

For a moment I quite literally was not able to move. Then I called myself an imaginative idiot and got up to make some coffee. As I took my first step, thunder bellowed like the voices of the Furies. The windows rattled and the walls shook and the almost-dark room flared white with lightning. Then there was an abrupt pause in this awesome display, a slackening of the rain, almost a silence, and out of this breathing space flashed a bolt so near that my ears stung with the snap of the gigantic spark. I thought the big pine was hit and, terrified and half-blinded, stumbled into the kitchen, which was at least farther from the tree. I saw smoke drifting past the kitchen window and grew dizzy at the thought of forest fire. Then the rain roared on the roof again and my common sense took over to tell me that the woods could not burn in such a drenching. What I needed was coffee—maybe some lunch.

I turned toward the range, only to see St. Elmo's fire tip-toeing on the lids, its eerie blue light intensifying the dimness. As I backed away from the stove I froze to listen to new splashing sounds from the flooded basement. I heard a snuffle and relaxed, feeling a fool. A stray dog had come through the open door looking for shelter. I was managing a shaky laugh when there was a scratching at the trapdoor. I knew it was nailed shut but as I slowly turned my head toward it, the hair lifted on my neck and arms and it seemed that an icicle was dripping down my spine.

Black claws were splintering the edge of the broken board and a paw groped through, all of five inches broad and covered with black hair. A bear—a big one—and not in an amiable mood if his deep-throated growls were any indication. A meeting between a scared bear and a scared woman held unpleasant possibilities, for me, anyway. I opened the door to the outside. A small tree snapped and fell almost across the doorstep and the air seemed full of flying branches. I couldn't get anywhere in such a gale and the bear could run out just as well as I could.

I pushed the door shut and leaned against it, watching the trapdoor in horrified compulsion. The bear hooked the claws of his left forepaw over the edge of the trap and began to push the broken board upward with his right paw. I remembered the barrel Ade and I had filled with junk. If I could put it on top of the trapdoor—but it was in the bedroom. I couldn't possibly force myself to almost jump over the bear to get to it! A gust of wind shook the windows and seemed to shake my wits into working order at the same time. I scurried around through the living room to the bedroom and, though the barrel weighed almost three hundred pounds, somehow I wrestled it across the floor onto the front part of the trapdoor. The bear hastily withdrew his paws and began to assault the broken board with his claws again. He was slowed down, for a while, anyway—and I had been annoyed when Ade first mentioned bringing in the barrel!

The bear stopped clawing, perhaps to consider his next move, and I was drawing a full breath for a change when I heard the sharp crack-crack-crack of breaking wood, ominously near. A tree was coming down. I held my breath through endlessly stretching seconds until it struck the cabin with an overwhelming crash and vibration.

When my ears stopped ringing I found myself sitting in the middle of the kitchen floor with no idea how I had come there. I was so weak I thought I couldn't get up but loud thumps near the basement door had me on my feet in a hurry. From the kitchen window I watched the rapidly diminishing rump of a bear who ran as though he was as frightened as I was. If I'd had the strength left, I'd have been glad to run somewhere else, too.

Later I sat in the living room as darkness gathered, a normal dusk now that the storm had passed on. I lit the lamp—blessed warm glow from that little flame—and felt spiritually wonderful if physically limp. All that was left from the strenuous hours was a sense of relief and a feeling of deep content that was new to me. Slowly I began to understand its source.

Here in the woods Ade and I were touching a way of life

very different from the one we knew in the city. There we lived within an unchanging framework, established largely by our chosen employment and by the lasting inflexibility of the corporations for which we worked. Here storms and bears and falling trees passed against the oldest background man can know, the natural one. Here both background and the framework that touched us were variable and full of the un-expected, as the ways of nature are variable and outside of human planning. Here men were as independent as it is pos-sible to be in our specialized society and could, if they were versatile and ingenious and tenacious, build a life based on their individual abilities. For a time I sat thinking that it would be good to live here, where we might test our strength against the unpredictable future.

Then I felt hungry and saw that the windows were black. I looked at the clock. It had been more than eleven hours since Ade left for town. I saw him crushed by a fallen tree, under the car in a rain-filled ditch, burned in a smash-up. The floor sagged again; the crack in the wall widened—and where was that contented feeling? I passionately wondered why anyone in his right mind could even *think* it might be good to live in the woods.

The door opened and Ade came in, fairly dry and smil-ing.

"My, you look cozy," he said blithely. "The place to be when it storms is safe at home, not sitting it out by the side of the road."

4

Once Ade had eaten, looked at the basement wall with his flashlight, and assured me that the breaking had sounded worse than it was, I was ready to sleep the clock around. Instead I woke three hours later to a rain so heavy it might have accompanied a hurricane. It didn't just roar on the roof. It splashed and thudded and splattered as though heavenly sluices were open in flood time.

Ade half-drowned himself closing the basement windows but still the water gushed knee deep from its open door. Even as he was changing into dry things, cement began to crunch as loosened stones worked their way out of the weakened foundation, and the logs jarred and settled in the wall above as the stones fell. The floor sagged little by little, more and more. We dragged the nail-keg wastebasket from beneath the desk, overturned it between the armchairs to hold the lamp, and tried to read, but gave up when we heard part of the north foundation collapse. There was nothing to say or do, so we went back to bed.

I don't know how Ade felt, but I was miserable. I told myself that he had made the decision to buy, but might not have except to please me. We had transferred Carl's insurance, of course, but it was inadequate and I wondered why we hadn't increased it at the time. If the foundation didn't collapse now it surely would during the winter or the next spring thaw. I'd seen what happened to poor foundations in the country when I was young, and southern Ohio winters were cool spells compared to what would come here. I heard water dripping and reached for the flashlight lying handy on the floor. Its beam picked out the spreading wet on the living-room ceiling, the water drops gathering and falling in half a dozen places. There had been no leaks here earlier. The tree that fell, of course. It had opened the roofing seams.

I got up to put pans under the leaks. The drips turned into streams and I put towels in the pans so water wouldn't splash all over the floor. Ade said "Don't worry about it," and I knew he meant that leaking water didn't matter in a collapsing house. The rain slackened at last and I slept.

Sunlight, slanting from the east window through the doorway to the sofa, touched my eyelids and woke me. It was eight o'clock and I couldn't understand why I felt so tired—until I saw the soaked ceiling panels, and the storm and the night came back to me. I shook Ade awake and stepped gingerly across the slanted, quivering living-room floor.

Food didn't interest either of us but strong coffee helped and I was pouring second cups when Sven hailed from the yard and Ade let him in.

"Hilda's been trying to call you," he said, accepting coffee. "I checked the phone line as I came down and it looks okay."

"Disconnected," Ade said, taking a small paper bag from the counter and stuffing it into a pants pocket. "No lightning arresters. I got them in town yesterday."

Sven looked at me. "Did you go with him?" I shook my head. "Where were you when that tree hit the house?"

"In there." I pointed to the bedroom. "Watching the bear try to get through the trap door."

"She put the barrel on it," Ade said.

Sven's eyebrows went up and he went over to heft the barrel and examine the claw marks. "Quite an initiation," he said.

"It was all right when it was over." I did my best to sound nonchalant.

"I'll have to revise my opinion of city women," he said, and I heard trumpets blowing in the distance.

The house shook slightly and there was a splash from below. Sven looked startled.

"There's been a lot of that," Ade said, getting up. "We might as well go and see how bad it is."

The ground was a mass of mud and washed-out vegetation, with a few of the plants I had seen still clinging by the tips of their roots under a clutter of broken twigs and branches. Rivulets were eroding their way to the lake. Almost all the fern sprouts were broken. Some raspberry canes lifted mud-coated leaves, but most still pulled upward in the silt that covered them.

The turn-around was a sodden pool of mud and, with the worst possible timing, I asked Ade what he thought of parking in the wood-chopping area.

Sven said, "There's a deeper mudhole than this halfway up your drive. Maybe a spring."

Ade laughed but without amusement. "I parked at the road

last night and saw the spring on my way down. We've lots of springs. So I park by the road from now on. You can grow petunias here if you want to."

We slogged under the sixty-foot fallen balsam that slanted from the edge of the big woods to the southwest corner of the cabin roof. There were foot-wide openings in the west foundation wall where stones had worked loose and dropped out, and the north wall had burst outward, making a gateway into the basement wide enough for Ade and Sven to walk through abreast. I looked into the basement to see floating planks, the washing machine wading hip deep so to speak, and the wash boiler sailing around like a half-submerged submarine. I turned away from this discouraging spectacle to notice that the rush of water had carried stones from the broken wall to the base of the pine stub that held the aluminum tower for the wind generator.

"The pine looks burnt," I said.

Ade and Sven walked over to examine it, then backed away to look up at the wind generator at the top of its hundred-foot tower. Sven shook his head.

"That lightning bolt of yours hit the tower," Ade said to me. "The generator's probably burnt out and there wasn't any fuse to the relay in the basement so that's likely shot, too. So no lights."

"We've managed without 'em so far," I said with resignation.

"Well," Sven said, "he used enough wire to hold it up. You won't have to worry about it falling on the house and when you take it down you can use the guy wire for something. But your foundation—it'll never hold through the winter."

"I can fix the phone at least," Ade said ruefully, and pulled the bag of lightning arresters from his pocket. Then we might as well see what's under the house."

I left them to it and went inside to have another cup of coffee.

They came in very soon and Sven went directly to the phone. When Hilda answered he said, "Call John Anderson and see if he'll come. The foundation's washed out." He hung up, shook the percolator, poured himself the dregs, and said: "She'll call some people who live near John—on the forestry line, I mean—and they'll call him on their bushline. It's a baling-wire system but it usually works."

I got out some cookies and found that, now that Sven's experience was being applied to our problem, I was normally hungry. Ade must have felt the same because he was on his fifth cookie when the phone rang.

"That was quick," Sven said, answering. He listened, said "yes" twice, and hung up. "No luck. John's working on his own house and won't take any more outside work this year."

"Is there someone else?" I asked.

"Nobody who isn't tied up for the season, and that means until heavy frost next fall."

There was a silence. My throat was so constricted that I was afraid I might cry. Ade looked white. He put down his unfinished cookie and said, "Any suggestions?"

Sven rubbed his chin. "Well, it's this way. The logs of this cabin are all spruce, tough and strong, and each log is notched on the bottom to fit over the one underneath, with the lowest log and the edge of the floor resting on the cement at the top of the foundation. As far as the cabin itself goes, if it was on level land you could set it and the floor on jacks and it'd stay there. But Carl wanted a basement and it saved digging to use the natural slope of the hill. He used a concrete and stone mixture to wall it in because it was cheaper than plain concrete reinforced with rods, although it isn't as strong. The basement walls formed the foundation, of course, and they ought to have been strong enough.

"But the thing is that the north foundation and part of the west had no support inside or out, and when enough water piled up in the basement, they gave way and the house twisted enough to let your floor sag. What's really holding the house up now is the northwest corner of the foundation, and that's cracked. Once it goes, the whole thing'll slide downhill and collapse into a pile of logs. We can try to brace it—I've some big timbers—but the ground heaves with frost here. I doubt it'll hold up. But we'll try."

I looked up. "Do you think it would do any good if we went to see this Mr. Anderson? We could ask . . . oh, I don't know . . . I'm just trying to think . . ."

"It won't do any harm to ask his advice," Sven said. "It'll be a lot better than mine and he may have some big jacks we can use. There's time enough today."

Armed with directions, we set out as soon as Sven left.

Thirty miles away on a side road much like ours we stopped beside the concrete foundation and rising supports of what would be a handsome two-story house, set on top of land that sloped gradually to a lake bordered by slender young birches. They got more sun than our trees and were already greening. The sound of a buzz saw came from behind a heap of birch logs. It stopped as Ade said, "I'll bet he cuts his own lumber," and a man rounded the logs and walked toward us.

He was tall, stubble-chinned, and white-haired, with the sloping shoulders of very strong men. Muscles rippled under his blue shirt as he stretched his arms and flexed the fingers of his big hands. There was sawdust in his hair and on his clothes, and his blue eyes were very keen. He nodded, sat down on a pile of bagged cement, and looked expectant.

"We're the Hoovers," Ade said.

John Anderson smiled.

"Hilda Peterson called you about us," I said.

John nodded.

"We thought perhaps you'd have time to give us some advice," Ade said.

John nodded again, leaned his elbows on his knees, his chin on his hands, and prepared to listen.

Ade found a stick and squatted to draw a diagram in the dust between them, explaining when he had to, letting the drawing do most of the talking. I sat on a log, making a determined effort not to fidget. Without warning, a squirrel shot in front of me, followed by a big, old brown dog, who was doing her lumbering best but losing ground with every lunge. I laughed.

Without looking up, John said, "She's been trying to catch a squirrel all her life. She won't get one, but she loves trying." And to Ade: "Go on."

When Ade had finished and straightened up, John looked from him to me and then at the sky.

"I think there's going to be more rain," he said. "I'll just cover my cement and ride up to your place with you. Mind, now—I won't do more than look."

John made the ride seem very short. He told of the cabin where he and his wife had homesteaded forty years before, and of fighting the great fire that had almost burned over the place where our cabin now stood. And I'll always remember how he laughed when a low branch slapped our windshield and I ducked.

When he and Ade went to look at the foundation and I was brewing the inevitable coffee, I realized for the first time that Ade and I were truly babes in the woods beside the people who had pioneered in this forest such a few years before that they were still here to tell about it. Again I thought it would be good to live here, but when the men came in I had to admit to myself that most of my optimism and confidence was reflected from John Anderson.

We sat at the kitchen table in silence and drank coffee. Ade's expressionless face told me that John had made no suggestions and when I had reached a point where I thought I must scream or throw my cup on the floor, John set his cup down and asked, "How much time d'you have left?"

"Just tomorrow," Ade answered. "We could stay Saturday but that'd make a pretty long run back to Chicago for one day."

"Too long. That's the sort of thing causes accidents. All right. Tomorrow get everything you want to keep out of that basement and throw your trash beside that west wall. I've got to pour some concrete at my place. When that's done, I'll bring my cat and my man and twenty bags of cement and fix this little house for you—and she'll stay fixed. It'll settle some —then you can fix up your inside trim." His eyes began to twinkle. "For the last thirty years I've been promising my wife I'd build her a nice house. I don't think she'll pull out too much of my hair if I make her wait a few days longer."

2 *The Decision*

I put the breakfast dishes into the cupboard and swept a last
look around the tourist cabin in the Village. Everything was
as it had been on our first stay two months earlier, except that
now the ruffles on the curtains were green, Lake Superior was
like zinc-spangled steel under a pattering rain, and the calendar above the sink said July 18. And, more important, when
Ade tooted the horn to tell me to hurry, I knew where we
were going.

As we turned onto the Trail I was filled with a wonderful
sense of anticipation and relief. The former didn't seem very
sensible, considering the problems we had met during our
earlier short acquaintance with the cabin, but the latter did,
because everything had gone wrong after we left for home in
May.

On the way, Ade developed a sore throat that led to a rush
operation. It wasn't particularly serious, but he recovered too
slowly and had to give up his job for an indefinite period. It
made me uncomfortable to come home from the lab and find
him starting dinner, and then came an evening when I
rounded our corner as he was returning from the grocery

three blocks away. He stopped at the foot of the four steps leading up to our apartment-building door. I thought he had forgotten something. Then, from the way he drooped, I knew that he was so exhausted by the short walk that he had had to stop to rest. That he had been fighting off colds and flu I knew, but I'd had no idea of anything like this, and it filled me with panic. When I could think clearly, it was all too plain to me that if something wasn't done to help him get well I was going to lose the only husband I ever wanted.

The next morning I went to the head of my metallurgical department, explained the situation, and asked for a year's leave to be spent in the woods. He said he'd have to talk the matter over with the company medical department. At the end of the week, I was told I had an appointment with one of the company doctors, who was familiar with Ade's case. It startled me to learn that he was a psychiatrist as well as a medical doctor until it came to me that it must seem very off-center to my boss for an engineer like me suddenly to want to go back to nature.

I enjoyed my talks with the doctor, a thoughtful, compassionate, and highly intelligent man. He felt strongly that the bitter cold of the northern Minnesota winter might be dangerous to Ade, and he was doubtful of my reactions to such an environment over a long period of time.

"You're a mental worker," he said, "and there won't be enough to keep your mind occupied. Don't you think you might be bored?"

"If you mean will I be pining for gears and bull pinions, I'm sure I won't. I'm pretty tired of being a man among men.

I'll have a lot to do in and around the cabin, all of it constructive, and if I've time to spare, I'll try to write. I've often
thought I'd like to go to the woods and write."

He looked interested. "When did you first get this idea? Of
writing in the woods, I mean. Lots of people have it in one
form or another, you know."

So I told him of the country town where I was born, a place
with elm-shaded streets, curlicued Victorian houses, and a tall
brick schoolhouse, in whose yard stood trees from the original
forest, shedding leaves on the building's peaked slate roof.

Miss James's seventh-grade class met in a brindle-yellow,
high-ceilinged room of that building. One afternoon I was
enduring the deathly hush of a study period, my attention
divided between keeping my long yellow curls forward so that
the boy what sat back of me couldn't dip them in the ink well
and reading *Flynn's Detective Magazine* behind the ample
cover of my geography text. I already knew all I needed to
know about "The Principal Products of the State of Texas."

With a snap, one of the long roller blinds took off and went
flapping up to the top of its window. In the exciting arrival of
the janitor with a ladder, I forgot about Miss James—until
her hand came over my shoulder and removed *Flynn's* to the
trash container. She said nothing, no doubt thinking the delighted or pitying looks from my classmates were humiliating
enough—or maybe she was planning something specially unpleasant for me. I decided not to worry about it.

Instead, I hung around after school until I thought the coast
was clear, then slipped back to retrieve the magazine, but
Miss James knew me better than I thought and was waiting

behind the half-shut cloakroom door. In the discussion that followed I made some ill-advised comments about my father's position, the school board and the responsibility of a teacher being limited to teaching and having nothing to do with selecting my private reading matter. Result: an extra-curricular paper of half-hour reading time on *Our Western National Parks*.

I started the composition with the idea that I'd hate national parks forever, but, as I read and compiled, my feelings softened. I would never know who robbed the fictional bank in *Flynn's*, but this world of trees and rocks and waters was far more interesting. Anyway, there were lots more detective stories.

When I read my masterpiece to the class I could not resist ending: "Some day I intend to live in one of the parks where there will be no one to bother me while I read, and write about what I see."

"The ending," I told the doctor, "was not as well received as the rest of the paper."

He grinned. "I can imagine. I'm not at all sure though that you aren't trying to escape your present heavy responsibilities by retreating into a childhood fantasy."

I sighed. "One man's fantasy may be another man's reality—isn't that so?"

He looked at me a long time, then said: "I can't take a chance on it. You do see that?" I nodded and he went on. "Nor can I take a chance on your husband's reaction to the severe winter up there. But I'm with you in that I think the disease-free atmosphere will help him by freeing him from these virus infections that are delaying his recovery . . . as long as he doesn't overdo and gets plenty of rest. I won't recommend a year, but I will recommend two months, to start as soon as possible so that you'll be back before it gets cold."

So here we were, rolling up the blacktop toward the narrow, twisty road, with the cabin and the beautiful woods ahead.

We were suddenly halted by a flagman, standing in front of something that looked like the excavation for a big building. A pickup truck was grinding toward us through a sea of red mud, generously sprinkled with granite boulders and threaded all over with ruts left by the road-building machines, which were pushing and churning the earth like giant eggbeaters.

When the truck had squeezed past, the flagman waved us on. Ade took a deep breath and the car wallowed into the truck's ruts. Surprisingly, we kept going, somewhat cheered by the driver of a bulldozer, who pointed to his blade and to the car and made gestures of pushing us out. I had visions of us rising from the muck in the maw of one of the gigantic shovels, something like mushrooms appearing from cream soup on a spoon.

This went on for the next fifteen miles. Sometimes we waited while trucks loaded with stone swam past us or the side of a hill fell away from a dynamite blast. We dodged boulders that would have torn away the underside of the car, dropped off declivities as straight and sharp as curbstones, passed over pools of water on built-up bridges of stone from which the edging boulders rolled away from our wheels, and forded other pools, depth unknown, but never too deep to get through.

In any other place this would have been thought completely impassable, but here it was the only road. If you wanted to go into the woods, or to come out, you went over it. That it was difficult and hazardous was unimportant; if you kept at it, you'd get where you were going. I liked that. It was what I wanted to do myself, although my goal was still a little hazy. I looked sideways at Ade. He grinned and pointed to the end of the construction just ahead, but I hadn't seen such an expression of triumphant glee on his face for a long time.

The old Trail looked like a highway by contrast and we didn't even mind when a pattering rain became a downpour. Our narrow side road's rain-slicked surface only slowed us down a little, and we thought nothing of leaving the car at the top of the hilly path and running through the rain to the cabin.

We entered to an overpowering stench of mildew. It reminded me vividly of an abandoned burial vault dug into the side of a hill in the cemetery of my home town, where similar odors of dankness and decay seeped out through the rusted iron gates and helped scare the daylights out of me and my childhood pals. The gloominess of the kitchen was vaulty, too. Ade sneezed.

"Let's get some air in here," I said between sniffles, and tugged at one of the French windows above the kitchen table.

"That was last time," Ade said, moving me to one side and

turning the latches he had put on to hold the window panels. I stepped back while he lifted them out and jumped when a drop of water hit the back of my neck. A leak? I'd thought all the leaks were in the living room near the corner that had caught the falling tree. Well, this one could wait while we ventilated the place.

Letting some fresh damp air in and some stale damp air out improved things immensely and I mentioned the dripping water. Ade turned a flashlight onto the ceiling and we saw that the main beam, which was also the ridgepole, was covered with drops that fell periodically. The Celotex panels glittered with mist. I peered into the dimness where the peaked ceiling met the beam at the end of the room.

"Throw the light over here. What on earth . . ." I leaned against the counter and whooped. "Mushrooms! Mushrooms on the ceiling!"

Ade studied the patch of twisted, wrong-way-up umbrellas. "Might be convenient if they're edible." He went to the desk in the living room and added a note to the list of things to do waiting there. "Ventilators," he said, "before we have moss on the walls." He picked up the empty water pails on his way to the door. "I'll put these outside, go to the car for a minute, and then tend to the ceiling."

"If we're going to eat we'll have to have some water beside what's already in here," I said patiently.

He beckoned me to the door to see him set the pails under streams pouring from the roof.

"Distilled water, straight from the clouds through clean air and caught by a rain-washed roof," he said.

Wondering if I was as capable as I thought I was, I filled the glass tank of the kerosene stove and upended it in its support. The oil glub-glubbed satisfactorily into the pipe that fed the burners and I lighted the wicks of all three. I was measuring water and dehydrated soup into a saucepan when Ade, standing on the table to wipe the ceiling, shouted, "For Pete's sake, turn it off!"

I whirled. Orange flames were shooting three feet into the air, their edges green and sparkling. I shut off the oil and we watched the subsiding fireworks. Gouts of soot began to drift about our heads.

"A little more soot won't matter," Ade said, perhaps with intent to soothe.

Out of a newly acquired well of resignation, I said, "Maybe it'll drift out the window. What's wrong with the fool thing?"

"Just damp," Ade said airily. "We ought to light the wood stove, anyway—to dry the place out. There's enough wood in the box for a while and I've some more outside, covered with birchbark to keep it dry." I lifted my eyebrows as he burst out laughing. "I was just remembering that note Carl left. He wished us good luck. D'you suppose he meant it two ways?"

Once we had closed the windows and eaten, the heat from the big range began to soak comfortably into our bones and to warm the house, accompanied by the little creaks and snaps of drying wood. A bit late, I remembered to put pans under the leaks in the living room, discovering in the process that one had developed directly over the now-soaked daven bed. Acquainted with this, Ade sighed. "There's no telling where the water comes through the roofing paper. I'll have to go all over the seams with patching asphalt. We can dry this thing in the sun—when there *is* sun—and in the meantime I'll find some boards to use as slats under that sagging spring in the bedroom."

Congratulating myself on having found a husband who not only liked to fix things but had the know-how, I unpacked the throws and paper drapes I had picked up at Chicago sales. Once I had these in place on furniture and at windows, the dull, grimy walls and ceiling and floor receded into the obscurity they deserved. That the throws were India print and the drapes baroque floral made no difference. They were light, bright, and colorful, and would look more so when the lamp was lighted. I glared at the dark, wet daven bed and then tried to ring Hilda to tell her we had arrived. The bushline was dead, probably shorted by a sagging wet branch. (I did not yet know that this happened often and usually when one felt an urgent need to call someone.)

It seemed a good time to start relaxing, so I searched the bookshelves and settled by the west window with *The Prisoner of Zenda*. I was so engrossed in this fabulous romance that I did not know the rain had stopped until copper-colored light reached from behind the clouds to reflect from the lake surface and shimmer on the living-room wall.

When Ade had put the makeshift bed slats to dry by the stove, we went out to see what John Anderson had done to the house and grounds. Along each side of the driveway were ditches which spread apart to follow the edges of the clearing, so that the whole was something in shape like a lopsided stemmed glass, with the unused driveway as the stem. The ground where the turn-around had been was several feet lower and the soil from there had been pushed under the cabin and against the west and north walls. Water gurgled pleasantly in the ditches that drained the bulldozed land, but it was still deep mud. The basement was filled, its outer doorway closed with concrete blocks and its windows now ventilators for the crawl space under the cabin. The trash we had laboriously piled against the walls was buried and the washing machine, copper boiler, and furnace were standing under a tarpaulin near where the basement door had been.

The furnace was a barrel stove, standby of the woodsmen, made from a fifty-five-gallon oil drum by attaching fittings. These consisted of a small door with draft slots below in front, a stovepipe fitting at top rear, a flat iron plate to hold a kettle at top front, and spraddled short legs. Years of service had given this stove the mien of an old campaigner. The replacement of a hinge pin by a bent nail and the door handle by a piece of twisted wire added a rakish touch. It was big, rusty, battered—and scowled at us with an air of grim efficiency.

I was impressed but not attracted. "How'll we get rid of it? It must be heavy."

"We won't," Ade said. "Suppose the cook stove burns out and we need heat?"

I looked at the barrel stove again. Esthetically it was a disaster, but I was getting a new idea of beauty as I remembered the waves of heat from the cook stove that morning. The old campaigner took on a charm beyond that of any decorative effect.

Just around the corner of the cabin was a sturdy wheel-barrow, home-built by Carl, with an engine I hadn't seen before on it.

"This," Ade said, making a gesture which might be interpreted as pointing with pride, "is a little 110-volt light plant Jim Herbert used as an emergency standby for his machine shop during the war. He gave it to me and I tucked it into the car trunk. I'm going to rewire the cabin. Then I can use my soldering iron and so on, and we can have decent light. Carl's plant is beyond repair. It was 32-volt, too, so we can't use any of his equipment."

I was happy about everything, especially the new security of the house, and said so.

"We'll have no more foundation trouble," Ade said. "A good workman does a good job."

He wheeled the light plant toward the icehouse, where Carl's old plant was set up. I wandered over to the spot covered by wood chips, thinking that we could begin to enjoy our surroundings, now that the house was solid and we had the hang of living here. Vegetation was spreading through the chip layer and, in the clarity of the sunset light, every leaf and twig stood out sharp-etched. The low plant with the creeping stems was covered with white flowers, like dogwood, and here and there tiny green berries were forming in the center of the browning and shriveling white bracts. I recognized it then—bunchberry. The little brown funnels had become graceful, shiny leaves, from which lifted tall stalks with clusters of greenish-yellow lilies drooping at their tops. Clintonia, of course, or blue-bead lilies, from the metallic-blue fruits that would follow the flowers. I dropped to my knees to better see the tiny buff spore caps on a delicate moss and almost fell flat as I jerked my right hand back. A brown wolf spider with a leg-spread of nearly three inches clutched her sack of eggs close under her body and reared in defensive position, ready to do all that nature permitted her to do in defense of her unhatched young. I got up carefully. I'd have to watch my steps here, where heavy feet could destroy so many small creatures.

We took sandwiches to the shore and marveled at the long summer twilight of the North, which far, far beyond the hills would give way to the Midnight Sun. We watched mosquitoes rising newborn from the now smooth water and dragonflies darting after them, lace-winged, iridescent, and accurate as missiles. Night insects began to fly in the forest and when the blue dusk hummed with the violin sounds of mosquitoes' wings, we fled to shelter in the cabin. Ade wrote "insect repellent" on our shopping list and I carried the lamp into the bedroom.

A preliminary poking disturbed a community of mice whose nest was cozily excavated into the mattress stuffing. They literally sprayed out and fled squeaking to all parts of the house.

"Mouse traps," Ade said, and made another note on the list. I decided that alternative methods of mouse management might be suggested but not at this particular time, and laughed to myself as I remembered hiding a dozen traps at the bottom of the barrel of trash on our first stay in the cabin. Meanwhile, with the daven bed wet, where did we sleep?

Ade, half-hidden behind blankets heaped on his arms, said, "Seems we've been here before, only this time we've got bedding. I'll toss you for the sofa or its cushions—on the floor, that is."

I "won" the floor and was drifting off to sleep when I felt a little touch under my chin, then an unmoving soft warmth against my throat. I lifted my hand very slowly and gently— and touched fur. The mouse who was enjoying a warm nap was not alarmed by the light touch, but uncurled and walked delicately on pinpoint-clawed feet across my face and on to the floor.

I remembered how Great-Aunt Anne, who wouldn't have a trap or poison in her farm home, left a plate with crumbs on the kitchen floor and shreds of soft wool or cotton near it. "If they have food and something for nests, they don't need to bother anything else," she explained reasonably. She kept her food enclosed and put mothballs in her linens, though. Well, if it had worked for her, it should work for me—but I fell asleep thinking that it would take a miracle to persuade Ade to go along for a trial run.

2

We had thought a lot about the interior of the cabin while we were in Chicago. The logs were too stained to be restored to their original color, but we still wanted them to look like logs and not painted imitations. After all, cabins built of real logs were no longer common. We had once brightened an ugly apartment floor by covering it with a light-tan undercoat and then using a maple-color varnish. It seemed this should work on logs, too, so we had brought along the leftovers. Ade found oakum and patching asphalt in the icehouse, of all places. So, while he alternated between stuffing up openings where you could see daylight between the logs and clambering around on the roof, I cleaned logs as a preparation for painting.

Sounds simple, doesn't it? Take a cleaner and a sponge and go after it like any other wall. However, these logs were coated with a layer of grease, turned sticky with passing time, so the cleaner had to be a solvent applied with a rag. Blobs of resin had run and hardened, to be scraped and filed off. Some knots were still oozing the gluey stuff. Splinters waited for my rag and fingers. Spiders peered out of cracks and scuttled back. And you have no idea how a surface is increased when it is corrugated.

The weather was sunny, breezy, and stimulating. By the end of the week Ade had stopped the most important air and water leaks and I pointed proudly to one living-room wall—the smallest one—cleaned, under-coated, and varnished until it gleamed like polished maple as high as I could reach.

The ceiling was another matter. The soaked Celotex had dried, but was hard, wrinkled, and cracked. There was extra Celotex, Ade said, also in the icehouse, so he put up a make-shift scaffolding of boxes and planks and went to work on the ceiling, cutting out the ruined paneling, fitting in patches, and tacking them into place with thin strips of wood. But the room was so jammed with heavy furniture that every night he had to take the whole contraption down so that we had a place to sleep and every morning set it up again. I tried to work on the bottom of another wall, but this meant moving furniture night and morning as well as the scaffolding. A week of this made it abundantly clear that we were unlikely to get even one room done in years. Ade was showing signs of overstrain and neither one of us got enough rest.

On a Saturday morning as we picked at breakfast in a sullen silence I decided I'd had enough. "Look. This scramble has lost its charm. I'm starting to nag, you're wearing yourself into a sick spell, and we're getting nowhere. Let's see if we can rent a cabin from Hilda for the rest of our time. That way we can sleep in peace and get something done here."

I gave no thought to our bedraggled and spotted working clothes until we walked into the lobby of the Lodge and I noticed the interested glances of the summer guests, every one of them the last word in magazine-ad outdoor people. Hilda was behind the desk and I started to apologize, but she waved her expressive hands. "Think nothing of it. It's good local color for the tourists." Sven, entering from the kitchen, added, "It didn't take long to wash the city off you two."

"No," Hilda said, "but you look tired."

"We are," Ade said, and went on to explain.

Hilda nodded and Sven said, "Sure. We can fix you up, but we'll have to move you around unless one of the advance reservations is canceled. Maybe I've got a better idea. Did you know the place next to yours is for sale?"

"You mean the steep, wooded place to the east?" Ade asked.

"No. The one on the other side." He stared at us. "Haven't

you even walked over to look at it? There's a path through the woods."

"Never thought of it," I said and Hilda murmured something about wishing more people had as little nosiness in them.

Sven went on. "It's beautiful. A Mr. and Mrs. Larimer built it and have been coming to it off and on for twenty-five years or so. They used to have a caretaker but he's too old to live up here now, so they really want to sell. My point is that they just might rent it to you. It'd be cheaper and handier than one of our cabins."

Ade dug a pen out of his pocket. "Do you have their address?"

"You don't need it. They drove in yesterday. It's a wonder you didn't see their car when you passed on your way here."

At what seemed a decent interval after lunch, we walked slowly through the woods. The path, soft with fallen needles, circled great tree boles, dipped into hollows, was ridged with roots of cedar. The stillness of the big trees soothed us, and their coolness and scent. Although it was still July there were signs of fall—here and there a pale-yellow leaf on the wild sarsaparilla, a few resin-frosted pine cones, red squirrels chirping to themselves as they hunted mushrooms for winter storage.

Beyond the trees, the path entered a yard so cleared that it received much more sunshine than ours. The ground on our left was carpeted with bunchberries, already loaded with scarlet fruit. On our right was a row of tall, slim pin cherry trees, where thrushes were gobbling the last of the crop. The house was directly ahead, low and wide, built of curved siding and painted the softest of grays, with cream shutters and gay vermilion doors. A roundstone chimney with a leaping stag atop its weathervane rose from the center of the blue-shingled roof, and beyond the house towered a huge black spruce. Voices came faintly from the shaded lake side of the building.

At the back, where entrances always are when a house lies between a road and a lake, was a flagstoned patio. From it curving steps led to the top of a mossy stone retaining wall, which marked the edge of a wild garden. Ferns grew waist-high in its beds, which were outlined with granite boulders and separated by gravel paths, now much overgrown by a riot of pink and white and red sweet Williams. Beyond the garden, a winding path passed small outbuildings on its way under tall trees to a big gray gate just beyond the carport. This was a dream house, in its own garden.

Ade lifted a wrought-iron owl and pounded him against his perch on the door.

The Larimers, no longer young but sparkling with graciousness and vitality, settled us on a homespun-covered couch on the screened porch, which gave a wonderful view of the lake through thinned small trees. After we had introduced ourselves, Mrs. Larimer took me inside while Ade talked business with her husband. There were two spacious rooms, gleaming with knotty pine and separated by a wall with a handsome double fireplace, built of varied and colorful native stone and with a mantel as high as my head.

"I went back and forth across the lake, selecting the

stones," she said, and patted the fireplace. "There wasn't any road and we brought everything down the lake. I love Victorian things, so we furnished with them."

Against the golden-pine living-room walls the walnut and mahogany and gilded lamp brackets were rich in the bright sunlight from the large windows. The Berlin-work cover on the music stool looked inviting before the parlor organ. The bedroom windows were smaller and high, so that the large room was cool and shadowy under its high ceiling. The drawer handles on the old chest, carved into bunches of grapes, and the prim wash-hand-stand with its pink ironstone crockery made me think of sachets and bustles and Langtry bangs.

We went out through a tiny kitchen with hand-perforated pie chests and a wood range so small as to be almost playhouse size, to find the men lying prone and peering into a foundation ventilator with a lantern. Mrs. Larimer looked taken aback, so I told her about the brook we had excavated in our basement.

"Dear me! I hope that won't spoil my brook for you."

She led me down a path partly overgrown with ground pine and bunchberries to a miniature rushing stream, spanned by a small red wooden bridge. A black-green frog sat half-submerged on a rock and stared up at us.

"In the spring it thinks it's a river and roars all over the ground, and in the fall it gets discouraged and dies down to a trickle, but it's a very personable brook, isn't it?" She sighed. "I think I shall miss my brook."

.   .   .

The lamp flickered late in our drafty log cabin that night.

"It always comes out to this," I said, yawning. "He won't rent it. It's so lovely it makes this place look like a bad example in a sociology textbook. It's cheap for what it is, and she said I could buy what I wanted of the furniture. I'd like some of the pieces—and we can pay for it. But it would practically clean out our funds."

Ade lit another cigarette from the butt in his hand. "If I keep on livening up after we get home, I'll be back at work in no time. Then it would be fine, but I can't see you . . ."

"Don't start worrying about me. I make plenty to handle everything and you won't be all that much better if you don't get some rest now. That's what we came up here for. We've started this thing, so we might as well finish it. We'll have a gorgeous vacation spot and we can shine this cabin up before long. Then we can sell it."

It seemed straightforward, reasonable, and foolproof—at the time.

On Wednesday friends of the Larimers arrived with a station wagon. On Thursday they left, hauling the furniture I did not buy. The Larimers, saying they would leave the keys at the bank and the signing to their agent there, headed for their home near Minneapolis.

On Friday evening we drove slowly back from the Village, happy but very tired, perhaps because things had required such fast decisions. In any case, the Larimer property was ours, along with a burl walnut wardrobe and matching Welsh cupboard, the chest with the carved drawer handles, a maple daybed, a walnut drop-leaf table, the wash-hand-stand complete with crockery, and *all* the lamps. Not only were they antique delights, but I had had a plethora of trying to read by the glow of one lamp.

The moon-silvered roof of the Lodge was brighter than its lighted windows as we slipped by in the deep shadows of the road. The headlights picked out two points of fiery topaz, and a deer, turned into a streak of leaping grace, crossed the road in one bound and crashed through thick brush that closed tightly behind. I had never seen a deer before, and this sight was bewitching, unreal—something trapped in the timelessness of the moonlight and kept from days gone by.

The sense of enchantment held as we went through the gates into the carport and, lights off, sat in a blackness made deeper by the blue brightness that spilled through the trees. We made our way in silence down the path to the waiting house—a strange abode drowned in a waving sea of ghostly ferns.

The silence went away in ripples from a ferocious squawl. I stopped, frightened of I knew not what. Ade grasped my arm and pointed above the roof. A big owl was flapping his noiseless way through the silver night. My heartbeat slowed and the owl seemed a fitting part of the shimmering dream.

Ade opened the door and I stood, watching the room come out of the shadows as he lighted the lamps. The walls picked up the glow so that the near-emptiness of the room did not matter. The Welsh cupboard watched us from its corner. Ade touched a match to a fire, laid ready in the fireplace. Before it, an unexpected walnut rocker invited someone to sit on its ruby plush cushion. On the mantel a sampler greeted us with its cross-stitched "Home Sweet Home" and a delicate bit of basswood scrollwork in a gilded frame said "Welcome." Between these was a small bottle, labeled "Cheers!" with two small glasses turned upsidedown beside it.

"I feel like Alice in Wonderland," I purred as Ade filled the glasses. "Are you sure that bottle doesn't have another label saying 'Drink me'?"

I dropped the cushion to the floor and curled up on it. Ade settled in the rocker. The flavor of the brandy lingered and its sting was unfamiliar because such frivolities had lost their attraction for me during the busy war years. I wondered if it would make me sleepy after so long a time, but it only drove away my weariness. I smiled at Ade, relaxed and rocking. The flames filled the corners with dancing light. A down draft forced a puff of fragrant smoke into the room. I leaned contentedly against Ade's knees.

But magic is ephemeral and I finally looked away from the fire. "Are you hungry?"

"Starved."

A numbness came over me. "We should have bought something in town."

"Yes. I suppose I'll have to go next door . . ."

I sat up abruptly. "No. I'd forgotten. Mrs. Larimer said she'd put any leftovers . . ."

I hurried to the kitchen where the icebox produced canned chicken soup, canned limas, some celery, bread, butter, and coffee, enough of it for the night and morning. The thoughtful Larimers had even laid a fire in the little range and filled the inevitable galvanized pail with fresh water. All went well until

I looked in the cupboard and saw the usual assortment of glasses. We had not bought the Larimers' dishes, and there was no silverware, either. If I asked Ade to drag dishes through the woods at this hour, he would probably sit down and howl—and justly. So we had soup in water glasses, limas in highball glasses, buttered toast and celery in turned-over pan lids, and coffee in cheese-spread glasses. It was all very festive, but you ought to try drinking lima beans out of a glass.

But this was only a bubble of laughter in the magic of the night. We sat a long time before the dying fire, thinking little, saying nothing. It is hard to leave the changing moods of burning logs. When there was nothing left but scarlet coals with flickers of purple above them, we went into the bedroom where the old mirror reflected us as greenish ghosts, lighted by spectral lamps.

The daybed, which looked large enough for two sleepers, did not prove to be. When I rammed an arm into the turned woodwork of the back of the bed for the dozenth time and woke as I had been doing regularly all night, I was annoyed, almost angry, that so commonplace an inconvenience had intruded after our perfect evening. Then I saw the first dawn light graying the windows and instinct told me that the cure for my irritation was outside. I put on a warm robe and carried the walnut rocker to the porch.

The light was a mistiness that revealed shape without detail. The lake was a sheet of gray satin, stretched tightly between our shore and some haziness beyond. The trees were tall, blurred pillars, topped by black-green clouds, and the ground was covered by soft shadows that seemed to have no source. The damp air carried a faint scent of honeysuckle. Abruptly, yet completely in place, life moved into the stillness in the form of a weasel, twisting his agile brown-and-white body among the roots of the big spruce beyond the porch, to reach a hole and vanish down it.

Slowly the lake changed from gray to violet and the false dawn gave way to a glow of rose, rising far to the northeast. The cool breath of the dawn wind rustled the high leaves of the birch and set the aspen quivering. The sky lost its paleness, a gull wheeled against cloudless blue, and the water began to roll in bands of mauve and azure. A chipmunk scurried up a dandelion's stem to pick winged seeds for his breakfast. A robin chirruped. A bee buzzed over a black-eyed Susan. Then the woods were green and the lake was cobalt flecked with gold, rimmed by the rippled hills of its distant shore. Far, far away loons laughed at each other, and the early sunlight pushed through the screening to fall warm on my hands.

3

The two-house arrangement worked perfectly. The Larimers had left a well-stocked woodshed and we ate morning and evening either before the fireplace or on the porch, depending on the temperature, because northern summers have their chilly times. To solve the sleeping problem, we carried the now dry daven bed through the woods from the log house. This made it plain that I *could* help move furniture, but had no flair for it, and also opened up considerable space in the log-cabin living room. With more room for us to walk around in, the repairs and decorating began to move right along. But the gentlest and most-treasured memory of those days is that of Mrs. Mouse's miracle.

On the Wednesday after we went to look at the Larimer house, I was trying to make some headway against the dust that crept in the log cabin's doors and windows and fell from the ceiling repairs. Ahead of my broom, something moved slowly across the kitchen linoleum, something that looked like an animated bit of dusty lint. I leaned down.

A deer mouse, her gray coat ruffled, her white gloves and face bedraggled, was feebly creeping along, useless hind legs dragging. I picked her up. She did not seem to be in pain, but she was pitiably weak. Her strongest attempts to bite my finger did not even dent the skin. She seemed to have been the victim of an accident that had broken her back and paralyzed her hind quarters. Looking for further injuries, I turned her over. The sad little mouse was a nursing mother.

I called Ade down from his scaffolding. No matter how he felt about mice, he was basically gentle and compassionate, and I needed advice. I explained the situation and asked, "What should we do?"

"I suppose," he said hesitantly, "we should put her out of her misery . . . but maybe if we feed her . . ."

Mrs. Mouse put out her miniature pink tongue and licked tentatively at my finger.

"She might recover," I said. "She's a pretty little thing."

Mrs. Mouse tried to prove this by washing her white-gloved hands.

Ade settled the matter. "We'll fix her up close by the stove. Nature is a great healer. I hate to think of the little ones . . . waiting somewhere . . ."

She lunched on oatmeal, bread crumbs, and diluted canned milk before she crawled onto an old wool sock and went to sleep. By evening she was much stronger and even moved one of the crippled legs a little. In fact, she moved about with astonishing ease and did not seem to be suffering physically, although her milk-swollen little body must have been acutely uncomfortable. But she spent every waking moment when she was not eating in the center of the doorway between the kitchen and living room, half-lying, half-sitting, her head low, her dull eyes half-closed, her soft fur ungroomed.

"She's the saddest-looking thing I ever saw," Ade said. "She looks like she's grieving—overwhelmed with despair."

"Mouse mothers and human mothers may have more in common than some people think," I observed. "But she can't tell us where her babies are, and she wouldn't, even if she could."

"I wonder how she was hurt?" Ade looked at the heavy storage drawers under the kitchen counter. "She might have been crawling around in there and been caught when a drawer opened or closed." Hastily he began to peer into the drawers. Then: "Here they are!"

On top of a wide-mouthed jar of crumbs that I had care-lessly put into the drawer without its lid was a nicely constructed spherical nest, soft as the finest silk, as carefully made as for winter quarters, with a round entrance on top. Lying on the chilly, bare wood of the drawer bottom were four infant mice, not more than three or four days old, who had crawled out of the nest. Were they alive? Timidly, I touched one. Such a fragile, helpless, tiny pink creature—and so cold. He squirmed in the way of all babies, and feebly moved incredibly delicate limbs, uttering a squeak so faint it was hardly a sound. I touched the others, one by one.

"They're all alive," I said happily. "Do you suppose we can give them back to her without injuring them? They're much too small and frail just to pick up with your fingers."

He handed me a sheet of thin, stiff paper. Carefully I rolled one of the little fellows onto it and carried him to the warm sock by the stove. Then I lifted Mrs. Mouse from the doorway and set her down beside the sock. She must have been utterly terrified, but she neither moved nor looked up. Then that whisper of a squeak came again.

Mrs. Mouse's ears perked up. Her eyes lost their dullness. She scurried onto the sock and stopped short, quivering all over. Slowly she reached out a paw and verified the reality of what she saw and smelled. Then, squeaking and chirping, she patted her child all over carefully. She licked him clean and tucked him cozily underneath her for his long-awaited meal. Courageous to the tips of her whiskers, she looked up at our huge bulks as though to tell us that this was her own, and that she was prepared to defend him at all costs.

Hastily we brought the rest of her family to her and moved the nest nearby. Mrs. Mouse was suddenly quite busy, settling

her family, examining her nest, popping over to get a bite to eat.

"I never saw so much happiness in one little body," Ade said. "It's like someone had turned on a light down there. She's . . . she's . . ."

"Transfigured is the word. That's what miracles do."

When we finished our meal, Mrs. Mouse was sitting in her old place in the doorway. Full of mousy high spirits, she was busily working out a technique for washing her face with one paw while she supported herself with the other. Her little eyes glittered brightly at us, clearly saying that if there had ever been a baby mouse it was news to her. She had hidden them cleverly indeed, and had even moved the nest piecemeal in the short time we had not been looking.

Now her days were full of housekeeping and mouse-rearing, but such free time as she had was spent sitting in her old place in the doorway, calmly surveying the kitchen as though she had not a single responsibility.

Some three weeks later, I awoke to the sound of outraged and urgent squeaking in the kitchen. Mrs. Mouse's children, all four of them, had fallen into the sink. I rescued them, dried them off, presented them with some cake crumbs, and sent them home. This happened regularly for the next five days, and at the end of that time the small, fat, gray balls were calmly waiting for me when I got up.

We partially solved their problem by leaving a short length of board propped in the sink corner, so that they could crawl out. But they usually didn't and, as soon as I appeared, they lined up in a neat row and waited to be fed. They liked chocolate cookies, which probably were much too rich for them, and corn bread, which should be fine for growing mice. They soon outgrew the sink game, but came regularly for their morning treat.

I had some onions that had sprouted, so put them upright in a glass on the windowsill until the tops should be large enough for Ade to eat as green onions. To my amazement, the young mice found onion greens a treat. The height of the shoot posed a problem but the youngsters managed well. One of them would climb from the bottom of the window frame to the top of the glass and up the onion sprouts. The added weight bent them down and the others pounced on the tender tips and nibbled. Then one of the three who had eaten changed places so that the first one got his share.

One day, when they were well grown, I was sweeping the kitchen with the door open and they hopped out, to hurry up the hill and go about the business of being independent woods mice.

Only then did Mrs. Mouse cease her quiet, diversionary vigils in the kitchen doorway. Without any attempt at concealment, she moved her nest from the old galosh in the clothes closet where she had reared her family to one end of the wool sock by the stove, which she used as a sort of patio. Her hind legs were hopelessly paralyzed, but she put this briskly aside and scurried about on her front legs almost as rapidly as a four-legged mouse. She hunted eagerly for crumbs that I dropped for her, and occasionally surprised us by climbing up one of the India-print throws and appearing in a friendly manner on a chair arm.

She often sat contentedly by her food dish, her head held high as with the knowledge of a task well done. Ade, who long before had scratched "mouse traps" from our shopping list, took turns with me in keeping her supplied with the food and water she was not able to find for herself.

It was not until the first red leaves were showing on the maple that her dish at last remained untouched and we knew that Mrs. Mouse's brave little days had ended.

4

For the first time in my life I found the early fall days sad, partly because I missed Mrs. Mouse and even more because it was almost time for us to return to Chicago. The trip had been a complete success as far as its main purpose, to improve Ade's health, was concerned. He felt fine and looked ready for anything, but instead of pining for the intellectual challenge of my research work, I longed almost to the point of weeping to see more of the forest and its changes and inhabitants. The work in the cabin had been satisfying, but it had not left me enough time for our surroundings. However, the free days were gone. On the last Friday, we packed, closed the cabins, said good-bye to Hilda and Sven, and drove toward the Village.

The Trail was a ribbon threaded through a loose-woven fabric in autumn colors. The verges were banked with the blue of wild asters and the white of late daisies and pearly everlasting. Wild buckwheat leaves and stems covered gravelly spaces with deep-crimson carpets. Beyond, the birches were gold and the maples like torches, shading from bright copper to flame red. The mountain ash trees, their limbs bent under the weight of clustered scarlet berries, had leaves of every shade from deep green to pale lemon to blood red. Behind these the balsam tops showed purple cones gleaming with resin and brown spruce cones decorated their treetops like exotically colored flowers. And always in the background stood the scattered pines—old, dignified, dark—rusted now with the needles they were discarding before winter.

As we moved through this blaze of color, I knew that I was not suffering from post-vacation blues. I wanted to stay here and if I never entered a laboratory again I would not miss it. I looked sideways at Ade. Aside from a rather too thoughtful expression, he looked better than he had since long before his illness, and his well-being—and mine—were probably due to our having been able, for two glorious months, to eat when we were hungry and sleep as long as we needed, something that time clocks and company schedules had made impossible during our city years.

"Do you realize how old I am?" I asked abruptly.

"Forty-four. Why?"

"Well . . . if I work another eleven years I can retire on a reduced pension."

"So?"

"I'm thinking that we'll both be too old by then to ever live up here."

He shrugged. "I've been thinking something like that all the way in. And that once I'm working again I'll have to go all the way . . . till I'm sixty-five . . . if I'm to get pensioned off . . . if I live so long. Because of this break now. And that'll be twenty-one years." He slowed down as a hare, feet already turned white, leaped across the road. "It's been wonderful, though."

His tone was noncommittal but he was humming "The Birmingham Jail"—"And twenty-one years, boys, is a mighty long time"—under his breath. I was pretty sure he didn't want to go back to Chicago any more than I did. It seemed I ought to at least talk around the idea a bit.

"Didn't Martin tell you he could sublease our apartment for the time we'd be gone?" I asked.

"Yes. Said he could get three hundred, maybe three fifty a month for it. I didn't think we'd want transients in there, though."

"Quite right," I said. "But we could live up here on the difference between that and the hundred fifty we pay for the place unfurnished. No utilities or daily transportation or expensive clothes or . . . oh, lots of things."

"We'd have food and taxes, and winter clothes and the like. And we'd have to do without a lot of things we've always taken for granted."

"There'd be others to take their place. I'm sure of it. And I've never minded cold."

"How about your job?" he asked. "You've worked hard to get where you are."

"I know, but there's no place to go now except into management, and that isn't for me, even if they'd put a woman on the staff. And I don't owe them anything. My big job is all set for the field testing and the patent. I'd have nothing to do with the testing and everybody has to sign away patents in a place like that. In the six years I've been there they've paid me maybe one per cent of what the device will bring them while the patent's in force, and the earnings won't stop when the patent runs out. I've not stabbed anybody in the back as I moved up, either. The people who do haven't got what it takes. So I could leave with a clear conscience."

"It's your job," Ade said. "You'll know what you want to do when you get back."

We hit the road construction then and, although progress must have been made, I couldn't tell it. Maybe there were less boulders strewn around in the mud. But even though I hadn't been over it since we arrived, it didn't seem to be anything to get excited about now. Probably I had already learned to take such things in stride.

We had a number of errands in the Village and, to save time for the miles we had to cover, we split up. Ade dropped me at the county building to get a plat of our land to use for planning during the winter and it was while I was walking from there to meet him in a restaurant that I came to the telephone building. I stopped and looked, first, across the Village to Lake Superior, gray and violet and smoking with mist, then back past the cleared hillsides to the edge of the forest.

There is a time for everything, and I knew with certainty that this was our time for moving to the woods—if ever we were to do it.

If we went back to Chicago and into our old routines, we'd

stay in them longer than we thought. In fewer years than eleven, pension notwithstanding, I'd be too old to leave a desk job and undertake the hard and even dangerous living the winter woods might bring. If we did not go back, we had a chance of working into the rougher way of life.

Money would be the biggest problem. We couldn't live off a sublease indefinitely because we'd need many of our own things if we were to be as comfortable as possible. But we would manage. We always had.

I was sure Ade would agree with me. He'd never been afraid to try anything, but he'd be doubtful as to how I would stand up under the hard work and possible periods of insecurity. Well, I'd have to show him.

So, on that golden afternoon in 1954, I went into the Village telephone exchange and, when my boss's voice came over the miles to me, said: "Hi. Uh . . . I just called up to say goodbye."

3 The
Unexpected . . .

In the middle of the week, when I might have been studying my graphs and data at the lab, I pulled out the last nail and Ade stacked up the last board of what had been the clothes closet and the cupboard over the trapdoor. I laid the crowbar on the kitchen table and sat down to rest before I scraped away the remarkable amount of dirt that had accumulated in hidden corners.

"It's a real improvement," I said. "More light in the kitchen, and a third more floor space in the bedroom."

"Even so," Ade said, filling the washbasin from the kettle and reaching for soap, "the next time the census gets to us we'll be classed as the underprivileged. No conveniences, no entertainment, no social advantages . . ."

"Oh fish! The more conveniences, the less exercise, and if all the things we have to see and do aren't entertainment enough, I'll eat my hat. As far as social . . ."

"Whoa! *I'm* not saying it. I personally feel very highly

privileged." He reached for a towel. "I doubt that we'll get a reply to the wire I sent Martin about the lease for a few days yet, but I ought to get your formal letter of resignation into the mail today, don't you think? It'll have to wait for Saturday if I don't. Mail twice a week now, you know."

"Oh Lord! I'd forgotten about it." I grabbed pen and paper from behind the crowbar. "I'm listed AWOL in the personnel files, I suppose," I added, writing.

He went whistling up the path and as soon as I heard him drive away I flopped on the sofa. Maybe I'd been the strong one during our last weeks in Chicago, but I surely wasn't here. I'd just rest a minute before I got the broom . . . and Ade was shaking me.

"I'd have let you sleep, but there's a letter from Martin," he said.

"What can he get for the apartment?" I asked, waking up with a snap.

"He's selling the building. He can either store our stuff or ship it. His mover has a trip scheduled to Duluth and Hibbing, to leave next Monday."

I felt as though I were suffocating. First we had had adequate money and a house we couldn't live in. Now we had two habitable houses and some money, not much. One might consider this a step forward, but I wasn't sure.

"With apartments like hen's teeth down there, this seems to close once and for all the way back," I said.

Ade nodded. "And it would take a fortune to store all our stuff for any length of time."

"We've got a house next door that needs furniture. You

might say both of them do," I said. "How much do you suppose it'll cost to move?"

Ade thought. "Based on what we've paid to move in Chicago and the extra distance . . . I'd guess around five hundred."

"Well, that'll cut into the money we thought we had for this winter, but there'll be quite a bit left, and there's still the money in my company pension fund. I was keeping it for a surprise. They'll send it as soon as they process the resignation. I don't know how much it is but plenty to carry us a year, maybe more." I looked at the letter. "This has been two days in the post office and it's Wednesday now. He must have got the wire you phoned to Duluth from the Village and rushed the answer. I don't see that we have a choice. Can you call long distance from the Lodge?"

"I'll try. If not, I'll have to go to town to call."

He was back in less than an hour. "The stuff'll be here Tuesday. Martin'll pay the bill and we'll reimburse him. Sven will get a couple of men to help, and Hilda says they're having some late vacationists next week and she'll give the movers lunch with her guests."

I called the Lodge to thank the Petersons and Ade went next door to measure the floor areas. Then, with roughly scaled plans and bits of cardboard to represent the furniture, we tried to fit things in. It was soon evident that our belongings from ten rooms and assorted closets couldn't possibly be squeezed into both cabins, even if we got rid of some of the furniture now in them. We compromised by assigning positions to larger pieces like the grand piano and the beds, and mentally storing small leftovers in the outbuildings.

The big van pulled in on schedule but was too heavily loaded to climb the steep hill just past our gate. There was no place for it to turn around. Result: it stood on a slant with everything inside threatening to slide out the back end. This complication was alleviated by using logs as props. The logs, of course, had to be readjusted as each item was taken out, so Ade tended the logs while the others carried in the furniture and I pointed out where things were to go. Then came grumbling thunder and the heavy, widespread clouds that mean a big rain.

The driver of the van had to be in Hibbing the following morning and was worried about getting stuck—and one could hardly blame him. So it all ended with some forty boxes and barrels, along with a studio couch and several chairs, tucked out of the rain in the carport. A washstand, removed from an apartment being remodeled and sent courtesy of Martin for some remote future with running water, was left standing beside the gate. All we needed was a sign saying JUNK. I don't think it was entirely the gloomy weather or the unfinished job that gave me a hollow feeling as the van, really our last link with Chicago, drove away.

Everything was beautifully packed but in spite of reasonable labeling I usually had to open at least three containers to find what I wanted. In a burst of energy, Ade unpacked all the books first, and they lay everywhere in foot-trapping heaps, the bookshelves being of the knock-down variety—and hidden in some carton. And it almost goes without saying that immediately useful things, like tools and tableware, were in the last cartons to be opened.

But things were taking shape by Friday night, and early Saturday I decided to wash my white Nylon curtains that had looked fine in Chicago but dust-gray in the clear light of the woods. Here I began to miss running water. It was easy enough to soak and squish them clean in a big dishpan, but rinsing was another matter. The only way seemed to take them to the lake and dunk them. That much soap wasn't going to disturb anything in a lake as large and deep as this one.

While I was kneeling on a rock, enjoying this ancient and airy way of doing the washing, a man and a woman approached in a boat, the vacationers from the Lodge, I supposed. They stared and stared, and finally cut to trolling speed and came in. I smiled.

The woman watched for a while, then: "What *are* you doing?"

"Washing curtains."

"But why here?" she persisted.

"My goodness!" I said, in as incredulous a voice as I could manage. "Why on earth should I do it anywhere else when all the water's down here?"

They more or less fled and I've never been able to decide whether they thought I was addled, rude, or only a simple backwoods type.

The day was one of those lovely ones after rain and the breeze had the curtains dry in a flash. I hung them and, while I waited for Ade to bring the mail, looked around me. The sun poured through the white curtains onto the yellow pine walls and the pale-green shag rugs. The shelves of the Welsh cupboard were really elegant with the gold-rimmed, pastel-colored floral plates that my mother had painted when she was young. Its top glistened with pressed glass and old silver. My mahogany baby grand held a tall cut-glass vase filled with long-stemmed blue beads and the last of the daisies. The rest of the furniture was maple, with ruby and green cushions. The assembled bookshelves held books wherever they could reasonably be put.

The bedroom had white ruffles at the windows and white lace I had made years before on the beds. My cross-stitched rugs with roses were worth all my labor, and really belonged with the old chest and wardrobe. I had put two matched rockers in front of the bedroom fireplace and it was going to be wonderful to sit and dream in front of the fire on chilly nights before we crawled into bed to watch the embers die as we fell asleep.

I stood a long time looking at a maple sewing table, made some two hundred years before by one of Ade's early grandfathers. I could see the man, patiently carving its spool trim, while his young wife cooked on their hearth. The things they had sought in the New World were, in a way, the same things Ade and I sought here. Perhaps the table was a talisman.

I went outside to sit on a handmade bench at the edge of a small flagstoned area from which the porch door opened. It was October now and the flaming red and glowing yellow that had decorated the Trail on our abortive start for Chicago had reached our sheltered spot, only here the dark evergreens were more prominent and the Lake made a background of deep, dark blue, edged by aspen gold on its far shore.

Ade came through the house, flipped a long envelope to me, and opened another.

"The insurance check," I said, glancing at the return address, then looked up at his sharp exclamation. "What . . ."

He handed me the moving bill. It was almost twice what we had expected. I felt my breakfast stir uneasily. "This can't be right, can it?"

"It's right," Ade said. "Our things weighed a lot—we might have expected that when we weren't there to throw out junk we don't need here. And neither of us had time to think how much it would cost to pack all the little stuff."

"What must be, must be. This'll carry us," I said, opening the letter I held. "Funds of your company's retirement plan are, as of August 1, administered by us. Your claim . . . delay due to changeover . . . settle in full . . . about four months from date of filing . . ." I shook my head and read it again, more carefully. "My God! That means sometime in January!"

"The fire insurance bill came today, too," Ade said in a flat voice. "Unless my memory's at fault, we can pay both bills and eat for two months, or ask the agent to carry the insurance and eat for three."

"But we'll have to have an oil stove in here . . . you can't get enough wood without help and you couldn't heat with just the fireplaces, anyway. And we've got to have heavy clothes. We can't grow fur like animals." I paused, then said inanely, "Something will turn up."

"Something will damn well have to turn up."

I shook myself mentally. "We both said that wrong. We'll have to *make* something turn up. First, I'm going to write to the man who's been after me for a couple of years, wanting to buy my biggest set of metallurgical books. They're no earthly use to me here . . . except to bring in four hundred dollars.

We'll make it to January with that and what little we'll have left otherwise, even with all the things we'll have to buy."

"What if you want to go back into the business?"

"I won't. Every technical library has 'em, anyway."

"Okay. I've an idea of my own about money. I was going to put it off until spring because there's still a lot to do to get us really settled. Besides wiring the log cabin so we'll have power. Now I think I'd better look into it right away."

"What is it?" I asked, much interested.

"Don't be nosy," he said, and I resigned myself to burning up with curiosity.

When I woke next morning I was stiff and aching. I even had chills. Hilda had told me nobody caught cold or flu here unless someone brought the bugs in, but maybe we'd moved them with the furniture. I crawled miserably out of bed, thinking that I didn't have *time* for the flu. Then I glanced out the window. The ground was sprinkled with frost and leaves were tumbling from the trees. The thermometer on the bedroom mantel read twelve above zero. I wasn't ill. I was half frozen.

Stove lids began to clank in the kitchen as I hurried into icy jeans and shirt.

"Wonder where that long underwear is I had left over from the Navy," Ade said as I joined him and rubbed my cold hands together in the warm air rising from the stove.

"I haven't had any since I was ten," I chattered, feeling the side of the lukewarm kettle.

"I'll get fires going in the fireplaces." He scooped up an armload of kindling and called back as he went out: "My heavy Navy blankets are probably wherever the underwear is."

"Just in the living room," I said. "A fire, I mean. We can save wood and build one in the bedroom later so the beds won't feel like they're lined with frozen custard."

The day was mostly a matter of trying to keep warm, and when the early dark came we were sitting in the rockers before the bedroom fire, eating spaghetti. The room was fairly warm. Ade had on his long-handled woollies, his pajamas, and a terry robe. I wore a hundred-dollar beige gabardine suit over my jeans and shirt. The heavy blankets were on the beds, along with some fuzzy red spreads.

"Did you call Sven and ask about the stoves and oil?" I asked, getting up to pour tea from the pot keeping warm on the hearth.

"Yes." I looked up and waited. Ade shrugged. "He said the mail order can supply any kind of stove we'll need but it may take a while. He and Hilda may go on a vacation this fall. If they're here when the stoves come, he'll bring them from town in his truck. If they're gone, we'll have to haul them in the car. This because they'll come by freight and deliveries drop dead up the Trail after Labor Day. And that means no oil."

"So we'll have to use wood?"

"Yes, but there's more—and I didn't need Sven to tell me this. We'll not be able to heat this house once it's really cold. It isn't insulated, and it's out of the question to do a big job like that now. I didn't realize it until this afternoon when it was thirty-eight outside and I couldn't get it above seventy in the other room. Sven didn't know. He was upset when I told him. The place was built for summer, and I didn't think of insulation or how it would be in winter any more than you did. There wasn't any reason to when we bought it."

I looked around the beautiful room I was not to enjoy until heaven knew when, and felt discouraged. "I'm fresh out of ideas," I said. "How about you?"

"We'll have to move into the log cabin if we don't want to freeze. This cold snap probably won't last long but it isn't going to warm up and stay warm."

"But there's no way to really heat over there until we get a stove. The range helps but . . ."

"Sure there is. Carl's furnace."

I thought of that grim-visaged barrel stove, as determined looking as I should be feeling, and began to laugh. "It just about matches the place, too, doesn't it?"

The next day we moved furniture and ended with the studio couch and the daybed in the log-cabin living room, the mattressless single bed stored in the little extra cabin, and the sofa on the summer-house porch, where we had already put the daven bed. This opened up space and gave us comfortable places to sleep, even though we had to make and remake the beds as though we were living in an efficiency apartment. By the time we got the barrel stove inside, I thought my arms would fall out of their sockets, but Ade went cheerily on, building a high shelf along the south living-room wall and screwing clothes hooks into the logs beneath it. I hung more of the paper drapes from its outer edge and we had a make-shift clothes closet. He was outside brushing rust off sections of stove pipe and I was putting linens into the heavy bedroom chest when Hilda called from outside.

"Things happen in such a hurry," she said, coming in and

setting a potted begonia on the counter. "It's full of buds. See? Pink ones. Put it in the south window. It'll bloom all winter and do wonders for you when you're down in the dumps . . . and you will be. Nobody's cheerful all the time."

"Not even you?" I asked, thanking her and carrying the plant into the bedroom. Its leaves shone like textured silk and Ade could build a little shelf inside the window, which had no inner sill.

"Least of all me! Well, anyway—my sister in Minneapolis fell and cracked a vertebra, so we're going down there for the winter. We'll be back a couple of times, I think, to finish up things . . . while she's still in the cast in the hospital . . . but we're leaving early tomorrow. We thought we'd see how you're getting along before we go."

"We'll be lost without you," I said, feeling lost already.

"Oh, you'll do all right," she said, leading the way into the living room. "It isn't as hard as some people make out to the tourists. You just have to fit yourselves to the weather. My, those curtains brighten the room."

I showed her our shelf closet with some small pride. "Of course, it's only temporary . . ."

She laughed so hard her face turned bright pink against her silver-gilt hair.

"Up here," she finally stuttered, "there's nothing as permanent as a temporary fixture. Just wait and see. Ten years from now you'll have something behind that curtain. And be sure Ade braces the shelf good or the whole thing'll come down . . . you'll pile so much on it. I know."

I smiled doubtfully and she dug a piece of paper from the

pocket of her brown ski pants. "I brought you my bread recipe. Up here you need one where you don't have to worry about drafts and temperatures. This bread'll raise in a snowstorm."

I was thanking her again and wondering what she'd say if I told her I'd never even seen anyone make a loaf of bread, when the outside door opened and Sven said, "We've got a little project for the next couple of hours. Have the coffee hot when we get back." The door closed.

"That man," Hilda said, shaking her head as she sat down. "He'd never think you don't run a lodge and mightn't have pounds of extra coffee. But everybody's always drinking it except some of the old woodsmen, and they get away with gallons of tea."

"We've plenty of both," I said, and settled to enjoy myself in the light of Hilda Peterson's great good will.

After they had gone and we had eaten, Ade suggested a little walk. This was so unusual after such a strenuous day that I wondered why and said, "Fine," even though my muscles had about as much spring as a blown-out tire.

We went slowly up the steep path to the road, where tough grass had begun to cover the newly bared earth and bright-eyed chipmunks popped in and out of doorways between the boulders that partially lined the ditches on each side. Halfway up I stopped, ostensibly to look around, actually to catch my breath. The bare branches of the maple brush were a scarlet fence against the sky and their drying leaves made a tapestry of muted browns on the earth. The road above and the house below were hidden behind curved walls of trees. It startled me to see how easily the forest hid the small works of men. Even the old driveway was quietly and slowly being made part of the forest floor again.

"I suppose it would be convenient to be able to drive down to the house again," I said, "but someday this is going to be the loveliest path in the woods. Even *that* will be beautiful." I pointed to the massive tangle of a big uprooted stump on the far edge of one of the ditches.

"I was thinking I ought to cut it up and burn it," Ade said as we walked on.

"No. Let it stay, and grow over with whatever wants to grow on it," I said, prompted by the beginning of a new understanding. "Natural things are never really ugly. It takes men to create a dump."

"I'll use the time and energy to build a toboggan, then. For hauling things down this path in winter—such as our wood. After it's split, that is." We stopped beside a neat stack of some twenty small logs at the side of the road. "Sven says we'll need about forty loads like this one."

"But how'll you get them? And where?"

"Along the Trail. Where this came from. Last year they cleared where they're going to widen next and stacked the logs in eight-foot lengths on the road shoulder. Some fellow bought it, but he isn't here now. When he shows up, we pay him a dollar a cord, which is two loads like this one. He'll come to the Lodge and Sven'll send him on. As to hauling it—I got a trailer hitch from Sven and we put it on our car. He's lending us his trailer. I also bought his extra chain saw—

on credit. I'd have to get one later anyway, and now I'll use it to cut up logs we can't lift."

"We?"

"We. Carrying logs isn't a one-man job unless you're bigger than I am or they're small ones."

"When do we start?" I inquired, trying unsuccessfully to picture myself as a lumberjack.

"Tomorrow, if this breeze from the south doesn't bring rain."

2

The breeze brought only warmth, so that we slept in the log cabin without needing a fire and started out in a morning that might have been a credit to June except for the bare branches. The Lodge was blanketed with that peculiar silence that covers untenanted buildings. Something whispered through me, akin to fear but different—a dim and uncertain comprehension of our aloneness. On my earlier day of trial in the cabin, I had been expecting Ade to return and I could have walked to Hilda and Sven if necessary. Now Ade was here, but we were the only ones of our kind living within many square miles on our side of the border. Every living creature around us was as incomprehensible to us as we were to them.

We rolled along a stretch of the Trail that extended beyond our side road toward where the Trail ended, deep in the forest. Here the tree-fringed verges rose higher and higher, first on one side of us and then the other, as the road wound through the hills. We seemed to shrink and grow less important by the minute. Then Ade stopped and broke the spell by pointing out a stack of birch logs near the edge of a high embankment.

"We throw it down into the ditch, carry it up to the road, and load it on the trailer. But first I'll find a spot to turn around where I can see at least a reasonable distance in both directions."

He found it, and we were directly across the road when a monstrous truck, bearing one of the enormous cats used in road construction, roared around a curve a quarter of a mile away. It came on like a locomotive while we backed, turned, and jackknifed. All I could think of was those old-time animated cartoons where some unfortunate animal was turned into a paper-thin wafer on a street by a steamroller. With a final swoop we pulled up on the shoulder as the monster rocked us with its air wave as it passed.

"I'd hate to meet that driver now," Ade said, mopping his forehead. "I'll bet he ruined his brakes."

Muttering something about the "damn road," he got out of the car and started up the embankment. I followed, trying to swallow what seemed to be a wad of cotton stuck in my throat. The slope was steeper than it looked and was composed of a particularly mobile kind of gravel that rolled underfoot like glass balls. I could only scramble along behind Ade, presenting a bent-over rear that must have been a treat.

When I reached the top I moved to the stack, doubtful but willing, and heaved tentatively on the end of one of the smallest logs. To my utter astonishment, it moved. Ade looked relieved when he saw that I was grinning.

"You take the rear," he directed. "We just lift it onto our shoulders and then you follow me. And don't shove! I don't want to go down the bank with it."

The log took up its position on our shoulders with such slight effort that I decided this was going to be pretty easy. Then Ade started forward without warning. The log was rough, caught the wool of my jacket, and yanked me ahead, but somehow my feet were left behind. While I flailed my arms and squealed, the log dropped from my shoulder and I landed on hands and knees.

"Did you trip over something?" Ade asked solicitously as he came back, apparently to check for broken bones.

"I did not!" I said with force. "And before we proceed, let me remind you that the front end of the horse ought to let the hind end know what it's going to do!"

I gave him high marks for not laughing.

After we had collected a dozen logs, Ade brought his newly acquired chain saw from the car and I sat on a boulder, wondering if my left shoulder really was pulp, and enjoying the satisfaction of watching someone else work.

His red shirt and the saw's yellow paint against the dark-green forest, the red-brown earth, and the banded gray logs, with the hyacinth-blue sky over all looked like a magazine ad for a lumber company. There was, however, no resemblance to those chain-saw ads in which some immaculately clad young man bends gracefully to snip off a small log section for the barbecue. Ade had a knee jammed against the stack as a

brace while the whirling chain snarled and back-spat fine chips and oil around his legs. His hands were tight on the supporting handle and the pistol grip that controlled the speed. Smoke and sparks and a deafening roar came from the exhaust of the little engine. But in a surprisingly short time the log was sectioned and Ade straightened, wiping sweat from his face and leaving oil streaks in its place.

"That's one load. Think you're up to another?"

"Sure," I said brightly, wondering if I could get to my feet without help.

"I'll push these off the bank and you can come on down and help me load up. Then I'll take them to the house while you stay here and rest. It'll be no job for me to shove 'em off the trailer."

When he drove away, I struggled up the bank and trudged out of the hot sun into the woods, to sit on a patch of moss with a convenient tree trunk, at least four feet thick at its base, as a back rest. It was cool and very quiet. I listened to the faint rustling of the forest and soon was half asleep. Then I heard soft chittering sounds. I opened my eyes.

Four young red squirrels were lined side by side on a log twenty feet from me. They clung tensely, fore and hind feet tight to the bark, heads stretched forward; from nose to tail base no longer than my hand and quivering with vitality. They stared at me, the white markings around their shiny black eyes adding to an impression of wide-eyed wonder, fear, and curiosity, such as I might feel if I opened the cabin door and saw an unidentified species of dinosaur in our clearing. I had the feeling that they had been watching Ade and me and that we were probably the first human beings they had seen in their woods, possibly the first they had ever seen at close hand.

I did not move and together, as on signal, they sat up. Now I could see they were not exactly alike, although I guessed they were from one litter. Two were the same size, but one of these had winter ear tufts and the other had not yet grown them. One was slightly larger than these two, and the last was considerably smaller. Then they moved, each according to his own bent.

The smallest one climbed down from the log and moved slowly toward me, not hopping as squirrels usually do, but walking—one foot, then the next, eyes fixed on me, ears alert, ready to retreat in haste at the slightest alarm. The largest one slid down behind the log and stayed there, watching the proceedings with only nose, eyes, and ears visible over its top. The one with the ear tufts jumped from the log and ran up a nearby tree, to cling to the bark and watch from a really excellent point for escape if necessary. The fourth remained sitting on the log, relaxed now with paws neatly crossed on plump white belly, a small buddha deep in contemplation.

The smallest one reached my jacket cuff after several minutes of circumspect stalking. The cuff didn't seem dangerous, so the intrepid little explorer climbed up my sleeve, watching ahead and around but not keeping his eyes on my face. In spite of the odd scent he must be noticing, he didn't seem to know I was alive. By the time he reached my shoulder, my eyes were burning from being held open and I was afraid I would start dripping tears, but before that happened or I could no longer control the reflex to blink, he hooked his claws into my neck as he prepared to climb higher. I didn't move, but he froze, staring at my neck, then went backward in a somersault and fled, chattering frantically. In squirrel talk, he might have been shouting, "Run for your lives!" The four of them disappeared before I could blink the tears out of my eyes.

I touched my neck and saw blood on my fingers. Then I wondered exactly what had frightened the squirrel. Perhaps just seeing the drops forming in his claw pricks, or maybe the bleeding had showed him I was alive, or it might have been something I knew nothing about. Idly I began to plan an experiment that might tell me, but I soon realized that no matter how carefully I planned, I could never find a reliable answer.

In the first place, such testing, whether in a laboratory or in the field, can only be designed, carried out, and interpreted by human reasoning. There is a concealed assumption that the animals tested react like people, although there is no basis for this. Squirrels act like squirrels. Thus, testing squirrels often tells more about squirrels as people than about squirrels as squirrels.

In the second place, although these squirrels had the common characteristics and appearance of their species, they differed in personality even more than they did in appearance. One hid, one waited, one started toward safety, one ventured out into the unknown. It was as unlikely that four young squirrels from another litter would behave exactly like these as it was unlikely that another four would have exactly the same differences in appearance. And no one could expect the squirrel who had scratched my neck to behave in the same way again in similar circumstances. Nor, for that matter, could one expect any other squirrel to duplicate this one's reaction to scratching my neck—if his alarm came from that —and the whole pattern of behavior would be distorted if captive squirrels were studied.

At this point I gave up the idea of doing scientific work on animal behavior in the wild. I'd had too many years of the scientific method not to know its traps: the preconception that is so hard to banish from the mind, the two things which appear together but which have absolutely no effect on each other, the temptation to ignore scattered exceptional results, which seem insignificant but which may hold the answer to an inquiry. And then I'd been working with steel and its reasonably predictable variables, not with living beings whose variables were as many and unpredictable as the patterns of rain on water and whose environment was even more complex. I'd study the wild ones as unique personalities, try to see how they and their environment fitted together, watch their reactions to our intrusion into their world, but I would never presume to apply generalities to them. And from that day, I have thought of our wild neighbors as "he" or "she" and "who"; stones and trees are "it" and "which."

3

The cabin was warm from the sun when we got home and the warmth stayed on after we finished our dinner. Ade brought an end table and three lamps from the summer house and we sat in the big chairs with the lighted table between us and read two Zane Grey Westerns we had found in the bookshelves. The wind hummed through the trees but I paid no attention to it until my feet began to ache from cold. Ade checked for the draft and I listened to the wind, a steady blowing that was beginning to whistle under the eaves. Our north windows were running with condensation and, as I wiped them, I felt the chill through the glass.

Ade made another note on his list, saying, "The joining between the foundation and logs is tight—John Anderson took care of that—but the wind comes in the foundation ventilators and gets up here between the floor and the logs. If I close the ventilators this early, we'll have mildew. I'll put in some kind of baseboard seal after the wood's in. That comes first in any case. Right now I'll get a fire going."

The barrel stove huffed and puffed, then settled down to roar softly and pour out heat. We read another hour or two, using kitchen chairs for footstools. Then Ade banked the fire, partially closed the drafts, and we went to sleep.

I woke coughing. I felt sick, weak, and dizzy, and my only thought was of fresh air. The wind pulled the open door from my fingers and slammed it. Ade woke. "Hey! I smell smoke!" And, somewhat revived by the gale from the again opened door, I did, too.

The air in the cabin cleared quickly and, once the door was closed and a lamp lighted, we could see smoke coming through pinholes all over the barrel stove. Ade opened the drafts and the smoke disappeared, swept up the chimney. He said, "My God!" and sat down. I simply sat down, my wits too befuddled to grasp the situation.

"This stove's burnt out," Ade said after a while. "No telling what kind of fumes you got, maybe monoxide. So we can't close it down because it'll smoke. And we can't let it roar to carry the stuff up the chimney all the time. It could overheat the chimney or burn through somewhere and drop fire onto the floor. Either way we'd have a fire." He rubbed his hands over his face. "I expected problems, but this is turning into a landslide."

I looked at the stove. "Well . . . we'll hear from my friend who wants the books as soon as he gets the letter."

"What's that got to do with . . ."

I interrupted. "What I mean is we can't order stoves until we get some cash."

"You wrote quite a while ago, didn't you? We ought to hear pretty soon—maybe Saturday."

I shook my head. "It won't even go till tomorrow. We're still thinking in terms of city mail service." I paused to think tenderly of heaters—electric, gas, and yes, even clanking steam radiators—then said: "There's nothing to do but move the essentials next door again and try to keep warm in front of the fireplace. That'll beat sitting here in front of the open oven door."

"I suppose so," he said and paused, looking thoughtful. "I don't want to go to town as long as the weather holds and we have enough gas to keep hauling wood, but when we do go and I can get to a regular phone line where I'm sure I'll be heard, I'll call about that idea I have."

So we spent the five sunny days of the next week getting wood and the two days of cold rain and all the evenings in front of the summer house fireplaces; but the days were nippy and our kitchen water bucket was skimmed with ice in the mornings. Ade's heavier clothes kept him warm but I was slowly congealing. I thought bitterly of the insurance people, sitting on my money in their nice warm skyscraper while I turned blue.

The check for the books came a week after my letter was mailed, accompanied by a heart-warming reply, wishing us success and telling us to get our fall work done before we sent the books, the writer having been born on a Dakota homestead and recognizing such problems. It was a miserable day, dark and cold with the spattering of blown rain, but the letter so cheered us that we saw the day only as perfect for Ade to start work on the baseboards in the log house and for me to tackle our first mail orders.

It is revealing how circumstances can change your interests. I ordered a pair of boot pants, water-repellent with flannel lining, with the enthusiasm I formerly would have turned to the purchase of a Thai-silk dinner gown. For Ade there were woodsmen's pants, thick, close-woven, almost waterproof, much like the pants icemen wore in the days when they walked their horse-drawn wagons through the streets and carried blocks of ice to flats where they had seen "ice cards" in the windows. For both of us there were red-plaid mackinaws and padded red caps with flaps to cover ears and the back of the neck. The reason given for buying all these red clothes is that they are essential for safety if you are in the woods during the hunting season, and, less often mentioned, if you are injured in an open spot in winter the bright color can be seen for miles against the snow. However, I freely admit that in my case these reasons were justification for dressing in the bright color I could not have worn at work in Chicago without creating a sensation among the more conservative members of the managerial staff.

Then came the pacs, boots with soft, flexible rubber bottoms and strong leather tops, bought large enough to wear over two or three pairs of soft, thick wool socks for warmth. And the inner soles and the socks to go in them and the snowshoes to go outside when the need might arise.

I ordered sleeping bags, great down-filled things, even though they were much more expensive than Hudson's Bay blankets. There is something wonderfully romantic about these blankets, sold for more than a hundred and fifty years, used for making parkas by the early fur traders and explorers, and each still bearing the four short, black stripes, or "marks," to indicate the four large beaver skins that once were their price. But the sleeping bags and their flannel liners would keep us from freezing even if the cabin burned down and we had to spend a night out in the bitterest weather.

Also on the side of not freezing were the airtight, an oval sheet-iron stove that will give more heat from less fire in a shorter time than any other type, and the iron log-roller, compact, low, and capable of burning unsplit logs.

I had finished making out checks of ominous size and was sealing the flap on the deposit to the local bank when Ade came in to remind me plaintively that it was long past dinnertime.

On the second Saturday after Ade mailed the orders, when October was ending in a warm and glorious Indian summer, the mail brought a notice that our stoves were in the Village freight office. The news didn't seem very exciting, now that sunlight ran in mellow streams between the long tree shadows and the soft air stirred springlike twittering from birds high in the branches. But we had already learned to take practical advantage of our lovely days, no matter how much they inclined us to dreaming. We'd go to town Monday with the trailer and pick up stoves, heavy underwear, food, and our other purchases if they had reached the post office by then. They and the stoves had no doubt all been shipped as soon as the mail-order houses had cleared our rather large first checks.

When I woke on Monday morning, I was conscious of extremely bright light and of Ade, sitting on the edge of the bed, yawning.

"I'm glad it stopped raining," I said. "I heard it whispering on the windows just before I went to sleep."

"Whispering? Rain?" He jumped up and went to the window. "Well, it came down anyway. Look."

Almost a foot of snow was spread evenly over the ground, glittering in the slanting light.

"But yesterday . . ." I began.

"Was yesterday."

"D'you suppose the road's open? We really need the stoves now."

"We can't get both of them . . . I'd be a fool to try to haul the trailer through this . . . but I think I can get the airtight into the trunk. If not, I can tie it outside some way. I'll put my chains on. If it isn't any deeper than this we can make it."

"The only way to tell is to start out," I said. "I'll get Carl's old galoshes. They'll keep my feet dry—if I can lift 'em, that is."

Our side road was so smoothly white it seemed a shame to leave tire tracks on it. There were no drifts. Tree trunks were tufted and laden branches hung low, with snow garlands draping from branch to branch, from tree to tree. Every bush top and twig carried its diamonded-studded edging. The pines towered majestically, unmoved by their heavy burdens. Everywhere the white branch tips made patterns against the darkness underneath, and steel-blue shadow patterns lay on the white ground. This was the fantastic forest of "Peter and the Wolf," the sentimental dream of "Winter Wonderland," the mysterious place that lies behind the picture on a Christmas card.

Ade stopped suddenly. A red fox had stepped daintily into the road. He examined us with the condescension peculiar to foxes, then crossed without hurry. A squirrel scampered, sure-footed, along a swaying branch in a cloud of disturbed snow-flakes, made the mistake of trying to run across a snow bridge, fell through with a squeak, caught perilously on a lower branch, and hung there, a sputtering mite of indignation, as the disturbed tree poured snow over him with a roar.

The illusion of mystery was gone. This was a real forest after a real snowstorm, utterly beautiful in its purity, but filled, not with elves and snow sprites, but with busy animals going about the business of the day. Following their example, we drove on.

The sides of the Trail were lost in slanting snowbanks and

the few cars that had gone over the road before us were all headed for the Village. Their tracks were superimposed near the middle of the right of way, where one could be sure there was road and not ditch under the snow. We drove for almost three hours along these winding furrows in the white splendor, and when we stepped from the car to a shoveled pavement I felt for a moment that I had lost something.

Our parcels were waiting in the post office and, while Ade loaded them into the car, I bought a coil of five hundred letter stamps, which cost so much less then they do now that I didn't feel extravagant. Then I realized that I had no money. The postmaster laughed. "Just make out a check to 'Postmaster' at this address. Everybody knows who you are." I must have looked surprised, for he added, "Moccasin telegraph." I wondered then and I sometimes still wonder at this wireless, instrumentless message service, which spreads news by word of mouth with matchless speed and, quite often, accuracy.

We ate hot-beef sandwiches at the bus station, then found a store whose windows were filled with shirts, boots, caps, gloves, and an assortment of practical accessories. We extracted two thick, rough, flannel workshirts—red and black, of course—from a heap on a bargain table, and while Ade pawed through marked-down wool socks, I looked around for underwear. There didn't seem to be anything but old-fashioned gauze vests and the harshest kind of wool undersuits.

"Can I help you, Mrs. Hoover?" said a voice behind me.

I whirled around, wide-eyed, then grinned at the gray-haired man who was standing at my elbow. "This moccasin-telegraph business startles me," I said. "I'm used to a comfortable anonymity."

He laughed. "It's very useful for us local merchants. Excellent for business, especially with summer people who feel they should be recognized. But what's your problem?"

I explained that I wanted underwear suitable for a log-cabin winter, but that wool made me itch.

"Then you start with fundamentals like these," he said, holding up a pair of men's underdrawers, gray cotton with thick fleece lining. "Some of the ladies use them and use the long matching undershirt to give extra warmth over the kidneys."

I bought some for myself and some for Ade, and left the store cured of the notion that my winter outfit was going to look like some little things I might pick up for a trip to Lake Placid.

After Ade had put these packages into the car beside the ones from the post office, he consulted his list. "I'll pick up the airtight, and some extra pipe and a roof saddle, and get the car filled up. I need more antifreeze, too. And I'll get the five-gallon can filled with kerosene for the lamps. When the road's plowed I'll bring the trailer in for the big stove and haul a couple of drums of gas for the light plant. I ought to have it going pretty soon, if it doesn't get too cold to work on it. Anyway, don't buy more groceries than will fit in there." He pointed to such space as remained in the back seat.

The largest grocery, not a supermarket but a nicely arranged self-service store, displayed fewer fresh vegetables than the stores I knew in Chicago—a shipping problem, no doubt—and an excellent selection of packaged groceries. I had not used canned meats before, and took a sample of every kind, to top off my large cartful. When I pulled up at the check-out desk, the blonde girl there raised her eyebrows. "Inherit money or aren't you planning to come back before spring?"

So she knew me, too, I thought, and smiled. "Oh, we'll be in and out but I'm an inexperienced cook. I'll have to try things."

"Starting off to live in the woods and you've never cooked much! Well . . . you've forgotten your yeast, and some bread to carry you till you bake."

When she came back with the two items, I said, "I've got a lot of things to do. Could I have bread mailed for a while?"

"You can, if you don't care how much you spend." She picked up my box of salt. "It costs more to mail this than to buy it."

"Oh. I'd better bake then. I've Hilda Peterson's recipe."

"You'll have no trouble. Got enough flour?"

I thought of the jar in the high cupboard and, out of my vast store of ignorance, said, "Yes."

As I was writing another check she said, "The Petersons'll get here from Minneapolis sometime this evening. They'll be staying in the Winters' house—the Winters' are in Florida —so they'll probably be up your way in a day or two."

I thanked her and left with a better knowledge of how the moccasin telegraph worked.

By the time Ade had played checkers with the parcels and managed to squeeze everything into the car, and we were strengthened by apple pie and coffee, dusk was shadowing the waters of Lake Superior. We saw the plows working in the Village, clearing the streets, but the Trail was still unplowed. The twin ruts were wider but slippery, and we went slowly, pulling our heavy load up the now icing hills.

I leaned back, with my legs stretched out and my ankles, aching from dragging the big galoshes, crossed comfortably under the heater. Beneath the clear sky, the snow-covered land still reflected enough light for me to see a snowy owl, white except for black spatterings, on a bush top beside a hill just ahead. As we ground up the hill he flew, his feet flapping awkwardly, his wings silent as clouds. I turned my head to follow his flight.

Ade swore and his right elbow jabbed painfully into my arm as he wrenched the wheel to the right. I didn't feel the bump when my head, protected by my instinctively lifted hands, smashed the windshield. I only heard a screaming of metal that seemed endless. I looked dizzily over the slowly rising and crumpling hood as the car swung to the left, and watched the dash moving relentlessly toward my face. Then my chin was resting on it, there was a painful pressure at the back of my neck, and everything was dead still except for the throbbing of the engine.

"Turn off the ignition," I heard myself saying.

The throbbing stopped and I knew that Ade had heard me. He couldn't be too badly hurt and now we oughtn't to catch fire. I thought I ought to be doing something, but instead I sort of drifted.

4 ...And Its Aftermath

I heard Ade's voice. It sounded loud and far away at the same time and he was saying, "Are you all right?"

Of course, I'm all right, I thought peevishly. Why shouldn't I be? But it seemed also that he had been saying this or something like it for quite a while, that he sounded distressed, and that I really ought to answer.

I wriggled a little. I couldn't get up or down or out or anywhere. Also, the pressure on my neck was beginning to cut off my breath.

"I don't hurt anywhere," I said, trying to sound calm but hearing the shrillness in my voice. "Only get the door open. Get me out of here!"

Ade wrenched at the car door and another man joined him. The door didn't move. I slid farther forward and the edge of the dash was choking me. Then the pressure left the back of my neck, I gulped in air, and the two men pulled me backward out of the open window. For a moment it seemed hilariously funny that they would open a window instead of the door. Then I collapsed in the snow but stumbled to my feet when I heard Ade say, "Oh God, she's broken her legs." He sounded so desperate that I felt I must reassure him.

"I'm all right," I muttered, just as the strange man, tall, dark, and young as far as I could see, developed something like hysterics. He shouted wildly that we'd have to put him in jail—that it wasn't his fault—that the very-much-censured county engineers ought to be sued for building a road full of these totally censored hills. This jolted me more or less back to normal and I saw another car, its left front end crushed and interlocked with ours. The excited young man must be the other driver. I was thinking that his performance wasn't much help when I saw a girl standing in the roadway behind him, blood dripping from her face. This was all we needed. I grabbed the man's shoulders and shook him. Maybe his teeth rattled. If they didn't, they should have.

"Nobody's going to put anybody in jail," I raged. "This isn't anybody's fault. Dammit, get hold of yourself and look after your wife."

As he enveloped her in a bear hug that would have completed the damage if she had been injured internally, I realized that Ade was very silent and was bent over, hands against his chest.

"I don't think it's much," he said in the same kind of voice I had tried to use to him, "I broke the steering wheel, I guess."

Suddenly I was utterly terrified. I couldn't think or speak. I stood and heard voices but I didn't understand a word, had no idea of the passing time. Then I was in a car and a woman was saying, "Your husband isn't badly hurt. Everything's all right now. You'll all be just fine."

I felt immensely better, but things were pretty vague for a while. I remember being led into the warm kitchen of a lodge and drinking some strong and very welcome coffee. There was a man who made loud noises about wild drivers. I didn't like him much and wanted to tell him it wasn't that way at all, that Ade had never so much as scraped a fender before in his thirty years of driving, and that neither car had been going fast or we probably wouldn't be alive. But this all seemed to require too much of an effort. I drank more coffee and began to get my wits back. The girl, her face bloody but no longer bleeding, had fallen into the heavy sleep of shock, but Ade and the tall young man were not there. I asked the woman about them.

"They're fine," she said. "They're out with flashlights so no one will run into the wreck. Do you want me to call anyone for you?"

I gave my head a good shake and seemed to feel all right.

"I'll call," I said. I rang the forestry-line phone and waited, listening to the humming wire. Then I tried again.

"Who are you calling?" the woman asked.

"The Petersons . . . at the Lodge."

"The Lodge is closed. Didn't you know?"

Of course I knew. Perhaps I wasn't as clear-headed as I thought.

"They ought to be in town by now," I said. "Staying at someone's house. Yes. The Winters' house."

"You sit," she said firmly. "I'll call Hilda and Sven. Try to rest."

I was glad to leave the phoning to her but listened anxiously until I heard her talking. When she turned from the phone and said, "They'll be right out," I fell asleep.

"How d'you feel?" Ade was saying as he shook me gently.

"Tired," I said, then considered. "I honestly feel pretty good. The nap helped." I winced as I stood up. "My knees hurt. You?"

"Chest hurts and I'm tired. That's all."

Then I saw Sven at the telephone and Hilda in the doorway.

"What a thing to happen," she said, waving her hands and managing not to spill her coffee, "but it's an old story on the Trail. Don't even bother to think. Sven's got flares by the cars and the wrecker's on the way. He's calling the doctor and the sheriff now."

"Sheriff!" Ade said. "I don't want to make a complaint."

"You're not in Chicago now," Sven said, as he hung up. "Here we don't have as many crack-ups so we report the lot. The sheriff'll meet all of you at Doc Jones's office. Then we'll keep you till you're able to go out to the cabin. We'll take your perishables to town so they don't freeze and I'll haul the other stuff for you once I've picked up the trailer at your place."

I tried to thank the woman who had been so kind to us, but I'm afraid my effort fell far short of what I tried to say. All the way to town I kept thinking that in the middle of a supposedly deserted wilderness we had been less alone than if we had cracked up on the Outer Drive in Chicago's rush hour. There we'd have been a traffic block to get out of the way; here we were people in trouble. I wondered if the time would ever come when we could repay all this kindness. I doubted it, but as we pulled up to a curb in the Village I knew that we'd repay it by helping someone—it didn't matter who—sometime. And, in turn, someone else would help the woman at the lodge and Hilda and Sven.

Dr. Jones was a big, jolly, no-nonsense man whose office was upstairs over the post office. He looked at the girl's face and said, "Mostly blood. Cheer up. You won't have even a *little* scar." He settled her to sleep in a waiting room, gave her husband a clean bill of health, and took Ade, who was now white with pain, into his office. At this moment the sheriff's big shoulders filled the doorway from the hall.

Like everyone else, he knew who we were, and I learned that the tall young man was George Wilson, who, with his wife, was on the way to winter in Arizona.

"Now," said the sheriff. "You sit here, Mrs. Hoover . . ." he pointed to one end of a big sofa ". . . and George, you sit on the other end. I'll sit in the middle and we'll get all the details cleared up." I got Ade's driver's license and insurance card from his jacket on the coat tree and settled down.

The sheriff filled in the accident report, which he said was easy because we agreed on everything. Ade was insured, so it didn't seem too important to me that George was not.

Then Ade came out of the office, smiling and saying he'd only detached a couple of ribs from his breastbone and was taped up for a couple of weeks. I was so relieved I wanted nothing but to get away and try to sleep. The doctor listened and thumped and said I was a pretty sturdy animal, and I said I had a bit of a bump on the shin but that was nothing. Everybody shook hands with everybody else, the sheriff drove the Wilsons wherever they were going for the night, and Hilda and Sven took Ade and me to their borrowed house.

We were ravenous now and stuffed ourselves with milk and sandwiches in the kitchen.

"How'd the sheriff fix the blame?" Sven asked.

"Snow and the blind hill. He wrote it down 'road defect.' Neither one of us was going ·fast and the road edges were covered. George noticed that the front wheels were cramped as far as they'd go to the right. The cars didn't respond on the slippery road, that's all."

"No argument?" Sven asked, and I shook my head.

"That's good," Hilda said. "I hate this business of two people trying to pass the blame back and forth for something like this. You'll just report to your insurance companies, and that'll be it."

"Not quite," I said. "We'll report. He hasn't any."

"Oh Lord," Ade said.

"What's wrong? If we're insured . . ."

"We've liability to cover him if I'd been at fault, but our car isn't new and its book value is low, so it didn't seem practical, either to me or the insurance man in Chicago, to carry collision insurance. It's pretty expensive. We'll have to pay for our own repairs."

I set my sandwich down carefully and Sven, looking very thoughtful, said, "So the state'll pick up his driver's license. Well . . . finish your food and get to bed. You can tell better how things stand after you're rested, even if you *are* going to feel like you've been beaten with ball bats."

Ade looked fine in the morning, but his ribs were so painful that he could hardly move his arms. I helped him into his shirt and laced his boots, then began to check myself over. Both arms were purple from elbow to shoulder and my hands were full of little slivers of glass, but that was better than having my face cut. The gouge on my shin was deep and tender and both knees were blue, swollen, and didn't want to bend.

"How'd I get so banged up? It didn't seem that much happened to me."

"It happened too fast," Ade said. "After you broke the glass you bounced under the dash, hard enough to break the heater with your legs. Those heavy old galoshes certainly saved you from broken ankles. Then the load in the back shoved your seat forward." He hesitated, then said: "I sup-pose you ought to have it all. If you'd been pushed another inch your neck would have broken against the dash, a little less than that and you'd have strangled." He was trying to be matter of fact but not succeeding very well.

"Maybe there's something to be said for seat belts," I said.

"In some cases, yes. Here, I'd say no. You'd have missed most of what did happen but your abdominal wall would never have kept you from internal injury from the belt when the seat moved."

I thought a minute, then tried to match his everyday voice. "If I'm on borrowed time . . . I'd better make good use of it, huh?"

"Do anything you want with it . . . just so you're here."

With that to keep me happy, I was entirely at ease while Sven drove us all to the garage that had done the towing. Then I saw the car, or rather what was left of it, and turned hollow inside as though I had lost a good friend.

I'm one of those people, and so is Ade, to whom cars are personal, and this one was especially so. It was an old Chevrolet, built when many roads were not concrete or even blacktopped, so it had extra clearance for getting over rough spots. Its low gear was designed, not for jackrabbit starts, but for pulling—in mud and snow and up steep hills. Ade had bought it for the Trail and our side road, and now . . .

"Hardly worth towing her in," the garage man said.

Ade was bent over, peering under the shredded left front fender. "How's the engine?" he asked, straightening with an effort.

"Good as new."

"Well . . . it could be fixed."

The garage man nodded. "It'd cost more than the car's worth, though."

"But you'll have to have transportation," Hilda said.

"I don't think we should try to buy another car right now," I said, not willing to tell the whole village we had less than two hundred dollars. "Things are too unsettled."

Sven rubbed his chin. "There's a fellow who can probably get it in running condition. Straighten the frame . . . put on an old fender . . . fix the wiring. He'd do it cheap."

I cheered up and Hilda and I treated ourselves to chocolate sodas while Ade and Sven looked into the matter of the car.

"I went through your groceries," Hilda said. "To be sure you've everything you need. How about flour?" I waved my hand airily. "You'll have to buy more eggs," she went on, "and your doughnuts just rolled away. The foxes will love them."

I laughed. "If that's all there was to worry about . . ."

"Oh, you'll make out all right, but you might as well know that some people up here have been betting—really betting, I mean—that you won't stay the winter. And before all this, too. They think a couple of city people won't last two months, or else you'll be singing like the birds come spring. It's because *they* can't stand the isolation. Isn't it queer how so many people judge others by themselves?"

"What do you think? About us and the isolation."

"It won't bother you once you're used to it. You've plenty to do and then you're a lot like Sven and me. So of course . . ." She stopped and looked blank. We were both laughing when Sven and Ade joined us.

I slept most of the way up the Trail and when I had my eyes open again we were turning into our side road. Snow still lay deep on the road edges and in the woods but the road itself was almost bare and water dripped from the trees.

"It must be forty," I said. "If we'd waited a couple of days . . ."

Hilda lifted her expressive hands. "Well, you didn't. It's just spilled milk. It's too bad we'll only be here overnight, but almost anyone who comes along will give you a hand if you need it. We're not without our sour apples up here—but they don't spoil the rest of us, the way real apples do. It's the only way you can live—to help each other, I mean—

when you're so far from everything." She hesitated. "I didn't mean that the way it sounds. We really aren't away from anything that counts."

"If we hadn't thought that, we wouldn't have come," I said.

Sven pulled up at the path to the log cabin. "We'll settle you here. It'll be fairly warm for a while, I think, but you can't tell when you'll need night heat."

"The barrel stove's burnt out," Ade said.

"Oh? That's not too much of a surprise. You just leave things to us."

The path was crazy-paved with soft snow, ice, and mud. Between Ade's efforts to keep from falling and further disarranging his ribs, my efforts to keep my increasingly shaky legs under me, and the combined efforts of the Petersons to keep us all upright, we must have looked like the end of a very gay night on the town. But it was good to be back, even though the little house was cold. For a moment I fancied that it had a withdrawn, almost frightened air, as though it feared we had abandoned it. Maybe this really was *our* house. Hilda must have felt something of this because she said, "Houses need to be lived in. Sit down, both of you. I'll start a fire in the cook stove."

Then things happened with dispatch. Hilda stored the groceries and Sven filled the woodbox. I made tea and Sven, after he finished his cup, went to the Lodge, saying that a man who was doing some work for him had picked up our stoves and parcels in his truck that morning. Soon he was back, hauling our supplies down the hill on a toboggan that he said ran as well on mud as on snow. While I put the clothes away and Ade, who by now was in such misery that he could barely lift his teacup, looked frustrated, Hilda and Sven pulled the barrel stove outside, set the airtight in its place, and left the iron log-roller in a suitable spot in the living room.

"That's everything except your oil," Sven said. "I didn't move the trailer. It's still in the snow and you'll need it later, when you get your car. I couldn't squeeze the oilcan into my car with the rest of the stuff."

"We don't need it right away," Ade said. "We've at least half a gallon."

So it was left that Sven's workman would bring the oil the next afternoon when he left for town. We both tried to look cheerful when we again said goodbye to Hilda and Sven.

Ade and I closed the door and looked at each other, a bit uncertainly. We really were a couple of crocks. At length he said, "After all, we're alive, and all things pass, given time. We'll take care of emergencies as they come."

2

The first of these arrived at nightfall, after I had gone to the summer house with a basket and brought back seven lamps. The brighter, the better, it seemed to me.

"Where's the kerosene?" I asked.

Ade pointed to a can.

"Why don't you label things? This says 'varnish.'" I was

feeling worse by the minute and I have a notion I sounded more than a little cranky.

"Where did you put the raisins?"

"Raisins? In the red coffee can labeled 'oatmeal' . . ." I did a double-take. The queer muffled sounds Ade was making were the nearest thing to hearty laughter that his ribs and tape would allow. "All right," I said, starting to fill the first lamp. "I walked into that one . . . My God, this *is* varnish!"

"So it is," Ade agreed, touching the viscous goo on the lip of the lamp's glass tank with a finger. Holding a flashlight in his teeth, he pulled out one of the big drawers under the counter with his toe and looked into it. "I guess there isn't any oil," he said after some time. "But there's plenty of turpentine."

I suggested that turpentine wouldn't be much use as a substitute for kerosene in lamps, and he explained in a superior manner that it would clean the varnish out. Properly subdued, I lighted our old lamp—with an inch of oil in it—and proceeded to clean up the varnish and make sandwiches and more tea.

Food helped but not much. We were sore and weary, now that all the excitement was over. Ade brightened a little when he got the idea that he could label bottles and cans without moving his arms much, but I yawned and made the beds.

After breakfast, which we had shortly after noon, I built a fire in the airtight, following Ade's instructions. We were reading and making acid comments on the ability of fictional characters to recover overnight from almost any kind of mayhem, when a horn blew long and loud on the road.

"The fellow with our kerosene," Ade said. "He'll be down."

As I put on the coffeepot, I heard a truck drive away. We went out. Through the bare stems of the brush the bright-red of the five-gallon can stood out plainly at the top of the steep path.

"Maybe they didn't tell him . . . ," I began feebly.

Ade sputtered, too furious to speak. Then: "Of course they told him. He just doesn't give a damn. If I ever meet that . . . what d'you think you're doing?"

The last was occasioned by my stepping into the kitchen and coming back out, pulling on my jacket.

"Going after the oil," I said.

"You can't! That can weighs fifty pounds and you're hardly able to walk!"

"Unless we want to go without light, I have to. The lamp we used last night is as good as empty. It's out of the question for you to carry anything, and there's nobody else."

"Take my heavy work gloves. They'll protect your hands. And brace yourself on the can if you slip." He looked utterly miserable as I started up the hill.

Going up wasn't so bad, even though the path had glazed during the night and the temperature was still below freezing, but coming down was another matter. I found that I could lift the can easily, but something unbearably painful happened to my gouged right shin when I stepped on the right foot while I was carrying the extra weight of the can. I had to work out a system. I put my weight on my left foot, set the can a few inches forward and leaned on it while taking a cautious step with my right. Then I shifted my weight, moved the can again, and so on. It took me more than an hour to get the kerosene down the hill and my feeling for the "sour apple" who had left it by the road grew less charitable with every painful step. And that trek blasted once and for all my innocent illusion that people in the woods are either born kind and helpful or become so when they move there. People are what they are wherever they are. When there are only a few, each one stands out, and the kind of person he is stands out, too.

Once we thought it over, we were glad that this had happened because it showed us that if one couldn't do something that had to be done, the other of us could, and that necessary things must never be considered impossible to do. But it wasn't until spring that the heavy scab healed away from my shin and the hollow in the bone under it showed me that I had managed to haul that oilcan with what was, for all practical purposes, a broken leg.

Maybe it is just as well not to know about such things when you are not in a position to do much, if anything, about them. If we had cracked up in Chicago, both of us would have been hospitalized, running up large bills, receiving sympathy, and indulging in disgustingly large helpings of self-pity. As it was, we were too busy to need or want sympathy and had no time to feel sorry for ourselves. We came out of it just as fast, perhaps faster, and with new appreciations of each other and of our own strength—and of our limitations, which is even more important.

No matter how you look at it, though, the ten days after Hilda and Sven left were an idiot's delight. I could use my arms, but walking got worse every day. Ade could tramp around normally, but couldn't carry anything. Between us we'd have made one fairly good man, if there had been any way to coordinate our useful halves. As it was, I learned a lot about hasty adaptation.

For instance, I had previously thought getting a bucket of water from the lake was a pleasant walk with a nice view, but one trial showed me that I couldn't manipulate my wobbly legs over the now icy rocks. This meant limping through the woods to the brook and back, a very long fifth of a mile in my battered state. We washed "around the edges" and did dishes only when we had to. Then we had a pouring rain and I hauled everything from kettles to the wash boiler into position under the eaves.

And there was the little matter of firing the airtight. It had a hinged lid on top and a front door low to the floor. The first time I added wood through the top the house filled with smoke and we lost all the heat while ventilating with the door open. Next time I squatted on my heels to look in before adding wood and my knees felt as if they were being crushed. The pain almost made me sick and I couldn't get up. While Ade stood helplessly by, I half-straightened my legs and hunched across the floor to pull myself up by hanging onto the kitchen table. After that, I fired the stove by flopping down from the hips. By the time the tape on Ade's chest made him complain of itching instead of pain, I could easily lean on the palms of my hands and was beginning to think I might take to walking on all fours, just as a matter of habit.

The second Saturday after the accident was a day of crisp, cold air, cloudless azure sky, and a light breeze that rattled the bare maples and rustled the fallen leaves. Ade, with his tape off and the zest of a boy out of school for the summer, walked up to tell the mailman to bring our mail on his next trip. When he came back, he handed me two letters.

"How'd he know you'd be there?" I asked.

"He didn't, but he heard what happened, so he's been carrying these with him each trip. He knew I'd come or somebody'd come for us, eventually. He also brought word that the car'll be ready Wednesday. I can ride to town with him and pick it up. Then I'll drive down to Duluth. I'd take you along but he doesn't like to carry more than one person with him. Any more crowds the seat in his station wagon."

"Duluth? Whatever are you talking about?"

"When we were in town I called the ad agency I worked for five years ago. This is confirmation." He waved a letter, grinning. "I'll meet one of their men at the Spaulding Hotel at two Thursday and sign a contract for artwork to do up here. We're all set."

I didn't grasp what he said. We had been on a financial seesaw for so long that anything smacking of a steady income seemed impossible. I watched stupidly when he walked to the south window in the bedroom and said, "I'll have to use this window. The trees block too much light from the north ones. The empty part of the shelf I made for your flowers will be handy, too. But how'll I keep the sun glare off my board?"

Board—drawing board—artwork! I woke up to the marvelous news.

"Your drawing table's in the storage cabin, isn't it? And use a venetian blind. It'll look silly against the logs, but it'll control the light. The blinds must be somewhere . . . the movers packed everything."

"And so are those knocked-down apple boxes," he said and went outside, leaving me to wonder what he was talking about.

But he knew, all right. He rebuilt the apple boxes into convenient storage cabinets for drawing paper and scratch-board, brushes and watercolors, pencils and pens and smudge sticks and charcoal. In two days the former bedroom had become a workable, if not conventional, studio.

On Wednesday morning Ade got into his city clothes, packed overnight essentials, and was having bacon and eggs before walking to catch his ride with the mailman, when the mechanic who'd worked on the car arrived. He'd brought the car, he said, because he had to come up the Trail and figured he could save Ade the trip to town. We thanked him, Ade gave him a check for a hundred dollars, and he left with a friend who'd come along in another car.

Ade drove up the road to tell the mailman of the change in plans and we spent the rest of the day relaxing to celebrate the end of our problems. Neither one of us gave a thought to the eighty-some dollars that was all that remained of our funds.

Ade left early the next morning and I settled at the kitchen table with the mail-order catalogs. There were many things I could do during the winter—paint and varnish, make proper curtains—but I needed the raw materials. I had just started the first list when Ade came in, perfectly white.

"The car's no good," he said.

I began to shake and sweat, all the strain of the past weeks piling up on me. "But it was all right yesterday!"

"It *seemed* all right. I didn't think to try the lights or the horn or I'd have known. There's a short somewhere and the battery's dead. The radiator's dry. It leaks worse than the one that got punctured in the accident, and the left front spring's ready to go any minute. If it's another one, it's no better than the old one."

I had a sudden and vivid memory of myself, washing engine parts in gasoline some twenty years before on a Sunday afternoon in a Chicago garage, while Ade whistled and tinkered and put another Chevrolet into running condition.

"But surely you can do something," I said.

"I could, if I could get parts and had a battery charger . . . and power to work it . . . and a week or so to spend on the job. As it is, I can't even get the car to town." He started to change into his boots.

"What *are* you going to do?"

"Take the field phone and hook onto the forestry line and call the Spaulding."

He was gone for hours, during which I paced and sat, lay down, and got up to pace again. He'd get through all right and the contract could be mailed, of course, I told myself, but then so many things had gone wrong for us already. It seemed unbelievable that Ade could lose out on this. It wasn't fair— but since when had the vagaries of fortune had anything to do with fairness? I was still trying to hang onto hope when Ade came back and one glance told me he had not been successful.

He dropped into a kitchen chair, looking pale and ill as he had not since we left Chicago. "I got the operator in town but she couldn't get Duluth. There's been a storm down there. And all calls have to go through there, so I couldn't call the agency, either. I tried to call the garage but she told me the man who owns it left for the winter a week ago and his mechanic stayed on to finish a job . . ." He choked and shook his head. "To finish a job and left yesterday for his home. He was only here for a short time and she has no idea where he came from."

"Bother the garage! Can you write the agency?"

"I can. I will. But it won't do any good. Madison Avenue isn't likely to understand backwoods problems. I'll just be written off as unreliable."

"Was it . . . was it a good contract?" I asked.

"Ten thousand dollars."

I got up and walked into the living room. I couldn't bear to look at his disappointment and I blamed myself bitterly. I was the one who had said we'd never know if we could make it to town if we didn't start out, and if I had been even hesitant . . . but I had not. And ten thousand dollars was a lot of money in the woods. By managing carefully we could have lived on it for three or four years, had plenty of time to organize ourselves and find other ways to live if Ade didn't want to go on with the contracted artwork. After a time I stopped this useless thinking and returned to the kitchen. Ade hadn't moved.

"We've got to see where we stand," I said. "We've got to figure out what to do next."

Ade took a deep breath. "First, how much money is left?"

I got the checkbook and looked. "Eighty-three dollars and thirty cents."

"We have to live from now until some time in January, when your check comes from the insurance company. Say the middle of the month. That's about eight weeks. We have food for how long?"

"Four, maybe five weeks."

"Yes, and no way to get more except by mail. We have wood for about ten weeks. We have a trailer but no car to pull it and we can't afford to hire anyone to cut more, so the only way for us to get fuel is for me to cut it and drag it out of the forest by hand."

"You can't do that. You aren't used to such heavy work or to bitter cold, and you've still got to rest. Maybe later on . . ."

"Now's what matters. We have no way to communicate in a hurry in case of illness, accident, or fire. I can walk to the Trail, or you could in an emergency, even with your bad knees, but that phone line might work . . . or it might not, as we've just seen. And we have no way to make a living. That's it."

"We still have a couple of bonds—a hundred and a twenty-five," I said.

"Keep them. They may be our getaway money."

There are times in life it is better not to dwell on, once they are past, and the next three days made up one of those times. Even now, a dozen years later, I feel weak and ill as I remember. I believe now that all that kept us from giving up was the certainty that if we went back and started over in the city, we'd never make a break again. Then, too, neither one of us had ever given up on anything we felt was worthwhile as long as there was the least chance of making a go of it.

Saturday's mail brought a letter from the man whom Ade had not met in Duluth. He had written it before he left and while he was very annoyed indeed. Its tone was totally unnecessary—insulting, verging on the scurrilous. It made us both so hopping mad that we snapped out of our depression.

We decided to ration our food, do what we could to the cabin with the paint the movers had brought along and the old drapes I might recut and sew by hand, wear heavy clothes inside and go to bed early to stretch our wood. Somehow we'd make it until the check came. Then we could start planning for the future again. And when next Wednesday's mail brought, among others, the canceled check for the car repairs, I put it away with the two bonds. I still have it—and the bonds—in a safety box, to remind me that any decision, large or small, may be vital, and that the road to good fortune may follow strange ways. I know now that if Ade had decided to junk the damaged car, he'd have gone to town with the mailman and taken the bus to Duluth. He'd have been there on time and signed his contract. We'd have had an easy life and another car. And it is very possible that I should never have written anything except letters to my friends.

3

The next day it snowed—heavily, magnificently, and for a long time. We weren't going anywhere—we couldn't—and we badly needed diversion, so we enjoyed watching the snowfall as we had done when we were children. We watched it slowly cover the bare ground outside the cabin and round the stumps into igloos. We saw it first touch every needle on every tree with white, then blur the needles into a twig pattern, and finally cover them, too, and start bending the laden branches down. It was wet snow that froze onto the trees so that the white layer on the ground grew deeper but was unbroken by the fall of snowballs from the boughs.

It was not uncomfortably cold so, when the snow stopped for a while, we went outside and started to make up for the busy months when we'd had little time for the land we had searched so long to find.

The old forest was a temple where white-fluted columns lifted a vaulted roof above a marble floor, but life was here, busy among these trappings of eternity. We found the tracks of hares, their big hind-foot marks like deeply cupped flowers with pointed petals. Deer mice had come from under roots and out of snow tunnels, leaving the marks of dainty feet beside their curving tail impressions. The wing marks of a big owl were superimposed on one mouse trail, but the mouse had popped into the snow and escaped. For the first time I was aware of divided sympathy—for the terrified mouse who had almost been eaten and for the owl who had gone hungry.

Later, in the blue light of early dusk, we kicked our way up the path, with new whiteness covering our shoulders and heads and touching our faces as lightly as gossamer. Halfway to the road we stopped and turned to watch the pale light from the cabin windows deepen to gold against the gathering dark, then stretch through the snowfall in sparkling beams. The little house still had a waiting look, but now it offered shelter from whatever the night might hold.

As we stepped into its welcome warmth, Ade looked around. "Pretty is as pretty does," he said.

Around nine o'clock we were sitting in the living room. It was chilly, the fire in the bedroom airtight being too small to heat more than its own area. Ade was lamenting that his injury had delayed him in setting up the iron stove. ". . . and I could have done it days ago. I know better than to put things off."

There was a knock at the door. Startled, we looked toward the kitchen. Someone here? At night?

"Maybe somebody's lost," I said.

I was just behind Ade as he opened the door and the light fell on a big man, a woodsman from his looks and clothes, but now gray-faced with fatigue and swaying slightly as he stood.

"I don't like to bust in like this," he said, "but I've had quite a walk and . . ."

"Come in," Ade said. "This is Jacques Plessis, Helen. I met him in the freight office when we were in town."

Ade took his cap and heavy mackinaw and I waved them toward the living room, picked up the can of tea and got the hot kettle from the top of the airtight. "Will you have something to eat?" I asked, poking my head around the door-frame.

Jacques smiled and no more answer was needed. In twenty minutes he was starting on a heaped platter of chili-mac.

When I took his empty plate, he grinned at me and said, "So now you've fed the hungry trapper."

I was puzzled for a minute, then realized that this was a situation to be found in almost all the old-time stories of the North. "Why . . . so I have," I said, feeling, and probably looking, slightly dazed by this entry of fiction into my life.

"It used to happen pretty often years ago," he said, "but not now . . . with the roads." His eyes were twinkling. "It'd probably bore you to hear how I got myself into this fix."

I looked closely at him. He knew perfectly well that we were both perishing of curiosity and that I was as thrilled at having him come in as if he had stepped straight out of the pages of Jack London. Also, he was all set to tell us his story.

So I lifted my eyebrows and said, "Of course, if you're too tired to tell us . . ."

He returned my serious look. "Nope. I'm not tired now. I had quite a walk, though."

Now, Jacques, whom we have come to know well, is a lumberjack from the days gone by. He has massive shoulders, a wide, deep chest, and arms and legs like the smaller logs that he lifts as though they were weightless. He moves carefully, as men of great strength customarily do, and speaks slowly, considering what he says before he says it. He is not a young man, but his deeply bronzed skin is almost unlined except for crinkles around his gray-blue eyes, born of squinting against the sun on winter snow, and of laughter.

Only such a man could have handled the situations he met that day as he handled them. If I had owned a recorder then, I would give you the story in his own words but, since I did not, I'll use my own and try to keep his flavor.

"About the end of October," he said, "I went into the bush

and set up a permanent camp on Kingfish River. It's a good place to trap mink, and the whiskey jacks kept me company. Every day when I started out on my trapline they came from wherever they had their nests, maybe a dozen or so of them, and followed along in the trees. I had the traps covered so they couldn't get at the bait and maybe spring a trap and get caught, but they followed me just the same, out from camp and back, whistling and warbling and sometimes coming right down to sit on my shoulders. I fed them at the camp and then, too, I only wanted the mink skins and whiskey jacks eat dead meat. They won't touch a wounded animal, though.

"Well, I'd been there a month when a fisher came down from his den in some high rocks and began running my trapline every night. He did right well—got the bait herring, and any mink that'd happened to have the bad luck to get caught. He was too quick and quiet for me, so I took it easy for a few days, waiting for the ice on the river to thicken.

"I'd come in by canoe and the only sensible way out was up the river ice, which should have been several inches thick by then, but wasn't because it hasn't been really cold. Kingfish River is more a long inlet between two lakes than a river. It's half a mile wide in some places, narrows into rapids in others, and gets deep just where you don't expect it. Its two lakes lie at the bottom of a gully with high, steep, sloping sides and a few nice little flats at the bottom, like the one where I'd set up my camp. The north slope wasn't too steep and if I'd had company I might have gone that way, but with a pack on my back and ice on the rocks I wasn't fool enough to try it alone. The cliffs and rock slides on the south were out.

"I puttered around following fox and hare trails, and put a broken-winged mallard that had frozen into the ice out of its misery. Last night it got pretty cold where I was and my tea ran out. I thought the ice ought to be safe by morning so I packed up my skins and what I'd need at home. I figured to come back later with a fellow and get the tent.

"But when I rolled out at five this morning, I learned all over again that it's no good trying to plan ahead on the weather. There was this snow, and it had warmed up enough during the night to make it stick. It's mighty pretty on the trees, but it's hell on snowshoes because it stacks on the toes and makes you feel like you're planted in quicksand. I almost unrolled my pack, but forty years in the woods hasn't taught me to follow some of the advice I hand out when I'm guiding in the summer. The snow stopped earlier there than here, but I knew I shouldn't start out. I was out of bacon—I'd have had some left if I hadn't fed so much to the jacks—but I could've eaten powdered eggs till a little wind blew some of the snow down and it packed on the ground. Anyway, I'd overstayed my time and if I didn't show up soon some of my friends would come trekking in to see if I was okay. I had a date for Thanksgiving dinner and if I hurried . . . what's the matter?"

"Good heavens!" I said. "Was today Thanksgiving?"

Jacques leaned back and roared. "You forgot it," he said happily, still laughing.

"Never thought of it," Ade said.

"What's so funny?" I asked.

"It usually takes an old-timer like me to get so wound up in what he's doing that he forgets the days. I was thinking some people are going to lose some bets this spring. Did you know . . ."

"We do," Ade said. "Know about the bets, I mean, and we'll be here in the spring. But let's get back to your story."

"Where was I . . . oh yes. Just about starting out.

"I didn't want to get hungry on the way, so I made myself some pancakes with a lot of powdered eggs in them. Then I cut a stout six-foot green pole and took off over the snow-covered ice, and the whiskey jacks dropped out of the trees and came right along with me. I wonder now if I'd've gone ahead if they hadn't, even though I knew all they were thinking about was a hand-out. Jacks are mighty encouraging—friendly and full of cheer.

"On my third step I felt the ice give and stopped to watch the water creep into the snow from the crack. I'd have to pound ahead of me with the pole every step of the three miles on the river. It wasn't very deep, but even with a pole to hang onto—you leave the bark on so it won't be slippery when it gets wet—I didn't like the idea of trying to get out if I broke through, or of drying wet clothes. With a fifty-pound pack I go better than two seventy-five, so that pounding has to be more than a tap. I hammered and thumped with my right arm until it wore out and then I wore out my left. When the ice broke under the pounding, I detoured up the steep banks and tried the ice along the shore until I found a spot safe to travel on.

"There were holes with water lapping the edges, and cracks where the wind had moved the ice layer in the night, and pools on top of the ice. Some were so deep I waded over my boot toes and slush caked between my boots and the snow-shoe hitches and froze solid. I stopped and dug it out a few times but the water froze all over the boots. I had to make the best of it and that wasn't so good, because the pressure on the tops of my feet got painful and pretty soon I knew I had blisters all the way across my insteps. They wouldn't get better with this kind of traveling, but it was only half a mile more to the trail I'd come in on, and it was two and a half back to my camp.

"This trail runs along the inner side of a ridge of hills to the end of an old tote road. My car was waiting by the Trail at the other end of the tote road, keys in a coffee can under the roots of a big white pine. I kept thinking of the side trail during that last half mile on the river to keep my mind off my feet and the beating my arms were taking as I thumped the ice. I'd helped open that trail years ago when there was a fire crowning the hills, and I've been one of those who kept it open since, so it was an old highway to me. But it didn't look that way when I got to it.

"When we cut the trail, the fire'd already burnt over the land, so that now it's grown up in young birch and popple. The snow had bent the little trees down into the narrow cleared space of the trail so that a fox would've had to stoop if he'd tried to trot through. There was nothing to do but chop enough branches and trees to make room to walk.

"I leaned against a biggish tree to rest and eat a chocolate bar, and the 'jacks perched around me, flying to get little bits of the chocolate I threw on the snow for them.

"I felt livelier pretty soon, and got my ax off my pack and started ahead, but my birds stayed where they were, whistling and teetering on the branches. And then, all together, they flew back to their home. I felt as alone as I felt once when I was a boy and got lost in a fog that settled in the woods.

"That trail's four miles long and I don't know how long it took me to get through it. I could taste that dinner I'd missed and I was getting tired, so I stopped when I got to the tote road and rested and tried to revive myself by thinking that the tote road was clear of trees and I'd only two more miles to go to my car. I'd dig out my keys and be back at my trailer house right quick. Then I remembered they wouldn't be plowing the Trail on a holiday except if somebody was sick, or the like. No way I looked at it made me like it, but I couldn't just stand there.

"So I walked to my car, but then I couldn't find the can with my keys. I knew right where they ought to be, but I couldn't find them. What made it worse was that I could've made it on the Trail—the snow wasn't too deep—but I'd have had to shovel my car out first . . . and I'd left one shovel at my camp and the other was locked inside my car.

"For a minute I didn't know what I ought to do. Then I remembered you folks. I'd heard you had some car trouble but you settled in anyway—so I just walked down."

After a long silence, Ade said, "You mean you came nine miles out of the woods and three miles here through this muck —and how far along the Trail?"

"About two miles."

"Take those boots off," I said.

Jacques looked at me, eyebrows raised.

"Yes. And I'll get whatever you need to fix those blisters, and then we'll fix you up here to sleep tonight. Just what were you thinking of doing?"

"Well," he said, with that infectious grin, "I kinda thought you might have room for the old trapper—like in the stories."

After breakfast, Ade and I walked up to the road with Jacques, who looked thoughtfully at our woodpile, then shook his head.

"How are you going to get your wood—without a car?"

"I'll have to cut it and drag it in," Ade said.

Jacques, who would make two of Ade, shook his head again. "Better let that go till you're used to the cold. Ain't as easy as it sounds." He looked up at the tree tops, thought, then said, "A fellow's hauling wood off the Trail, where you got this, I reckon. A truckload for four-fifty, and that's such a good price I don't know how he can do it. If he's got time— maybe ten loads?"

I looked at him, knew that he wasn't fooled about our financial situation, calculated mentally, and said, "That'd be wonderful."

Jacques grinned again. "And if he hasn't time, I'll get you some wood. In my spare time."

"But . . ." Ade began and Jacques broke in. "You didn't let me freeze, did you?"

"Well . . . no. Thanks."

"Would you take a note to Steven's grocery?" I asked. "Whenever you go to town again? It won't take me a minute to run to the house and write it. Just to say we'll have to have groceries mailed later."

"Don't bother," Jacques said. "I'll have to go in for supplies today and I'll tell 'em."

So he swung away down the road, yesterday's long, hard struggle behind him. As I watched him out of sight I reminded myself that we were going to have to push ahead as he had, step by weary step—and there would come a day when we, too, would find the struggle behind us. This we must believe, no matter what came.

4

The next day's mail brought a note from the grocer, saying he would sell to us in case lots so we could get set for the winter, that he'd have his truck bring the order, and that he'd figure the discount and bill us at the end of the month. And, P.S., I'd better get hundred-pound sacks of flour, sugar, and potatoes. I looked at the calendar. The next mail would go December first, so the end of the month would be the end of December. With my check due in January, that would work out perfectly.

While Ade hammered together something that resembled a ladder and went to work fitting the roof saddle for the iron stove in the living room, I began the grocery order. I had an idea that a case usually held twenty-four cans and soon saw that if I ordered all the different fruits, vegetables, and meats we might want we'd have canned goods for years. I cut down the variety and was worrying over the meat when Ade came in to fit the stovepipe.

"It's going to be awful," I said, "having to eat canned meat for months."

"Why?"

"We can't keep fresh meat. No freezer. Not even ice for the icebox."

He sat down and laughed till he choked. Finally: "How were you ever so good in science? Look." He waved a hand at a window. "Out there everything is frozen and will stay that way, in the shade at least, until spring."

"Oh," I said meekly. "Of course. We can put things in cans . . ."

"We can do better than that. The barrel stove may leak smoke, but it's plenty strong enough to keep out mice and foxes and whatever. I'll set it north of the cabin. You can put a hundred pounds of meat in it and have plenty of room to reach in and get things out."

So I ordered a ham, and two huge pot roasts, lots of ground beef, and slab bacon, which I'd noticed was cheaper than sliced when I'd been in the store. I longed for sirloin steaks, but ordered thick-cut round instead. I was getting the hang of things, I hoped. I added a case of canned milk. Then I thought of eggs. How could we keep eggs? Jacques had mentioned powdered eggs. I knew nothing about them, but if he could use them, I'd learn. I kept on the list an extravagant case of boned chicken and a case of Vienna sausages, which I thought Ade liked particularly. I was wrong, and this was unfortunate for me, because the case held forty-eight cans and it takes one person a long and increasingly trying time to eat that many cans of anything, even though they are small.

While I finished and refinished the grocery list, Ade built a toboggan of old boards salvaged from the yard, with a little log in front as a bumper, and sheet metal wrapped around that end to prevent wear. He waxed the bottom with candle stubs the Larimers had left in a drawer and said he was ready to haul the grub down the path when it came. This toboggan was temporary—until we could buy one—but it is still doing fine, although now it is splintered and wobbly in spite of many bracings. It always had a tendency to go where it wanted to without considering our wishes, but it has faithfully hauled our wood and oil and food through the years.

On the following Friday evening we were settled in bed, reading by the light of two gilded bracket lamps with their original silvered-glass reflectors—bought from Mrs. Larimer and attached to the logs by Ade—when there came a clattering and banging from the road. The racket reached a climax at our path and subsided into a series of shouts.

"Somebody's cracked up," Ade said, grabbing for his clothes while I pulled on my robe and slippers. He opened the door and was almost knocked down by the headlong entry of a thin, wild-eyed man who, from his breathlessness, had come down the hill at top speed. Ade was trying to get him to sit down while I lighted the kitchen lamp, but he shook his head.

"If I sit down . . . go to sleep . . . been working twenty-four hours a day for two days . . . Jacques sent me . . . I've got your wood."

He paused for breath, his bloodshot eyes, whiskery chin,

and haggard face bearing out what he said about sleep.

"My men are at the top of your path with the first load," he went on more slowly. "There's a little cleared space. Do we put it there?"

"Fine," Ade said, and our visitor opened the door and bellowed, "Go ahead!" which started a fresh series of noises in the night. "How much can you bring?" Ade asked when the closed door made it possible to hear again.

"Eighteen loads—two cords a load—if you want it. I can't stack it all up the hill, though."

"Put some in the turn-around across from the gate next door," Ade said, and the harried man was running up the path almost before he finished speaking.

"At this rate he'll have a lively life but a short one," I said, peering into the iceless icebox. "Where's all this fanciful North Woods leisure?"

"Make my sandwich peanut butter," Ade said, sitting down at the table and leaning his elbows on the red-checked plastic I'd bought for shelves in Chicago but never used. "I'd guess he works like fury and then does nothing much for a while. Everything's seasonal up here."

"I think I'll have smoky cheese," I said, opening the box of crackers. "Let's go watch when they bring the next load."

The full moon was high and frost was sparkling on the snow and in the air. The lumberman's truck looked, at first glance, as bad off as our car after the accident. More careful study showed that although it had only one feeble headlight and no fenders and showed signs of many abrupt contacts with firmly resisting objects, it had four wheels, a cab, a small crane for loading just behind the cab, and a sturdily chugging engine. Its bed was large enough and strong enough to hold roughly the equivalent of a four-by-eight-foot stack of eight-foot logs, loaded crosswise and held on by stakes and chains. A cord was four-by-four-by-eight, so eighteen of these big loads would be thirty-six cords. Sven had said we'd need up to twenty cords a year. If we used this, and the wood we already had, carefully, it should last three years.

It is a matter of interest to watch a machine unloading heavy goods; it is a matter of wonder and astonishment to see two men doing the job with comparable speed and in a skilled coordination of irregular movement that a machine would find difficult. As one man atop the load slid the logs from the truck with a hook-tipped pole called a peavy, a man below effortlessly, and with a litheness few people have any more, avoided the heavy butts crashing toward him, balanced lightly on the unsteady logs of the growing stack on the ground, and slid the first log into place as a shout announced that another was shooting down. The harried man drove the truck, inching it forward as the ground stack increased in size. In less than fifteen minutes, the entire load of two hundred "sticks" had been neatly placed and the truck clanked away.

Sleep was sporadic that night, what with the uproar that came again and again every time I got more or less settled, but at eight o'clock I was giving coffee to the weary lumberjacks, while Ade wrote out a check for eighty-one dollars. The men left and I slumped in my chair.

"Peace and quiet, my hat!" I said, pouring some coffee. I

lifted the cup . . . and a hail came from the path, followed almost at once by a young redhead with a happy-go-lucky manner and the name of Jake.

"I've brought your groceries," he said cheerfully, "and your mail to save you the walk. Boy! With all that wood and all this grub you won't have to come to town for a couple of years."

He and Ade began hauling the cases down the hill on a metal cart and the toboggan and piling them in the middle of the kitchen floor. They were just through when a tall, gray-haired man with a reserved manner stepped up to the open door.

"Hello, Jake," he said, and came in.

Jake, with an embarrassed stiffness, introduced us to Mr. Glenn, which meant absolutely nothing to us. Mr. Glenn wouldn't have coffee, thank you. Mr. Glenn just stood by the wall and did nothing with fidgety dignity. Jake finished his coffee and left in such haste that he forgot the invoice. We expected Mr. Glenn to go along with him, but he stayed by the wall, his eyes moving back and forth between Ade and me.

"Are you looking for someone?" I asked when the situation began to grow ridiculous.

"Mr. Adrian E. Hoover," he said.

"I'm Hoover. What is it?"

Mr. Glenn handed Ade a paper. "You'd better read it."

Ade glanced over it. "It's some legal thing—has to do with somebody named George Wilson. Who's he?"

I shook my head. "Never heard of him."

Glenn was looking as puzzled as we were. "You *were* in an accident in November, weren't you?"

"Sure," Ade said, and I saw light.

"Wilson's the guy in the other car," I said, "but what's this thing?"

"It's a summons and complaint." Glenn looked at our blank faces and went on. "I'm a deputy sheriff. Wilson's suing you for eight hundred dollars damages." We gawked. "Get in touch with your attorney right away." We didn't move. "That's all you have to do. Just send him these papers."

Glenn went out. Ade and I stared at each other.

"He must be nuts!" Ade said. "There's no basis for a suit on either side."

"I know. The fellow went over everything with me and the sheriff. Anyway, we've less than three dollars now and won't have eight hundred left after we pay for the groceries out of the pension fund."

"Oh yes, we will. The property."

That frightened me. The property was, quite literally, our future. We didn't know anything about Wilson and I'd heard of some pretty sticky things that had happened when accident cases were tricked up for gain. I got hold of my thoughts. "I'll write to Joe Elliott. He's a good lawyer and he wrote our insurance and handled the property sales. He'll know what to do."

So I drafted what I thought was a reasonable letter, looked for the summons and complaint to put in the envelope, and couldn't find them. I was sure I had put the papers in the top left-hand desk drawer, but they weren't there. Ade convinced himself that I had, in a moment of madness, dropped them into the airtight as waste paper. I said "top left-hand desk drawer." He said . . . and so on for hours until I gave a yipe, pulled out the top left-hand desk drawer, and found the papers, slightly creased, where they had fallen after being pushed over the back of the drawer into the space behind.

Ade sent the letter after a miserable Saturday-to-Wednesday wait for the mail, and then we waited again—a week— ten days—and the expiration date of the summons was only twenty days after date of serving. I think we both got our first gray hairs during those days before we got a note from our attorney saying he had entered a counter suit for ten thousand dollars. We doubted that George Wilson had ten thousand cents, but comforted ourselves with the thought that this would slow him down a little.

Being dragged into court was abhorrent to me and I was sitting at the typewriter trying to distract myself by writing long letters to my friends when Sven strolled in.

"How come?" Ade asked. "We thought . . ."

"I had to come back on business and Hilda's with me. We just got to the Lodge a half hour ago and were coming to see how you were doing when . . . but what's this I hear about you suing George Wilson?"

Ade told him—at length and in colorful detail.

"Something's screwy," Sven said. "George is at the Lodge now. Said you'd sued him and would I come down and see if you'd settle out of court."

"Why did he start all this, then?" I wanted to know.

"That's what's screwy. He didn't say anything about suing

you." Sven scratched his chin. "You don't want to go to court. He doesn't want to go to court. And you've both filed suit against each other."

"Is he still there?" Ade asked. Sven said he sure was and would be until the people who'd brought him up the Trail picked him up around six on their way back to the Village. Ade reached for his jacket. "Then let's go."

The lobby of the Lodge was, for the next couple of hours, the scene of an impossible farce. Hilda fluttered behind the desk while Ade and I shouted, argued, and cajoled, fruitlessly trying to convince George Wilson that he had sued us first. He was absolutely sure this wasn't true. Finally Sven took me back to the cabin for the dated carbon of the letter I had written to Joe Elliott.

"But I don't know a thing about it!" George shouted, waving the carbon in air. "All I want is my driver's license."

"What've I got to do with that?" Ade asked.

"You have to sign a release before the state'll give it back to me."

"The state? Why'd they pick it up? You weren't to blame for the accident any more than I was."

"It's routine," Sven said. "A matter of financial responsibility. You don't have to have insurance, but in an accident with personal injury, if you haven't that or pretty valuable property of some kind they hold your license until things are settled."

Ade rubbed his temples. "I thought it *was* settled. What do I have to do?"

"Sign a release, you and George both, if you want to settle everything," Sven said.

Ade turned to George. "I still don't see why you sued me. All you had to do was ask."

George waved his arms. "Somebody told me to go to a lawyer, so I did and he said he'd write to you. That's all. I didn't do another thing. I haven't even heard from him. All I want is my driver's license."

Hilda smiled and said, "I don't suppose there's a man alive who could talk about an accident he was in without making himself look just a little bit on the abused side." Sven opened his mouth. "That means you, too, Sven. And George is only human." George turned a beautiful crimson. "I think it's all a misunderstanding."

Sven spoke into the momentary stillness. "George, why don't you call your lawyer and tell him to get together with Ade's lawyer—that's Joe Elliott—and draw up the releases. When they're ready, I'll bring Ade and Helen to town so you can clear up this fuss about nothing."

George looked hopeful. "And then can I . . ."

"Yes," Ade said with great restraint. "Then you can get back your driver's license."

5

Life had not been exactly routine during the days we waited to hear from Joe Elliott, but any unusual occurrence, good or bad, was welcome as a distraction from our main worry.

First came the problems with the stoves. To spare the airtight as much as possible because these thin-metal stoves don't last very long if they are always kept at top heat, we had planned to use the log-roller in the living room for much of our daytime and all of our night heat. However, it would handle only a small fire, just enough to give off a little heat once its thick walls were warmed up, but slowly died if we fed it a big load of wood. We decided that if we had to we would set the alarm and get up in the middle of the night to tend the stubborn stove. This idea was so unattractive that we allowed ourselves to blame the wood—maybe it wasn't dry enough—and bypassed this really urgent matter, telling each other that at our present ten to twenty-five degrees above zero we didn't need heat at night, and it wouldn't get really cold for some time.

In order to keep some heat in the living room, I trotted back and forth from stove to stove all day, while Ade split wood so that we wouldn't be any colder than we had to be in the future. Consequently, very few things outside of chopping, firing, cooking, and eating were done.

It was then that I learned the difference between clean and dirty dirt. The kitchen linoleum had paths like mud roads across it from Ade's boots, melted snow, and the ashes from the stove, and there were always twigs and chips and bits of bark scattered around. I could have scrubbed the floor a dozen times a day, and had I been one of those women who put newspapers down to keep the floor clean, I'd have been quietly taken somewhere for a "long rest." I didn't have the newspapers, anyway. We soon learned that we could ignore a dirty floor, which might not be a joy to the eyes, but which was in no way dangerous to our health. I saved my scrubbing energy for the dishes and pots and pans, because uncleanliness there could be a serious matter. As a Victorian housekeeper I would have been ostracized, for my lamp chimneys were sometimes smoky and, between the smoke from the stoves and the condensation from cooking and the light tracings of frost, my windows usually resembled those seen in an abandoned warehouse. The fogged windows worked to our advantage in one way, though. If we wanted a clear view of anything we had to go outside, where we breathed air as fresh as on the earth's first day.

I had little time for small chores like washing socks and polishing silver, so I took special satisfaction in doing them. One evening when I was drying the dishes I remembered a co-worker in a Chicago laboratory to whom I had said, "I never do anything I don't want to do." And she had replied tartly that the world would be in a sad state if there were many people like me. This startled me, because she wasn't the sort of person to be either rude or offensive without good reason, and I didn't see the reason for her insulting remark. I was hanging my dish towel in the cabin when I realized that it was all in a different point of view. She looked upon many necessary things as duties that *must* be done. It had never occurred to me that anyone with brains—of which she had plenty—wouldn't *want* to do the necessary things first.

I said something of this to Ade when I called him to haul the drain bucket from under the sink, finishing, "You have to bake the cake before you can frost it."

"It'd be hell up here for anyone who didn't think work

came first," he said. "We spend six hours a day just keeping alive," and he staggered into the wind with the bucket.

I was trying to forget the impending suit by reading one evening when I heard . . . something. "What's that?"

Ade listened. "Sounds like seals barking."

"Well, it does," he said. "I think it's ice floes rubbing together." He went outside and came back fast. "There's wind as cold as the Ninth Circle of Hell and it's five above. It's ice all right."

By the time we went to bed it was ten below and we knew we'd have to have some kind of overnight heat or our food would freeze. "Let's try the airtight," I said. "You use green wood and cut the draft almost off, they say."

This worked well—for two nights, that is.

Then I woke in the dark, covered with perspiration. I sat up, smelled hot wood, and heard the airtight roaring. I rushed into the other room. The airtight wasn't just red hot, it was white hot, and the pipe looked ready to melt. The logs beneath the chimney were smoking and dripping resin.

Ade tells me that I screamed and woke him, but I don't remember it. He glanced at the stove, grabbed the dishpan as he ran through the kitchen, and bolted outside, barefoot and in pajamas.

"Snow!" he yelled. "Put snow on it!"

I snatched my largest kettle and dashed after him. We ran back and forth, dipping snow and pouring it over the stove, on the pipe, around the feet, until it was cool enough for us to grope our way through the clouds of steam and drown the fire.

I dropped onto a kitchen chair while Ade lit a lamp and started a fire in the cook stove.

"I couldn't think. I kept trying to remember the melting point of sheet iron," I said, and burst into tears.

By the time Ade had soothed me and given me warmed-over coffee and got both of us into robes and slippers, I was shaking. "Is it awfully cold in here or is it me?"

"It's not you," he said. "Look at the windows."

The frost traceries were now a thick layer. He scraped a space and turned a flashlight on the thermometer fastened to the outside window frame. I was muttering something about my feet feeling as if they were frozen to the floor when he said, "No wonder. It's thirty-five below." He pulled off one of his slippers. "Better check for frostbite."

But neither one of us was nipped in spite of our barefoot dashes for snow. We had moved too fast and not been out long enough at a time to freeze.

Ade swept the light around inside the airtight and said, "The liner's burnt to a clinker. I'll put in another, thicker and double, when there's light enough for me to find something in the icehouse junk. You'd better get back to bed while I see what I can do with a fire in the log-roller."

In the morning Ade bundled up to look for sheet iron and I started to mop up the flood left around the airtight by the melted snow. He opened the door and called me so sharply that I dropped the mop and ran to him. Outside was a world of wonder.

"Frost," he said in an awestruck voice. "It's *frost*."

I pulled on my heavy wraps and we went out together.

I'd always thought of frost as something white on roofs or

sprinkled on grass like sugar, but this was a feathery miracle. Every twig was fringed by it, every branch festooned, every bud tufted. Delicate ice plumes hung inches long from our eaves. The windows were barley sugar and the cabin logs were netted over by tiny ice fans. The snow surface had grown what might have been grass from some fabulous realm of the North Wind. The needle clusters high on the pines had turned into sugared popcorn balls and the tops of the balsams and spruces ranked against the sky like distant mountain peaks, snow-covered, remote, and jagged.

Deep, deep into the forest reached this white fantasy, where, head and shoulders framed as by a valentine oval of lace, a deer watched us, beautiful beyond dreams in her setting. Then she twisted her ears to catch small sounds we could not hear, nipped some twigs from her white-lace frame, and disappeared.

I was still savoring this marvel when the sun stretched rayed fingers from below the hill on the south to touch the top of a birch, transforming its crystals into a corruscating veil of purest silver, which seemed to move in the breeze and take on ephemeral rainbow hues as the crystals shattered and sublimed into the air.

Unfamiliar voices sang around us—the snap of a whip, the whine of a ricochet, the cry of strained thin steel. We followed these sounds to the shore where rime clung to the trees and rocks, dense and of the whiteness of sand-blasted marble. The lake had closed during the night and was an unbroken plane, smooth and sparkling white with the frost, its thickening ice creaking and snapping as it fitted itself around the rocks and into the bays. Occasionally it heaved a little from the pressure of water underneath. Sometimes a crack streaked across it, leaving a short-lived trail of silvery water.

Then wind swirled from the south and we saw the hoarfrost vanishing from the yard as we went back to the cabin. Ade labored on the airtight and, as though to help us with our heating problem, the temperature began to rise faster than I would have thought possible. At three in the afternoon it was fifteen above and snowing heavily. Then water began to drip into the log-roller, so much of it that steam puffed out of its draft slots into the living room.

I called Ade. "This thing's being drowned from the inside. Your screening over the pipe keeps out birds all right, but the snow piles up on it and melts. At this rate, the fire'll go out."

"I'll cut a big can or something and make a tin hat for it." He went out and clanking came shortly from the roof.

"How's that?" he asked, coming in and shaking snow around the kitchen like a dog.

"Listen!" The stove roared gently and was pouring heat into the room. "My heavens! All it needed was a cap on the chimney."

He tried to look as though he'd planned it that way but couldn't quite do it.

"Let's not mention this," he said. "Everybody around here expects us to be dumb . . . but not this dumb."

The snow stopped before dark, as suddenly as it had begun, and Ade and I stepped out to look at the fresh white. The silence was so deep that I could hear my blood throbbing in my ears. The air carried a scent like the taste of snow. A feeling of being watched from the white forest was very strong.

"They're all around us," I said. "The natives. We're a minority of two."

"You can really feel them out there."

"Yes. We're entering on an entirely new experience."

"You might say we entered on it some time ago," Ade said drily.

"Sure, but I mean we came here to find seclusion and beauty and instead we've found a kind of isolation few people of our time and country will ever know. At least in winter. Think about it. The nearest people are the Indians three miles away across the lake. The nearest grocery and doctor are forty-five miles away in the Village. The nearest telegraph and airport are in Duluth . . . that's a hundred fifty-five miles, and the railroad . . . I think a branch line ends about thirty-five miles closer."

"There's a bus to Duluth . . ."

"But it's only once a day or something like that in winter. We've no transportation, no daily newspaper, no radio, no TV, no telephone. We've no communication at all except the mail, and that's three miles away and it'll only be once a week after the first of the year."

"And we've no services," Ade put in. "You know, we're set apart like pioneers, only you can't live off the land any more. Not that I'd want to, except to have a garden."

"We wouldn't do very well playing at being old-timers, anyway. We've always made our living by thoughts and pencils and we can't change to muscles and guns overnight. Oh, we'll use our muscles more, but we're really making another kind of change. I think we'll have it made when we do what we have to do without thinking of the things we no longer have."

"Could be." Ade grinned. "For my part, it'll be when I don't wonder what I'll do wrong next."

6

Three days before Christmas Ade left for the mail and I sat at the kitchen table. It wasn't strange that the holiday had almost caught us unaware, considering the confusion of the recent past, but it was strange that, with things reasonably calm again, I couldn't feel in the mood of the season. Here I was, in the ideal Yuletide setting—but I couldn't get the feeling of Christmas! And it wasn't because we hadn't received the usual cards or because I was away from friends and familiar places. Ade and I had always enjoyed having a quiet Christmas Day to ourselves. I walked outside. It was sunny and crisp, a perfect winter day, and it was quiet, with a sort of brooding silence. Nonsense. I was brooding, not the woods. But the needles did not whisper and the lapping of water was held under the ice . . . and then I knew what I was missing. The carols blaring from loudspeakers, the office groups wondering about early closing on Christmas Eve, the exciting preparations for a day off.

It came to me first that "days off" had vanished from my life and next that the whole holiday season had been for me a series of outside activities, which, in the rush of Chicago's business world, had taken the place of the warm inner joy I missed now. It must have been missing from my Christmases for years, but I had been too busy to notice.

I looked toward the road and saw the rays of the low sun reaching up from behind the hills as rays sometimes reach down from clouds at sunset. I remembered that the day just past was the shortest of all the year and that now began the slow lengthening of the hours of light that would bring warmth and green leaves in the spring. Everything around me was waiting for that, and I had forgotten the wisdom that had placed Christmas Day so near to the ancient festival celebrating the even more ancient return of the sun.

Then I thought of the forest—stretching south to the farmlands, west to the plains, north to the tundra, east to Lake Superior and beyond. I began to tremble as I saw my smallness and inadequacy against the vastness of the natural world. I went into the cabin because inside I was important enough to control my surroundings. I sat down, wondering why I'd never felt a need to run home for shelter in the city. Then I knew that cities were, although not unnatural, far removed from the indifferent forces of nature. Aside from man-made trouble, only such things as great storms or floods or earthquakes disturbed their artificial complacency, and the people in them were all rulers of their domain. I got up and went to the window. This was all very reasonable but I still felt terror growing, something I might feel if I had just learned I was the

last human alive. This was completely witless and I knew I'd have to break it up at once. I got scarf and gloves and jacket and headed for the road.

Ade's boot tracks were the only sign of life on the light layer of fresh snow and I had a dreadful moment when I imagined that he would keep on going—and never come back. I remembered the doctor's reservations about his reactions to cold . . . and he would have to trudge back and forth all winter over that empty road! I'd share the trips if he'd let me, but there were my still uncertain knees. I started to follow him, realized that this was giving way to my fear, stood very still until I had control of myself, then turned and walked in the opposite direction.

The undisturbed beauty of the snow was frightening, so very empty, until I saw the heart-shaped tracks of a deer along the roadside. I caught movement high in a tree ahead of me and, with a flourish of gray wings, a whiskey jack lighted on a low branch in a cloud of disturbed snow. He cocked his head, gazed at me with a bright, dark eye, and trilled softly. I stopped and answered in my best low whistle. He rocked on his branch and replied in a friendly warble. While we continued this pleasant if unintelligible conversation, I again sensed movement ahead of me. Half-hidden in the brush a doe, probably the maker of the tracks, had her eyes and ears turned in my direction, testing this creature who stood in her roadway. She and the whiskey jack left at the same time and I turned back.

When I came to the path and looked at Ade's tracks I merely wondered how far he had gone. I thought of Jacques' long, long walk, and again of the vast wilderness around me, but I was no longer afraid. It didn't matter that the forest dwarfed Ade and me. It only mattered that we should recognize our smallness. As long as we remembered that, we would know our limitations, as all men should know their own, and we could live here as safely and naturally as though we had been born with wings or paws.

I looked back along the snow-trimmed road and knew that I would never feel lonely here again. The whiskey jack and the doe had come at the critical time to remind me that I was linked to them, not only by our common flesh and blood, but by the very earth from which we had sprung.

5 Snow Scene

1

We moved warily as the days marched toward the end of the year. Things had been so hectic that we were conditioned to expect anything, but I went about my chores and Ade cut wood without interruption. Then he decided to build a wood-shed. When he announced that he had found a good, flat spot where he could remove the snow easily before he began notching logs, I smelled quite a project and went out to look things over. The location was sixty feet from the house and, considering the length of the weathered but sound logs he had moved from an old stack of Carl's, he was going to build another cabin.

I moaned inwardly and said, "This'll take ages, and you can't get a proper foundation for all that weight now. Besides, I can just see myself staggering all this way through a snowstorm with an armload of wood. Better still, I can see you doing it. Why don't you build a shack close to the kitchen door?"

He thought this might not be too bad an idea and it would certainly be easier. In two days he completed a shed of weathered boards, open to the south and protected somewhat from rain and snow by pieces of Carl's discarded blue roofing. It stood on the northeast corner of the cabin and all I had to do was step out, turn left, select my wood, and pop back in. Purely by accident it broke the north wind and prevented snow from blowing across the doorstep. We couldn't have planned it better and when, later on, people complimented us on our cleverness, we looked suitably modest and said nothing. This shed was temporary, you understand, but Ade re-roofed it for the second time last year.

Next day's mail, the last midweek delivery until spring, brought my long-awaited pension-fund check, unexpectedly early but well timed—the grocery bill arrived with it—and a stack of Christmas cards, forwarded in a bunch from Chicago. The check wasn't as large as I'd estimated—such things rarely are—and the grocery bill was larger, as I might have expected. I did some hasty figuring. After we paid the grocer, and Sven for his chain saw, and the taxes and fire insurance —even if we increased the latter to a reasonable amount— we'd have enough of a balance to cushion things slightly until we could earn some money, and that couldn't be put off much longer. What we needed was a bright idea, but we'd think of something, now that we had passed through the first stages of getting settled and had some free time. We'd have to think of something.

I put this aside and began to open the cards, only to stop short. What could we do about these Christmas greetings? We couldn't let all our human contacts die just because we were out of reach. We'd made our own cards several times and still had plenty of envelopes but nothing else.

Ade came in with a pail of water, saying that the ice was thick enough to walk on and he'd cut a water hole and nailed some boards to make a cover for it so nothing could fall in; it also might slow down freezing under it.

"Mmmmm," I said, and handed him the cards I had opened. "We ought to answer these some way. I'd type up a New Year's letter if I could get to a mimeograph machine, but . . ."

"I've been thinking," Ade said. "If we're going to make a living here we'll have to do it by mail, for a while, anyway. We could use a mimeo for advertising."

This sounded practical to me, and we also felt, not very reasonably, that our thinking of mimeographs at the same time, even though for different reasons, might be a good omen. Ade remembered that the movers had even packed our Chicago telephone directories. After he found them and a Chicago dealer's address, I typed a letter asking for prices on used hand-operated machines—with a mental reservation as to whether they still existed—and of accessories and paper. Ade took the letter to the mailman on New Year's Eve, and came back through snow that fell straight down, fine and thick and heavy.

This seemed as good a day as any to try to bake some bread, all the mixes being used and biscuits having lost their tastiness through continual eating of them. I got out Hilda's recipe. It made four loaves . . . and called for eggs, milk, and shortening. I didn't know how to substitute powdered eggs and milk and we were not well supplied with shortening, but I had a feeling that many loaves had been baked without those ingredients. I halved the recipe for my maiden attempt and decided to use only yeast, flour, salt, and water.

I climbed on the sink and took down the big jar of flour Carl had left in the cupboard, but when I began to stir it into the dissolved yeast it, too, dissolved. Flour dissolving? Then I saw a tip of cardboard in the jar and pulled it out. Cornstarch! I emptied the bowl and started over, silently thanking the grocer for telling me I needed the hundred-pound sack of flour.

The mixture puffed up satisfactorily and when I dumped the dough onto the floured counter and began to work it— rather timidly at first—I found that I liked this. I watched big blisters form in it and pop, and when the dough was as springy as soft rubber, I shaped two loaves . . . and looked wildly around for something to bake them in. Finally I found bread pans in the kitchen things Carl had left behind. By the time I had washed and greased them, I had to work the dough over, of course. I had no way to tell oven temperature, so I let the loaves rise and put them to bake—hopefully.

I found such satisfaction in the whole process, uncertain though I was, that I believe there is something basic about making bread, handed down from mother to daughter through all the centuries since one of my ancestors first pounded wild grain in a hollow stone and made cakes of it to bake by the fire. And where was that fire, I wonder? When I took the loaves from the oven, brown and crusty, I was as proud as if I had invented bread. I called Ade to admire my production and, when they were cool enough, we cut off a heel, thick and fragrant, and divided it between us.

"I haven't tasted bread like this since my grandmother used to bake," he said.

Aside from my delight at the time, I think I know why. That was the kind of bread our grandmothers did bake, bread to go with eggs and milk and not necessarily to contain them. In any case, our bread is still baked as those first loaves were.

We spent the evening more or less reading, but mostly talking over past New Year's Eves—and there is a lot to remember when you've spent so many of them together, with only the break caused by World War II. I got out the last of the cheese and made toasted sandwiches, served with a flourish and a hitherto concealed bottle of stuffed olives.

"Very luxurious," Ade said, chewing.

"Luxury," I said sententiously, "is like a lot of other things —all in the point of view. Once it was an extra car; now it's an olive with an onion in it. It's midnight. Let's go outside."

We walked away from the cabin into the darkness that comes with a heavy snowfall and stood in the muffled silence, remembering the shouting, glittering city we had left behind.

"I suppose a lot of people would feel sorry for us," I said, softly so as not to break into the stillness too much. "Poor souls spending New Year's Eve all alone in a wilderness."

"No doubt. And if we were where they are, we'd be making a lot of noise and three or four hours from now we'd be going home and wondering whether we'd be hit by some celebrant on the way. We'd have spent enough money to keep us for a couple of months here and have nothing to show for it tomorrow but a big head. We've walked into 'the good old days.' It's not a matter of time—it's a way of life."

Later I woke to the sound of wind whistling and moaning under the eaves. A tree cracked like a shot under the inexorable pressure of frost. I sat bolt upright. How could we possibly be here? The whole idea was preposterous! Pretty soon I'd really wake and hear the hissing of a radiator as the janitor got up steam in our apartment building. But a log fell in the stove with a thump and the glow of rising flames lighted the foot of my bed. It was real, all right, and it was also very cold in the room. I groped for my slippers and pulled them into the bed. When they were warm, I slid them on and hurried across the cold and drafty floor to lug a big birch chunk from the woodbox and push it through the door of the stove. Then I crawled gratefully into the down-soft warmth of my sleeping bag.

Stretching and relaxing in the primitive animal pleasure of getting warm I recognized this as only one of many simple things I had never appreciated or even thought about in the outside world. Suddenly the moon slipped from behind the clouds and its light slanted in the west window so that the curtain of icicles hanging from the wide eaves glowed as with its own pale-blue luminescence. The storm was over. The stove breathed steadily. The varnished logs shone dimly in faint light reflected from the fire. Drowsiness came to me with the warmth and I fell asleep again.

I woke next time with the tantalizing scent of coffee in my nostrils. I jumped up to look out of the window, which seemed to be nearer the ground; instead, the snow level had risen a full two feet. The sky was a clear, pale blue, the air seemed made of light, and there were as yet no little trails on the snow. Deep wind rings were hollowed at the base of every tree and drifts as high as my head were edged with sharp folds of snow, like waves frozen into immobility just before the moment of their breaking.

"I'll tramp some snowshoe paths," Ade said. "Shoveling all that doesn't appeal."

I went out and stood on the step—almost snow-free thanks to our woodshed—and looked up the sparkling slope toward the road. The path was obliterated—I could not even tell exactly where it had been—and a snow wall had built itself along the edge of the clearing.

"You can't walk over that," I said. "I'll help you shovel."

When we had cut through the drift, we saw that the rest of the path was travelable, just.

"If the road's drifted like that—can they get the plow through?" I wondered.

"I think so. It'll pack. If they don't get to this road for a while, I can tramp over it for the mail. The system is to roll with the punch."

"I'm learning." I looked closely at him. "This light certainly shows up your whiskers. Why don't you shave?"

"Lost my blades. I'll find 'em. They must be somewhere."

"You could grow a beard." (This was, of course, long before beards began to sprout as symbols of individuality and then went on to mark the individual as one of a group.)

"You mean you wouldn't mind?" He was incredulous.

"Not only that. I've a sneaking liking for beards—unless they're scraggly. Besides, it'll keep your face warm."

Ade, shaking his head, looked me over carefully. "I guess you mean it. You'll never cease to surprise me."

On that note we turned away from the snowbank.

"Look," he said, stopping as we neared the doorstep. "Our tracks."

Out from the door they came, gray and dusty from our floors, but in only a few steps the snow had wiped our boot soles clean and we had left only blue-shadowed hollows behind us.

"In the city you track dirt in," he went on. "Here you track it out. It's symbolic."

2

All day there was a ceaseless fall of glittering frost, like snow from a clear sky, ephemeral and enchanted, spreading a thin veil over the movements of birds and animals brought into the open by the snow to seek food. None of them came to the cleared area west and south of the cabin where the snow had buried the barren, bulldozed earth, but three ruffed grouse came to the tips of the undisturbed raspberry canes north of the cabin. They wallowed and floundered through soft snow, righted themselves and walked briskly up wind-packed snow waves, only to tumble over the crests, land in a flurry, then pick themselves up with much puffing and rearranging of their finely patterned gray and brown and white feathers. They went from prickly cane to prickly cane, burrowing their heads into the snow to nip off buried buds. Their alert black eyes watched everywhere and their crests, swept back and down, lifted only when they were alarmed—by my movement in a window or the approach of a squirrel. When they froze they were hard to see even against unbroken snow, because their irregularly striped black-and-white sides blended into the white and their other feathers took on the appearance of stumps and stones.

Once a squirrel came very near and two of the birds puffed their feathers and spread their tails. The squirrel retreated in haste—they must have looked very large to him—and I noticed that one bird's tail had a continuous band near the rear edge while the other had a band broken in the middle. Since then I have seen male grouse strutting in the spring, tails like lifted fans, wings drooping, black neck feathers raised to form the ruff for which these birds are named. Every one of these strutting birds had unbroken black bands on their tails and I assume that the individuals with discontinuous tail bands are females.

The squirrels were leaping about in the cedars, cutting down bunches of cones that decorated the snow, small, light-brown wooden flowers, grown in graceful clusters with an intricate leaf or two to add to their beauty. When each squirrel had cut several clusters, he scampered down to his own cones and sat, gobbling seeds and scattering bracts while carrying on a noisy argument with any other squirrel who might happen to be nearby. There were eight squirrels now, all eating and arguing in a manner that would have brought a tableful of people to ulcers in no time. Now and then two of them stopped eating, folded paws on creamy vests, pattered furiously with hind feet, and yelled at each other until one leaped out and the fight started. The flurry of claws and teeth usually ended in seconds, the victor returning to his own cones and the vanquished removing himself a short distance, to return to his original place after a discreet wait and take up eating where he had left off.

Suddenly all the squirrels were in an uproar. There was such a hubbub that I went out but didn't see anything unusual. Then a squirrel leaped from an observation post on top of a snow mound that hid a stump and rushed after what seemed to be a white flash. The white flash kept an easy distance ahead of the squirrel, circled widely, and stopped almost at my feet to look up at me. This was an ermine, exquisitely graceful, fluffy as whipped cream and as creamy white, too, with black tail tip and ear touches, eyes like polished jet, a pink nose and rounded ears pink-lined. He sat up, all of eight inches high, lifting dainty forepaws and twitching a fine spray of long whiskers.

At this point birds began to circle and swoop—blue jays, whiskey jacks, chickadees, each screaming in his own way. The ermine considered this onslaught for a moment, dropped flat to avoid the beak of a dive-bombing jay, then shot between my feet and plumped into a snowbank where he no doubt had his own secret passageways. The birds scattered and I went inside to hear a frantic squeaking and scurrying in the double ceiling where some deer mice had found shelter for the winter. A few minutes later I again heard the blue jays' sharp alarm call and the ratchety sound of disturbed whiskey jacks. I looked out to see the ermine bounding away, a large mouse dangling from his jaws. He stopped once and sat up to scan the snow surface, holding his head proudly as if to show everyone his fine dinner.

"That's the handsomest little animal I've ever seen," Ade said from behind me. "I hope he sticks around."

"The mice'll keep him for a while. Unless I mistook the sounds overhead, he caught that one in our ceiling."

Ade thought a minute. "We've some bacon rind. He might like that."

"The birds will, whether he does or not. You could tack it down somewhere so it doesn't get carried off."

Ade nodded. "And we ought to put it where we can see who comes for it. There's that bench outside . . ."

It was in the shape of a bench but was too high, too narrow, and too wiggly for anyone to sit on. However, it made a fine small feeding bench and Ade placed it outside the south window at dusk. The cabin protected it from the prevailing northwest wind and the big eaves would keep it free of snow, while we could stand inside and watch in comfort. We didn't expect visitors until the next day, but in the middle of the night I was wakened by a heavy sound—something striking the cabin wall.

I couldn't see anything from the window but the noise stopped when I looked out. Some creature had seen me. We were conserving the weakening flashlight batteries for emergencies, so I went cautiously into the outside darkness, remembering that the noise had been rather loud and wondering what kind of animal might be out there. As my eyes grew accustomed to the starlight, I saw the bench tilted toward the wall and the ermine standing over a strip of rind, braced as though ready to defend it against me. I stood without moving. At last the little animal, not half as large around as my wrist and only a foot long, tail and all, jerked at the rind with such strength that the whole bench moved and struck against the wall. I walked slowly toward him, but he didn't run. When I was almost within touching distance he retreated to the ground and, partially protected by one of the bench legs, squeaked angrily.

I was filled with admiration for him and his courage. He should have his bacon if I could arrange it. I pulled out the nail that held the strip, took the rind in my fingers, leaned down slowly, and held the tidbit out to the ermine. He drew back, making a melodious, warbling sound that might have been a warning. I stayed as I was and after a long wait he inched forward nervously. I was a bit nervous myself because his teeth were needle sharp and he was lightning fast. Then he leaped for the rind, pulled it from my hand, and streaked away.

Only then I remembered that ermines are weasels and that someone had once told me that "weasels will jump at your face." This didn't make much sense after what I had just seen. My ermine had jumped at the rind because he wanted it, but he hadn't even looked at my face. As I recalled it, the woman who had been "jumped at" was bending down, holding a piece of meat in her fingers, moving the food about so that the little animal could not get it. So, hungry and tormented, he had jumped at her face . . . and I don't blame him.

The next day birds came to the bench and Ade and I did little but sit inside and watch. There were more than a dozen chickadees, so lively I couldn't get an accurate count. They were energetic little feather balls, most of them with gray-and-white bodies and black-velvet caps and bibs. Two, a little darker all over than the others, had rosy-buff breasts and dark-brown caps, and softly slurred voices that said *zhee-zhee-zhee* instead of *dee-dee-dee*. They darted and dipped and picked the tiniest morsels from the rind and bench, making almost as much noise with their small, pointed beaks as woodpeckers. Flocking with them were nuthatches, slate-backed, black-masked, and rose-breasted, hopping upside down on the bench legs before they flew up to take their share of the bacon fat.

I remembered the black-capped chickadees from my Ohio childhood, as well as the two species of woodpeckers that came periodically to monopolize the bacon: the long-beaked hairies, a little shorter than robins but much slimmer, and the smaller downies, with rounder heads and shorter beaks. Both are black and white, with nearly identical feather markings, and the males have almost fluorescent red patches at the back of their heads. Somehow, downies always look like young hairies to me.

The blue jays, too, were old friends, with their turquoise and black and white, their violet-washed heads and backs. Beside them the whiskey jacks, gentle-voiced and modestly clad, reminded me of Jane Eyre in gray bombazine. At close view they were comical because they had been drinking somewhere—perhaps at an unfrozen trickle from the brook—and the protective feathers around their beaks were frozen like upright hairs and made them look as if they needed a shave. It was a year or two later that I learned they were relatives of the blue jays and very aptly named gray jays.

The red squirrels came, too, scattering the birds. They sampled the fat, liked it, and nipped off small pieces which they ate at once. This was contrary to a common belief that they will carry meat away but never eat any. They do, however, take food home, perhaps for very cold days when they are less active.

I looked away from the squabbling birds and squirrels. Hopping around the trunk of a pine was a pileated woodpecker, unquestionably the most spectacular of the birds that frequent our particular type of forest. He was the size of a large crow, but longer of body and shorter of tail, with a proud scarlet crest, black-and-white-striped face and neck, and black back and tail. He visited several trees, then flew out of sight, stiff wing feathers creaking rhythmically. That one of his kind would prove helpful to us later on, we had no idea.

And then the nine deer moved across the face of the hill between the cabin and the road, four does and five fawns, not hurrying, nipping a maple twig or nosing some tidbit from the snow's surface, stopping to curl a long neck back to lick an itchy spot, ambling on again, unconcerned and relaxed, following a trail we had seen indented into the snow but had not recognized for what it was. The shadows of the brush were soft, so that the deer stood out clearly, especially those whose winter coats were more brown than gray. One doe in particular was almost a golden color. She was small and slim and had no fawns, and I know now that she was a yearling. The other three does were larger and had, respectively, two pairs of twins and a single fawn.

One pair of twins were very small, with bright brown coats and pale faces. They stayed close to mother, although they watched the cabin with wide and wondering eyes. The second pair were grayish and plump, with larger ears rimmed inside with fine hairs like black velvet. They seemed inclined to do some investigating and moved nearer and nearer the clearing until recalled in some way by their mother. Once they were back on the trail, she walked toward the cabin, ears laid back and nostrils spread. When nothing happened, she returned to her children, glancing back occasionally and sniffing as though we contaminated the air—which, to her sensitive nostrils we probably did in fact. The other doe and fawn stayed close together and hardly looked toward the house.

I thought again of the four young squirrels and of the individuality in behavior they, too, had shown, but mostly I was breathless at the beauty of the deer. If you thought of them piecemeal they seemed awkward—big ears, long neck, blocky body, short tail, legs too thin and hoofs too small—but to watch them was another matter. They turned and twisted and stretched in almost impossible ways, but no movement was without grace. They moved their ears together or singly into unexpected positions, and these movements gave expression to their slender, large-eyed faces. And when something startled them and they flipped up their white flags and ran, they moved with such sureness and precision, such lightness and rhythm, that their elegance held Ade and me spellbound.

I sighed as they went out of sight and Ade said, "We aren't

going to lack for entertainment. I hadn't thought how interesting this sort of thing could be."

I hadn't either, and it came to me that this was my first
opportunity, and a remarkable one for the times, to learn
something about wild animals. There had been some in the
country around my childhood home, mostly fox squirrels, cot-
tontails, raccoons, and muskrats, but my father thought of
them only as something to hunt and my mother was afraid of
anything but a horse, a chicken, or a dog. Cats might scratch,
birds might fly over her head and create an embarrassing
moment, cows were huge creatures who might be expected to
charge without warning. Hunting was not in me and, by some
fortunate chance, I did not catch my mother's fear. When I
met the wild citizens of the North Woods I was ready and
willing to accept them as friends.

3

The snowplow cleared our New Year's snow from the side
road so early on the following Tuesday that we were not
awake to hear it go by. We did not see how it could have
reached us so quickly until we considered that the Trail
stretched a long way and the snowfall might have been much
lighter in the Village and on the part of the Trail near there.

So, in spite of our heavy local snow and the Saturday-only
mail, the mimeograph plans rushed ahead. Ade's letter
brought a reply from a Duluth representative who could ship

a hand-operated machine two days after receiving our order. We ordered the machine, stencils, ink, paper, and styli, the latter in case Ade wanted to decorate whatever we sent out. That meant a mimeoscope, which was too costly for us even to think of buying. Ade said he'd make his own and, while I got the order ready, he hunted up glass and wood scraps and assorted hardware. The result worked perfectly, even though lighted by reflected sun or lamp light instead of an electric bulb.

The mailman offered to bring the parcels from the freight office for Ade to pull the last three miles on his toboggan. He waxed it thoroughly on the Thursday before he expected the shipment, and it began to snow that evening. It was still coming down the next morning, adding steadily to the deep layer already on the ground. Ade went out, put the toboggan away, came back in.

"From the direction this is coming it'll be deeper toward town. Nobody'll get through till it's plowed."

The snow covered the frozen waves left by the New Year storm, smoothed over wind rings and stumps, piled up like white sand level with our window sills. Ade kept a small space outside the door shoveled clear and walked back and forth on showshoes—to the shore, to the outbuildings, up the hill to the road—packing the snow so that we could move around easily.

The clouds moved out on Saturday afternoon. We thought the plow might reach us late Tuesday, more likely on Wednesday. When it had not come by Wednesday night we began to feel, not exactly worried, but uncertain. It was our understanding that the road would be plowed, *if* the plow could get through. We really didn't know much about such things and there was nothing we could do about it, anyway. Ade could always snowshoe down the side road, but what if the Trail were blocked? That meant no mail and the mail was our financial life line.

If we couldn't get the mimeo, we couldn't start work on our tenuous ideas until spring and, although we had resolved not to touch our small reserve funds during the winter except in a real emergency, we suddenly felt that we needed things—to come by mail, of course.

This wasn't entirely imaginary. We were running short of oil for the lamps, the flashlight had glowed its last, and we had finished our meat three days before. The last was very upsetting to me at the time, but, looking back, I see that considering my lack of experience I had ordered fairly well. Considering also our finances, I doubt that I could have done much about it except cut out the few luxuries, and their psychological value was important during those early days of our adjustment.

On the brighter side, we could be thankful that we had bought plenty of warm clothes and the sleeping bags, and that we still had lots of canned vegetables, flour, sugar, potatoes, tea, and coffee, and the helpful but monotonous dry milk and powdered eggs.

When the plow had not arrived by Friday noon, we decided we were snowed in and stopped dithering. If we were without contact with the outside until the spring thaw, we were—and that was that. Ade went to the storage building to measure and ration the lamp oil so that we should not be without light. I sat down to my first long-distance food rationing, glad that I didn't like meat much and so would probably get to like the dry milk and eggs.

Then I heard Ade yell and opened the door. The plow was rattling and roaring its slow way toward us and Ade was already halfway up the hill, dragging the toboggan. The mail would follow the plow, of course, and he could ride to the Trail on the plow. I caught glimpses of red lights, on in the day as a safety precaution. When the plow stopped I heard loud voices and was startled by their strangeness. Only people are habitually noisy in places where a murmur can be heard a long way, and why they are is still as incomprehensible to me as are many of the doings of the wild animals.

The coming of the plow brought contradictory feelings. I found that I had liked being cut off from the outside or, to put it another way, being enclosed in our small domain. There had been no sense of imprisonment, only an awareness of being part of a secluded world, gratifyingly separated from the confused one we had left. But still it was good that the plow had made outside contact possible again. It was not a sense of relief; I was no longer afraid here and we could have managed well enough until spring. It was that our living must come from the outside, and we were dependent on it as the cave men had been dependent on their native earth. I was a part of two worlds, and always would be.

The arrival of the mimeograph completed the change of the erstwhile bedroom into a multifaceted workroom. Ade's jig-saw had been installed earlier for doing odd jobs, with a motor and a small gas engine to power it, the engine exhaust going outside through a hole in the frame of the east window. His workbench was beside it, with tools neatly hung in a wall cabinet that had once seen duty in someone's bathroom and which Ade had dug out of the mud of the basement floor. His drawing table still waited in front of the south window, and the mimeograph was established on top of the heavy chest that had once held Carl Johnson's clothing. The effect was somewhat spoiled by the big sacks of potatoes, flour, and sugar between the base of the drawing table and the wall under the window, and by the apple-box shelves of canned goods along what wall space was left, but when space is limited you do what you must with things.

New Year's greetings at the end of January would be ridiculous. I sat down the next day to write a general letter about our sudden move.

"Can you make some kind of decoration or drawing for it?" I asked Ade.

"Hand drawing on stencils is simple cartoon stuff. I don't know how it'd look."

"Does it have to be that—crude, I mean?" I was thinking of Ade's delicate pen-and-ink drawings.

"Did you get a fine stylus?"

"Yes."

He shrugged and reached for a sketch pad. "Maybe I can do something different. No harm in trying."

By the time I had finished the letter, he had a sketch. A snow-laden balsam stood tall at the left. A doe with her fawn and a snowshoe hare looked curiously down our path to the cabin, beyond which the lake lay flat and white, bordered by the Canadian shore.

"It's perfect," I said. "Mark off a space for it in the bottom left corner of a sheet of paper and I'll type the letter to fit."

"You might wait to see whether I can get these fine lines on the stencil without tearing it apart," he suggested.

As it turned out, he had less trouble with his drawing than I did cutting a stencil on a Remington portable given me for Christmas in 1923, but I typed that stencil, and many more, and hundreds of articles and four books on that typewriter. Now, at the ripe old age of forty-five years, it only needs a good going over to have it in shape for its next million words.

The letters brought a flood of replies and I noticed two things about them: almost everyone commented on the beauty of Ade's design and asked similar questions about our move and new way of life.

"These people really like your drawing," I said. "They wouldn't have to compliment you out of politeness, and if they didn't think it was striking they wouldn't say anything."

"So?"

"Why don't you think up some more designs and see if you haven't salable notepaper? It'd be a lot better than making wooden things to order."

Ade looked thoughtful. He had done woodworking and hand painting in Chicago as a hobby, but the mail-order market for such things was very uncertain. It was impractical except as a stop-gap source of income, anyway, because of the large amount of time involved. "I think you've got something," he said after a while. "I can still do a little jigsaw work—any port in a storm and all that."

So he went to work on the designs for the notepaper that was to be our first regular source of income, and I wrote another general letter, answering the questions that had been asked. Through the years many others have asked the same ones and those questions were the springboard for this book.

4

We knew at the start of the year that our financial situation was dangerously shaky and might well get worse before it got better, but it never occurred to us that there was anything disgraceful in being in the class of church mice or, as Ade put it, deer mice. That some people feel it is almost a moral lapse not to have a lot of money seems unreasonable to us. We learned during the depression years that having too little was not important in the material sense as long as we could get enough to buy the bare essentials for survival, but it was extremely important in the sense that stretching it to get those essentials tried our strength and ingenuity as nothing else in ordinary living could.

Now, we were up against the problem, more important than it sounds, of having only so many books for evening relaxation, not enough for both of us. Buying more, even paperbacks, was out of the question. Suddenly I was inspired. I plowed through the snow to the summer house and came back with *David Copperfield* and a large box full of thread, linen, and other appurtenances for needlework. So started the evenings when Ade read aloud and I crocheted or embroidered by the light of a wall lamp and its old-fashioned reflector. This is a better light than you might think and resembles the lamplight, concentrated by a bottle of water, that was used for generations by the pillow-lace makers of Bruges. *Copperfield* was a fortunate selection, too, because from it came the motto that for several years was tacked onto a log in the kitchen:

SOMETHING WILL TURN UP.

J. Wilkins Micawber.

And something did, in the form of a sizable order for jigsaw work from one of Ade's former Chicago customers. We decided to buy ground beef and bacon with part of Ade's windfall and he walked back to the Trail to "make that damn phone line work, at least as far as the butcher's."

There was also a letter from Hilda, asking if we'd like some baby chicks to raise. It seemed that one of the summer residents always had some for chicken dinners and she'd be glad to bring us a few. I wrote Hilda that we'd love to rear some chickens. The thought of possibly keeping some hens through the winter and having real eggs was heavenly.

When Ade picked up the meat next mail day, there was a second package filled with fresh suet and some rather doubtful bones, along with a note saying that we might enjoy feeding the birds, and maybe we could attract a fox. Foxes, said the note, were very entertaining and fine mousers. This was not only kind but cheering, because so many people think foxes, along with all other meat-eating animals, are villainous from birth. It was also important because it ushered in the time of our learning to know some of the animals instead of just admiring them as they went by.

Ade tacked a hunk of suet onto the bench and laid a meaty bone near it, where it would be available to any fox who might pass our way. The birds arrived *en masse*, the whiskey jacks and blue jays monopolizing the suet while the chickadees and nuthatches buzzed around uttering cries but getting no food. Even the woodpeckers hung back. The birds prudently took to the air when two squirrels approached the suet from opposite sides. Without warning, one squirrel bounced up and over the suet to send the other backwards off the bench. Before the winner could more than sniff at the prize, the loser climbed stealthily up a bench leg and bit the other's tail. Both squirrels seemed to shoot into the air before falling to the ground in a noisy ball of violently agitated fur. When drops of blood began to fall bright on the snow and the combatants separated, probably to get their bearings and start over, one sported a torn ear and the other pawed at the tip of his nose, which was ripped loose and flapping. Ade went out, shooed the squirrels, divided the fat into several portions which he tacked firmly to the bench, and scattered crumbs of suet on the snow. This didn't exactly bring "peace in our time" but it reduced the warfare to vocal protests and let all the visitors have a share, the squirrels getting the most by the simple expedient of gnawing portions free from the nails and carrying them home with all speed.

After they had made three trips, Ade said, "At this rate we won't have suet very long. I'll cover it with some of that half-inch-mesh hardware cloth I found in the basement."

He removed all the suet except one long piece, which he enclosed in a tight-fitting wire cage nailed firmly to the bench.

This did not hinder the birds' feeding and allowed the squirrels to gnaw off some fat, while completely foiling their attempts at grand larceny. Eventually they hopped away in opposite directions, muttering and grumbling and perhaps thinking dark squirrel thoughts about big animals who put out delicious food and then fix it so that squirrels can't have it all.

Next morning I looked out the window at the bench, didn't believe my eyes, went out to look again, and called Ade. In the snow were tracks about three inches across, the rear footmarks being noticeably longer than the front. Every print was blurred by fur at the edges and showed five rounded toe marks, each preceded by the marks of short claws. They didn't resemble tracks of members of either the dog or cat family, the bears were asleep, and we were completely at a loss.

The remarkable thing was the way our visitor had fed. To get the suet he had drawn the front nails, laid them neatly side by side, and turned the cage back as though on hinges. The bone was also gone.

"Nice of him not to damage the cage," Ade said. "You'd think he had hands."

Because I get sleepy later than Ade, I volunteered to watch for the stranger. The first night we left a small piece of suet on the bench but the weasel came for it as though he had been waiting. After that we left a small portion in the cage. It disappeared that night, and the next and the next, but I did not see the stranger, not even when the moon was bright. He bided his time and moved like a shadow among the shadows.

Meanwhile, when Ade was busy with his woodwork and plans for notepaper, I spent happy hours weasel-watching. When I heard the blue jays screaming, the squirrels chattering, the nuthatches' nasal cries almost drowning out the frantic *dee-dee-dee* of the chickadees, I knew it was time. And across the snow came the weasel, in his precious ermine white, loping along with such grace and lightness that he made me think of a plume rolling before the breeze. To me, he was a fairytale animal, lovelier than life, but to the small ones of the forest he was a dreaded hunter.

The more I saw of Walter—and when or why we started to call our weasel that I don't remember—the more I wanted to see, so I decided to try to persuade him that I was harmless. This took great patience and much time. Like many carnivores, he was essentially a creature of the night and shy by day. It is not easy to overcome such instinctive shyness, nor should it be overcome to the point where any wild creature loses his sense of caution. If this happens, he is a tame animal and no longer safe in the presence of unfriendly humans.

The next time our birds and squirrels raised their warning clamor I went out—well clothed against a twenty-mile-an-hour breeze and a twenty-below-zero temperature, which together give a wind chill of around sixty-eight below—and sat on the step where the woodshed partially protected me from the wind. I put a bit of frozen ground beef on my boot toe, and waited.

Walter approached with grave caution. He stalked me from all sides, moving low to the ground, so tensed for instant withdrawal that his wiry muscles quivered. He disappeared into one of the entrances to his tunnel system in the snow, reappeared from under the shed beside the step, slipped out of sight behind a box waiting to be discarded, and then came toward me from the rear. I watched as well as I could out of the corner of my eye, while he bit the folds of my coat experimentally. He went through this approach, with variations, several times, because the cold made it difficult for me to remain perfectly still and he was gone in a wink if I so much as twitched. Finally he darted at my boot and snapped at the sole, then retreated a foot or two, waiting for a response. When none came, he made several more approaches, nipping the edge of the sole or flashing in to snap at my coat. At last he snatched the meat and darted into his snow-tunnel entrance.

As Walter gained confidence, I held the meat in the palm of my hand near my boot toe, wearing one of Ade's too-large leather gloves. This proved wise because occasionally, as a matter of caution, he nipped a glove-finger tip. After a time I held the gloved hand in my lap and he ran fearlessly up my pants leg to get his meat. Then came a day that was almost warm and I forgot the glove. Walter took the meat from my bare hand with care and daintiness. I absentmindedly held the next bit of meat so that my finger extended in front of it and he took hold of my finger with his teeth but jumped away, frightened, when I pulled my hand back. It seemed that he mistook the finger for food because, when he made a similar mistake later, he held on, sat down, braced himself, and pulled strongly, then let go and looked puzzled as if wondering why that particular bit of meat was attached to me. I

should add that his teeth were not pressed tightly enough to break the skin.

After Walter had so overcome his fear of me that he climbed weightlessly up my shirt—ermines only weigh two or three ounces—to inspect my ears and nose and eyes, I hid bits of beef and raw bacon in my pockets. He quickly nuzzled in to the beef, but seemed to locate the bacon by chance. I thought at the time that he did not respond to unfamiliar food scents, but questioned this after the incident of the boned chicken.

I found the can under the icebox where it had rolled when we were storing the groceries. When we used it, I put a piece of white meat and the fat into the juice-lined can for Walter. I doubt that he knew anything about chickens, live or canned, because the summer people who kept chickens lived quite a distance away and Carl Johnson hadn't seemed the type to buy canned meat. But when I opened the door with the can in my hand Walter dashed from under the shed and almost danced as he sniffed the air. I set the low can in front of him and he cleaned it with concentration, going over it so vigorously to get the last traces that I feared he would cut his fuschia-colored tongue on the sharp edge. But even this wasn't enough for him. The can must be taken home.

On his first attempt, he grasped the near edge with his teeth, so that the can overturned and extinguished his front half. He hissed, pulled his head free, and sat back, considering the can, which was now bottom up. He didn't try to grasp it but after some minutes managed to paw it over so that it was as it had been. This time he reached across it, caught the far edge with his teeth, lifted his head high, and pattered away with his treasure.

If he did not discover morsels hidden in my pockets in a few minutes, he refused to waste more time and simply went away. He had great energy and there was never a sign of languidness about him. Sometimes when I was feeding him he lifted his head, sniffed, listened, and bounded away from my pampering to hunt his own dinner.

There were times when I wished he did this more often, because he had several food caches around the yard, under roots, woodpiles, outbuildings, and boulders, and would have put our entire meat supply away if I had given it to him. The squirrels tried to reach these hoards and Walter, although he did not reveal their location by approaching any of them when the squirrels were sniffing and nosing nearby, watched carefully and gave all the indications of being worried about his stores. This tendency to store for future use may be an explanation for the weasel's unsavory reputation as a killer of more than he needs.

Suddenly he stopped coming by day and arrived in the small hours of the morning, running up and down on the screen door to attract my attention. I gave him his bit of meat as soon as I heard him so that he might get away quickly because he seemed unusually cautious. Then came a night when he was plainly afraid of something. He timed his visit to avoid the moonlight and stopped between my feet to look and listen and sniff the air before he darted into the small space between the woodshed floor and the ground.

This was six nights after the last visit of the stranger. The suet was again gone from its open cage in the morning, and this time the big tracks did not lead away into the woods but were thick around the woodshed. Our unknown had returned and was hunting Walter.

In early evening Ade made whispering sounds from the workroom. Outside, paws on the bench, intent on chewing a bacon rind fastened flat to the bench top with roofing nails, was one of the most beautiful animals I have ever seen. He had the long, lithe body, the short legs, the inquisitive pointed face of the weasel family, and he was at least three feet long from nose to tail tip. He was so dark a brown he looked black where shadow touched his long-haired glossy fur. His nose and feet might have been swathed in black velvet. A sparse layer of long, white-tipped hairs over his head and upper back gave him a frosted look. He was very like a large mink and even had a small white throat patch, somewhat smaller than the mink's chin patch. He sat up and looked in the window at us without alarm, but made many trips to the corners of the cabin, looking cautiously around the log ends to assure himself that no danger was approaching unseen. And when he did this, his bushy, tapering tail and sinuous body flowed as one, glossy as black river water against the snow, and his haunches rippled with leashed power. This was a fisher, reserved hunter of deep woods, brought to our clearing by hunger.

With some idea—not a very practical one—of protecting Walter by keeping his large and hungry cousin away from the house, we covered the bacon rind at night and wound the birds' suet into balls with heavy cord, which we hung from low branches and took down at dusk. For the fisher, we nailed pieces of suet firmly to trees at the edge of the clearing, and we knew he got them because the nails were pulled out of the tree trunks. Our other animals would have simply chewed off as much suet as they wanted.

One night I opened the door to breathe the snow-scented freshness and, from a nearby cedar branch where I could dimly see a forgotten suet ball, came a tiny *tcheek-tcheek-tcheek*, a mere whisper of sound. I thought some night bird was there until there was a soft thump under the tree. I longed for a flashlight but the starlight showed the fisher as a black cutout against the track-riddled snow. He still made his querulous sound. I closed the door behind me and stood motionless. He retreated some thirty feet and turned to watch me. I waited a long time before he returned, moving slowly and watchfully, to crouch at the step, ready for any hostile movement. At last he inched nearer, sniffed at my feet, U-turned, and flashed up the cedar trunk.

His first attempts at the hanging suet ball set it swinging widely, and his louder squeaking showed his annoyance. Then he nipped the string with his teeth and dropped, like falling water, to be on the ground almost as soon as the suet. He ate it there, pulling the string aside with his paws and not interrupting his meal when I went inside, although he watched me until the door closed.

Our suet was getting low and we didn't like to ask the butcher to go to the trouble of mailing more unless we ordered something else so next day Ade hung one large ball of suet from a clothesline, propped high, saying, "We can leave that out. I don't think he can walk a wire."

And he couldn't, but shortly after dark we heard faint squeaks and thuds. The fisher was jumping for the suet, launching himself from a high spot and trying to catch the ball with his paws. This only set it swinging and he tried to snatch it on the fly with his teeth. His jumps were fifteen feet long and five feet at the highest point, which was just under the suet. He did not pause for a half hour and twice he almost had the prize. Then he began to tire, resting between jumps which were increasingly lower and at longer intervals.

I was entirely on the fisher's side by now and was thinking that hunting animals must be very hungry when their prey is scarce. Ade opened the door, walked to the wire, and cut down the suet while the fisher hissed and sputtered halfway up a tree. Ade looked at him, said, "You earned it," and came inside to stand beside me and watch the persistent fellow eat.

Walter had fared very well, even though his arch-enemy was sharing his restaurant, so to speak, but when we had nothing more to give the fisher he dug out Walter's store-houses, one by one, and then went after Walter. Came the time when we did not see Walter or his footprints for three days and I tried to convince myself that the fisher would have caught Walter whether we had fed them both or not.

Then I woke in the night, with Walter trembling on my sleeping bag and patting my face with his paws. A wide gash extended from his right brow to the tip of his nose and his right eye was apparently lost in a welter of black swelling and blood. The fisher's slashing claws had seriously handicapped him but he had found his way into the cabin through some hidden crack to ask for food. I hurried to get his frozen beef from the drum outside. In the bookshelf corner unit, where the three baby mice had once played, he hastily ate *four* pieces of meat which altogether weighed as much as he did. Then he went to the inside of the door, accepted another piece of meat to take home, stood back while I opened the door, and waited on the sill until I threw a moon shadow across the step with my robe to protect him while he dashed under the shed.

For two days the fisher moved in daylight, back and forth across the clearing in regular paths like sine waves, hunting carefully and thoroughly. Several times he crossed Ade's snowshoe path to the road without even looking at the cabin. But he didn't have any luck and moved on, I hope to richer hunting grounds.

The afternoon after he left I heard scratching on the screen and there was Walter, lively as ever, his right eye narrowed to a slit by a magnificent and incongruous black eye and the gash already closed to form a scarlet band a quarter-inch wide. The days went by and Walter came every day but did not take much food for storage, which was a good thing because our meat supplies were nearing the vanishing point again. The red band on Walter's face faded to pink, narrowed, and was lost in a line of twisted fur, and both his eyes were bright again.

Having once come inside, he often scooted past my feet into the house. He poked an inquisitive nose everywhere and showed great interest in certain places around the floor edges beneath which mice were probably shuddering. We had to keep our eyes open, though, to be sure he did not start a meat-

storage locker under the bookcase or some other suitable place. Then he discovered the begonia Hilda had given me. It was lush and leafy, not being a plant to mind short hours of daylight or chilly nights. Walter put his forepaws on the pot, smelled the dirt, and looked around as though confused. Then, with a lavish indifference that seems to be the weasel's way of accepting something completely impossible, he jumped up, curled himself around the plant stems, and dozed, nose on tail. He did this every time he came in after that and I've often wondered if he might have been remembering the summer earth.

Then came more snow, not as much as we had had at the year's end but enough to bend the trees. Under the added weight, a small cedar on the edge of the ditch John Anderson had dug when he rescued the cabin pulled loose what remained of its roots and toppled into the yard. It was not in the way so Ade decided to leave it there until the snow melted.

The next day two does came timidly from the woods, one of them the golden yearling we had seen earlier. She stood on the bank, watching and listening, while the other fed on the leaves of the fallen cedar. Then they changed places so that the yearling might eat while the other guarded. The pale doe had long eyelashes that she used with unconscious coquetry and Ade named her Blondie because, he insisted, she acted like a blonde.

One afternoon we saw a tall, handsome young buck coming cautiously down the path from the road. Some distance behind him was Blondie, hanging back and watching his every move. He blew, studied the house a long time, came a little forward, stomped, retreated—then repeated the whole sequence. Then, and only then, did he turn and in some way signal to Blondie, who was hiding behind a bush. She came slowly forward, as though she had never seen the place before, and allowed him to lead her to the cedar. Ade swears she was batting those eyelashes at the buck—which I doubt—but it did look as though she were working the universal feminine trick of letting him think *he* was in full charge of their affairs!

Shortly after this, Walter again began to come into the house at night for his supper, slipping through his little entrance, which, by the way, we never found. He was just as watchful when he left as he had been earlier and Ade and I were sure some danger threatened him. We suspected another fisher but found no tracks and decided the animal, who is very agile in trees, might be hunting from above.

On a blue-bright night when wind was talking in the evergreens, I sat very late, reading. I shivered. The room was chilling rapidly. I put aside my book to check the temperature, but stopped short in the living-room doorway.

The outside door was wide open. In the kitchen a fisher, nearly four feet long, rose on his haunches, then stood straight up on his hind legs. He was almost pure black, with the smallest of white throat patches and very little frosting. As he arched his sinuous body to one side, his eyes, catching the beam of light from the reflector behind my lamp, exploded into green stars. He thrust his head forward and hissed—and, involuntarily, I hissed back. This must have been bad language because he dropped to all fours, swung into a U-shape to look back, and was gone, bounding gracefully across the blue pools of moonlight under the trees.

According to some old-timers and outdoor writers, I should have feared for my life or, at least, my limbs, but all I could think was: How did he get in? We had seen evidence of the fisher's mechanical skill before in the way he emptied the suet cages on the bench, but a closed door!

A glance showed me how easy it had been for him. The door handle had a thumb latch. He had stood up against the door, possibly to look in through the glass panel, possibly attracted by the smell of food. His paw had depressed the latch and, when the door swung loose, he had strolled in. If he had the quick intelligence of his small relative, Walter, he could come in again any time he wanted to.

Ade put a slide bolt on the inside of the door and exchanged the thumb latch for a knob. Not that we objected to a visiting fisher, but the havoc he could create, leaping from bookshelf to lamp bracket to mimeograph, would be too much. However, because we thought the fisher must be very hungry to venture into a house, Ade nailed two pieces of suet to the cabin logs, trusting that Walter's clever ways of getting food would again protect him.

In the morning the suet was gone and there were two fisher trails, from the difference in track sizes, those of a male and a female. The male—larger track—had come from the east and left in that direction. The female had come and gone from the south after frost had blurred the other trail. We concluded that the male had been content with one piece of suet and the later-arriving female had taken the other. The animals lived up to their reputation as loners and we never saw them together.

After several nights of this feeding, when we felt they would be accustomed to the house and its odors, we put out no food and watched from a window. The small female came at dusk, weaving along the wall, looking for the suet. When she had given up and was moving away, I opened the door and put meat on the step. After a thorough reconnaissance, she snatched the meat and squeezed under the woodshed. The male came later, behaving as the female had, except that he reared and hissed when the door opened.

We were fascinated as the animals rapidly gained confidence, but wondered, since we felt we should not spend more money for food, where we could get enough meat to feed them. Then something turned up again, in the form of another order for Ade's woodwork. With the barrel-stove freezer liberally restocked, we were ready to try to hand-feed the fishers.

When neither of the animals showed up by the next midnight, we gave up and I was just dozing off when I heard a bumping at the door. When I opened it, the male fisher fell flat across the threshold, recovered his balance, placed his black-velvet paws on the sill, and lifted his head with begging, open, pink mouth. We were completely surprised and his manner was so catlike I almost expected him to mew.

Very slowly I crouched and held out a piece of meat. Just as slowly and with care not to touch my fingers, he took it with his teeth. He backed off, chewed, swallowed, and returned for more. When the cold was penetrating too deeply into the cabin, I gave him a large piece of suet, which he carried away. After this he announced his arrival by pushing repeatedly against the door and Ade still says that he trained us to answer his knock.

The female also learned to hand-feed but she attracted our attention by running back and forth on the roof, the soft padding of her steps unlike the sounds made by the small nocturnal flying squirrels. As soon as we began to move audibly inside, the footsteps ceased and, when we opened the door, she was peering down from the edge of the woodshed roof, waiting to have her supper handed up to her. Then she disappeared, perhaps to prepare for young ones, and two nights later the male did not "knock" and I thought that he, too, had taken to the trail—until I went out in the morning.

On a shoulder-high shelf attached to the logs outside the kitchen door we had a breadbox, the kind that opens by sliding up the front like the lid of a rolltop desk. It was handy for freezing leftovers. I had accidentally left it open, or so I thought then, and our fisher had taken his meal from it. Two hamburger patties had been unwrapped, their waxed paper intact (perhaps having been licked free of the meat), and a half-empty can of powdered eggs was gone. I followed the fisher's tracks two hundred yards into the woods before I lost them in thick brush. There were several rings in the snow where he had set the can down, no doubt to rest his tired jaws, but he had not spilled the smallest bit of the yellow powder!

The next night I heard scratching at the breadbox and looked cautiously through the door panel. This time the fisher had managed to push the box cover up three inches before it slipped sideways and jammed. Inside was a glass of half-frozen pineapple juice. He tipped this over and poked his head under the cover to lick up the unexpected treat. I should have been more surprised if Walter had not already showed me that weasels like sweets by his special fondness for cookies, the sweeter the better.

Our real expert for opening animal-proof—in a manner of speaking, that is—containers was a heavily frosted old male fisher who arrived shortly after our first thaw.

The barrel-stove freezer had no means of entry except a stovepipe fitting, covered by a lightly weighted piece of sheet metal, and the firing door, beneath which was a draft slot, six inches long and two and a half inches high.

One morning Ade found fisher tracks and an open stovepipe hole. An inventory showed that the fisher had taken a three-and-a-half-pound dinner: two four-ounce beef patties, half a pound of liver, half a pound of frankfurters, a pound and a half of round steak, and half a pound of suet. Everything had been neatly unwrapped and the waxed paper left behind, not even ripped. We rescued the untouched bacon and four wrapped beef patties, leaving the chewed remains of the liver for weasel and fisher food. Ade weighted the metal over the stovepipe hole with heavy stones.

That night we heard a crash and from the window saw the fisher enter the stovepipe hole and come out a half hour later, carrying suet in his mouth. The liver was gone. Ade weighed the stones and metal in the morning. The fisher had dislodged fifty-eight pounds! And he could not have weighed more than fifteen.

Ade bolted a metal-covered piece of board across the hole.

This foiled our fisher, but he looked so discouraged after struggling with it for two hours that I put out some bacon grease and leftover meatloaf to reward his effort.

Next morning the draft grating was open. It seemed too small to have admitted the fisher, but he had lifted the door from its slot and squeezed through. His appetite was less and he had taken only two beef patties. Ade wired the grating shut.

That night there were soft sounds inside the freezer and I went out to watch through a gap in the woodshed wall. Although the door was held shut by its spring, the latch was not in place. By now I was not surprised that our fisher had opened the door and slipped past the spring, but it seemed incredible that he would voluntarily stay inside after the spring had clanged the door shut behind him. While I was wondering about this, the door was pushed partly open and a watchful head appeared. After reconnoitering, the head withdrew, to re-emerge with a large mouthful of suet. Carefully the fisher slipped out, keeping a paw in the door until his tail was safely outside.

As he dropped to the ground, I saw that one foreleg ended in a stub. At some time he had chewed off his paw to escape a trap.

All this resulted in a spring-and-bolt closure on the freezer that takes a wrench and a strong man to open, but Ade and I both felt that this fisher, so ingeniously and bravely making his handicapped way, deserved to be helped. We retained for ourselves the right to select the best of the meat, but put out a good meal for him every night.

He accepted this, but limped away if we opened the door.

A man had set the trap that had crippled him and, for the rest of his shortened life, he would be wary of creatures with the man scent.

The day after Blondie had allowed the buck to lead her into our yard we heard the first outside human sound, aside from snowplow noises, since we settled in for the winter. A saw was working, not a chain saw but some other kind. When Ade came in with the day's pails of water he said that someone was cutting ice a quarter mile down the lake, for some summer people, probably.

There was a note in our next mail from the man who had been cutting. Some of the cakes he'd cut, he wrote, were too thick to fit properly into the Greenfield's icehouse but they'd do fine in Carl's. We could have all we wanted and we'd better get it soon because we might have a big thaw any time and when things froze up again the melt water would freeze the cakes solid to the ice sheet.

"It would be wonderful to have iced tea next summer," I said wistfully. "But how can you get it?"

"This fellow probably thinks I can drag it down the lake with my car," he said, and laughed without humor.

"Drive on the lake? You'd break through! And it isn't even February yet. What's he talking about . . . big thaw?"

This time Ade laughed normally. "That ice is three feet thick and strong enough to march an army across, tanks and all. And where've you been recently? This happens to be Saturday, the nineteenth of February."

"Are you sure? It doesn't seem . . ."

"I'm sure. Who's been walking for mail every Saturday since the first of the year? And it was almost February when we sent the letter that should have been for New Year's."

I shook my head. "You're right, of course. But how could I lose so much time?"

"You didn't. You've just been too occupied to think about it. But as to getting the ice . . . since I haven't a car, I'll walk and haul it on the toboggan. And I'll do it first thing. He knows more about the weather here than we do."

I went to the shore with him in the morning. He had hammered together a skid from two little dead trees and some scraps of board, and this reached from the lake ice to the open end of the icehouse, which had been built high on the rocky bank.

"There's plenty of sawdust inside to pack the ice in," he said, fastening on his snowshoes. Then he grew smaller, dwindled to a black toy man as he moved away, trailing his toboggan.

The sun was not yet above the trees and the moon still hung high and bright in a faded, pallid sky. In the distance, the low, hummocky ridge of ice cakes was thrown into relief by purple moon shadows. They faded as the rising sun put out the moon, and the glare of light from the whiteness of the lake made me squint. The wind blew from the northwest as it almost always does along that shore in winter. Little snow devils lifted and whirled. Wisps like cold, thrown salt powdered against my cheeks. Ade was starting back now, head bent, shoulders hunched, tugging like a horse in harness. At last he pulled up, puffing, with two ice cakes upended on the toboggan, and slid them off in front of the skid.

"I'll get two more," he wheezed. "Then four tomorrow and so on to make five days. That'll give us about two tons. It'll be all we'll need." I looked from the ice to the high door of the icehouse and started to speak, but he cut me off. "I'll use a pulley to haul 'em up the skid. I can do that after I get it all down here."

And before I could protest, he was gone again.

I stood looking at the ice cakes. "Blue ice" was the term for it, but it didn't begin to describe this brilliant and beautiful color—blue and green at the same time, clear as finest crystal, shining as though it had captured the bubbling of a brook. It held within itself all the bright warmth of a summer sky. In the months to come, it would hold for us the memory of the black-and-white cold of winter.

Then I realized that the cakes were very large, much larger than those the iceman had fitted into the big icebox in my childhood home. I translated two tons into four thousand pounds, and four cakes a day for five days into twenty cakes, and divided. Ade, himself not 140 pounds, was dragging something like four hundred pounds in each toboggan load. Only the slickness of the packed snow made it possible. I looked again at the ice. It was enchanting and I was glad I had seen it, but never again would Ade labor like this so that I might have iced tea on a hot day.

I looked up and across the lake to the clear blue above the far hills and thought about my distorted time sense that seemed to have lost me three weeks. But it wasn't really distorted and I hadn't lost anything. I'd just been seeing things in a way that was new and different to me, a way that I'd probably known in early childhood and forgotten. Once the mimeograph had come and I no longer had any reason to think in terms of the outside, my eyes and mind and heart had turned to the forest dwellers and slipped into their kind of time. Time that measured itself by light and dark, by moons and seasons, by sunshine and rain and snow. Ade had watched the hours and days so that he could get the mail, but I'd had no need and so had forgotten the clock and the calendar. That I was weeks off in my thinking was unimportant. What mattered was that my days had seemed long and happy, rich with living.

This wasn't the "simple life." It was the natural life, lost to urban man for many centuries. It would come to me whenever winter drove other people away. My eyes followed the profile of the hills and I knew that there would be a time when I would look at the point of sunset, the length of shadows, and know that the time of thawing was at hand.

6 *Time of Thawing*

1

On the morning of March seventh I woke, sticky with perspiration, dizzy-headed, hot. For a moment I thought I had had a nightmare, then I decided I was catching something. Or maybe the stove had overheated again. The log-roller was all right. I hurried to look at the airtight. It was out and this was not surprising when I recalled that it had had no fire in it the day before. I turned vaguely to the window and lost the lingering remnants of sleep. Water was dripping from the icicles and the trees on the hill were waving before a south wind.

So came the first break in the winter—a wind change, a night temperature rise from zero to forty-five, water glistening on the snow. The air held the moistness of spring, and the wind breathed and swirled, its sounds and touch very different from those of the determined, steadily blowing winds of winter.

"It's so exciting," I said, when Ade joined me. "D'you suppose we can make a garden?"

"There's plenty of winter left, and Sven told me we can have frost till the end of May." I sniffed and he went on. "What I like is that you can really feel the seasons here. They change and we have to change with 'em. Stirs us up. I'm more and more convinced the reason so many people can't stand to live away from towns is because they try to live apart from the weather."

"If we'd tried to make an isolated bubble of this place we'd be half nuts already from getting nowhere. There's no sense in trying to buck the weather. It's too big, too uncertain. It's easier to cooperate—and handier. I mean things like our freezer . . ." My mouth stayed open and Ade raised an eye brow. "Our meat! If this keeps up it'll spoil."

"I could cover the drum with snow . . ."

"It's melting too fast. Why don't you take the perishables next door and set them on the fireplace hearth? That stone'll hold the cold for a long time."

"All that dead air in the house won't warm up for a long time, either."

The copper wash boiler, polished to a brightness that both pleased the eye and reflected heat away from its contents, had been filled with food in packages that were not mouseproof. I hastily moved such packages as were left to the high cupboards, which were reasonably mouseproof when the doors were closed. Ade repacked the boiler with the perishables from the freezer and pulled it next door on the toboggan. He came back rubbing his fingertips.

"Believe it or not, it's only ten in there, and me without gloves. We can leave the meat there in case there's another warm spell. You won't mind . . ." He made the mistake of pausing to gloat.

"I won't mind asking you to run over for things at all," I assured him.

Three days later the temperature began to drop and an east wind brought clouds. In the evening the snow began, heavy white balls that struck the window panes with a sound like sleet. Off and on during the night I heard it rattling against the metal of the roof saddle where the log-roller's pipe went through the living-room ceiling. In the morning it was still snowing and did not stop until early afternoon.

"I think I'd better get the snow off the roof next door," Ade said. "It'd be all right if it melted like it does here, but this new stuff's solid and heavy. Much more and that roof might collapse." He sighed deeply. "I should have shoveled it off earlier."

"By now we both ought to know better than to put things off," I said and he didn't bother to answer.

The sun was warm and the air pleasant so I made sandwiches and a thermos of tea and took them to the summer house for lunch. This was less easy to do than it sounds. The new layer of snow was firm but that underneath had been weakened by the thaw and I broke through to my knee at every third or fourth step. This didn't do much for my still-weak knees so I tried walking in Ade's footprints, but they were so far apart that I teetered and wavered and ended up flat in the snow a few times. I managed not to squash the sandwiches and the top of the old thermos fitted tightly enough so that I managed not to spill more than half of the tea.

I found Ade, not casually shoveling snow off the roof, but cutting the three-foot layer laboriously into blocks with the shovel, then pushing them from the roof. It was slow, hard work because the snow was packed so firmly that some of the big blocks did not break apart when they hit the ground.

As he climbed down and kneaded the muscles of his arms, I stretched an aching, wrenched leg. But then we had expected to use our muscles more, hadn't we?

When I entered the log cabin after we ate, I was welcomed by the sound of dripping water which seemed to come from the living room. I stood in the doorway from the kitchen and a drop plopped onto my head. The whole lintel was wet and trickling. This was something new. Ade had fixed the roof seams opened by the falling tree, and there'd been no leaking during the thaw. As philosophically as possible, I put pans in the doorway to catch the worst of it . . . and waited for Ade.

"Whew! I'm glad that's over," he said as he came in. He stopped and looked at my rapidly filling kitchenware. "Now what?"

"Something leaks," I contributed helpfully.

He reached up to feel the ceiling panels along both sides of the north end of the wall between living room and kitchen. "Wet. This is how they got all those dark stains. But why didn't it happen before?"

"I kind of remember John Anderson saying those stains came from snow packing on the eaves . . ."

"Of course," Ade said. He wearily shrugged into the jacket

he had just hung up. "There's ice on the eaves. The snow melts on the part of the roof that's heated by the stove and the water that doesn't run down to make icicles freezes when it hits the cold eaves. It's so thick now that the melt from the new snow is backing up behind it and pushing under the roofing paper. Where's the ice pick?"

I handed it to him. "What're you going to do?"

"Chip a channel and let the water drain. Tomorrow, when I'm not so tired, I'll start getting all the ice off."

"There's a hatchet, isn't there? Wouldn't that be quicker?"

"It would, but I'd probably cut off some of the roofing with the ice."

Fortified by a cup of hot tea, he went out. Chopping sounds ensued, followed by a rush of water and a spate of words that must have been left over from Ade's Navy days. I looked out, careful not to be seen. He had opened a channel, all right, and the water was spouting from the roof, but his ladder was so placed that he was directly in the path of the flood. I laid dry clothes on the kitchen counter and discreetly withdrew to bury my face in a book. The growling in the kitchen petered out after a while and Ade strolled into the living room.

"What's for dinner?" he asked, and burst out laughing.

I howled. "If I'd had to keep a straight face much longer, I'd have burst," I said when I could manage to talk. "You've no idea how funny . . ."

Still giggling, I set out to fix the best dinner I could, and even went next door for the hamburger myself.

"This was a queer snow," Ade was saying as we sat back with our coffee and cigarettes. "It packed so tight it didn't even close the road. While I was on the roof next door I saw a forestry truck drive right over it. Sign of spring. Well, the roofs are fixed—for the moment. Now I can relax."

"What's that sound?" I asked, listening to a heavy roar that seemed to be in the cabin.

"I don't . . . my God! The chimney's on fire!"

Some instinct told me to close the drafts on the cook stove, which was feeding air to the offending chimney, before I went out. It was already dark and blue flames, shooting ten feet above the chimney, cast a weird mantle over the house and yard. Ade swarmed up the ladder he had left in place after chopping the ice channel. The blaze was too far above the roof to be a danger to the cold, damp roofing but the chimney might get so hot that its masonry would crack or the wood of roof or ceiling catch from contact with its heated stones. After the flames subsided, we spent three hours opening the stove draft to let the flames flash again, closing them until the flames died, letting things cool a bit, and then repeating the cycle. It was after ten when we went back to drink our warmed-over coffee.

"What caused it?" I asked. "Soot?"

"Creosote, distilled from green wood. I can't think of anything except maybe gasoline that would burn hotter. Sven warned me about this, too. I guess the only way to learn is by experience." He yawned. "I'm sure ready to call it a day."

There was a knock at the door. Ade looked at me and groaned. Probably someone on the wrong road, stuck. Poor Ade. He'd have to give him a hand, of course.

I opened the door. A young man in a gray topcoat asked, "Is your name Helen Hoover?"

I admitted that it was.

"I'm from the FBI," he said. "Sorry to bother you so late, just to ask some questions about a former co-worker of yours, but I've had a rather hectic day . . ."

Maybe he still wonders why I laughed in his face.

2

Even before the thaw there was a change in activity around us. In mid-February a whiskey jack was stripping strands of the cedar's inner bark and flying away with it. The first birds to nest, I thought, unconcerned about snow and cold, or perhaps the barred owls were first. Their cackles and hoots had been breaking into the night silence more often than before and Ade had seen a pair of them making owl eyes and little bows to each other on a pine branch.

In March the squirrels were pairing off, chasing each other over the snow and spiraling around tree trunks, leaping like acrobats from branch to distant branch, the female keeping ahead, but not too far—just far enough that she could be certain not to lose her pursuing swain.

Walter did not come every day for food and twice I saw him trotting over the snow carrying a small mouse; the mice had started to produce their big crop of youngsters. One day I noticed a darkening along his spine and thought he had squeezed under something dusty, but the darkness widened into a brown band that extended over his head to come down above his eyes like a flat cap. Brown hairs increased and spread over his upper parts and tail until he was correctly attired to match the brown duff the melting snow would reveal.

On March fifteenth the crows arrived to flap above the cabin and complain noisily from tree tops whenever we went outside. Then the wild geese passed over in their high, trailing wedges, their shrill cries coming down to us like bugles blown far away, stirring an ancient restlessness from days when men moved from hunting ground to hunting ground with no barriers except those of mountains and waters and canyons they could not cross. Ade and I felt a special kinship with the geese and with those nomads of long ago because we, too, had moved from one hunting ground to another and, different though our methods of hunting might be, our ultimate aims were the same.

Cars began to move on the road, seemingly going nowhere since no one was in residence beyond us, and with their coming the deer went away. Robins sang out warnings against invasion of their forest territories and flocks of darkly hooded juncos and elaborately patterned though modest brown sparrows—I had not known there were so many kinds of sparrows —stopped in the yard to pick cedar seeds from the ground for a few days and then move on.

The feeling of movement all around us made us acutely conscious of all the things we had not touched during the winter—my mountain-high pile of mending, for one thing— and the sunlight that now came over the trees and through the trees and into the house showed us a cabin suffering from winter hangover. The dust lying gray on the upper part of every log made the rooms look dingier than they were and the thought of lint collected under furniture reminded me all too vividly of the uncleanable cupboard that had once stood over the trapdoor. To properly clean so crowded a place we'd have to move out, but it was still too cold. Instead, to banish a growing feeling that we hadn't accomplished anything, we dusted the logs and polished the frost patterns off the windows, and had just started to play checkers with the furniture so that we could reach into the corners when there was another of those unexpected knocks.

Just as I was, straggle-haired and streaky faced, I opened the door to a smiling and poised young man who carried an assortment of leather cases.

"I would have let you know I was coming," he said, "but I counted on your having a phone. I'm the photographer from the Magazine."

For a moment I didn't know what he was talking about. Then it flashed through my mind that I had written to the Magazine months earlier about a possible story on our woods life. I had had a brief reply, asking if I owned a camera—specifications given—for taking pictures to go with the typescript. I'd answered "no" and when nothing more developed had forgotten the whole thing.

I did a double-take and distinguished myself with, "You look so civilized."

Fortunately he had a sense of humor, but he did look civilized, and this was to be expected of such a cosmopolitan sophisticate with so much charm. Hat from Brussels, shoes from London, coat by Brooks Brothers, sweater from Norway, and, as he incidentally mentioned when Ade asked him if he was dressed warmly, Angora underwear from Vienna. I still think there is something fabulous about Angora long johns, whether they come from Vienna or not.

As the photographer asked questions and looked for picture possibilities, something was made very clear to me. I had gone after this too soon. Ade supplied excellent color with his piratical sandy beard but I was ordinary and dumpy and the cabin was still its dingy self. I'd hoped to contribute to the fund for improving the cabin, but I'd tried to take a way that more or less depended on having the cabin improved first. So we talked and laughed, and many pictures were taken. The pleasant young man went away with his negatives and shortly thereafter I got a letter saying that it seemed there was not enough variety to make a series.

I wasn't disappointed because I had gained something very valuable from the experience. I would keep hearing the young man say: "My editor thinks from your letter that you'd have no trouble writing the article."

A blizzard blew in, blotted out the trees and hills for an hour, and then turned to rain. The snow level dropped inches, and kept on doing so from day to day after the sky cleared. Drops plopped into puddles under the eaves. You could hear water from the deep melting gurgling and bubbling under the snow. The white glare was gone and the surface of the winter blanket turned to pock-marked gray. A skim of fresh snow showed small tracks one morning, coming from the side of the ditch, then turning back as though their maker had come out on a scouting expedition. In the afternoon he was running around in the sun, the first chipmunk out of winter retirement.

Although everything froze over at night, spring was here— the smell of it on the wind, the feel of it in the air, the promise of greenery all around. The afternoons were in the forties and fifties. This seemed very warm to us after the deep cold and we were outside every day, breaking through the weak snow crust, with the enthusiasm of puppies let out of a pen. The rotting, filthy snow of the city spring flashed across my mind and was forgotten. I had a great desire to dig, and never tired of poking through the snow to find last year's bunchberry leaves still rosy with autumn color or sweet Williams tenderly green under their covering.

But the vanishing snow left behind an earth smothered in debris as though a flood had receded. Rivulets piled clumps of leaves at the most inconvenient places on our paths. Dead stalks from last year's growth waved forlornly above such green as had stayed fresh under the snow, and this was muddied and bedraggled until rain came to wash it into freshness. The garden at the summer house was covered by a two-foot layer of dead vegetation, evidently the accumulation of the years when the Larimers no longer had had a caretaker. Trash heaps we had never suspected stood stark in the woods around the log cabin.

"I'll gather all these old sawhorses and cement troughs and such stuff and cut them up," Ade said. "They're wood and they'll burn."

"And I'll clean out the garden."

This turned out to be a matter of doggedly pulling and cutting my way through the tangle. I had known the garden was laid out in beds but I hadn't been able to see that the granite pieces that outlined them glittered with mica flakes. A graceful path came out from hiding in the center of a dense mass of fallen weeds, and flower pots built of granite fragments held the dark corms of ferns. Underneath a mat of the dead leaves of large-leafed aster were struggling sweet Williams, columbine, chives, daisies. If I never planted a seed, we'd have flowers all summer.

During these days the lake surface was as we had first seen it, covered with gray and rotten ice, dotted here and there with melt-water pools that reflected the sky as azure and cobalt. A pair of mergansers had already found the stretch of open water where the flow from the brook had helped the ice break away from the land. We heard the welcome cries of gulls again, and waited for the wind that would start the water and ice moving.

3

I was rattling the coffeepot on the first May morning when Ade stopped me with his hand. "Listen!"

The wind was soughing through the pines and spruces and there was a heavy, grinding undercurrent of sound—the gritting of a giant's teeth. We ran to the shore. The ice was moving eastward in a pack, giving way wearily before the west wind. Misty light fell in dull-gold patches on the dying gray layer. Little ice islands, pitted and honeycombed, glistening and black as wet licorice candy, clinked and ground together along the shore. By noon there was only a tinkling mass of melting crystals in the wavelets lapping over the stones, and in the evening the lake lay clear and blue, ready to reflect another sunset.

Next day as we finished the corn cakes and brown-sugar syrup that had become our regular breakfast, I sighed. "A grapefruit would taste good—a pink one."

Ade laid down his fork. "You must have spring fever."

"Not yet but . . ."

Shouting and halloos came down the path ahead of Hilda and Sven. I was showing her how well the begonia had done when Ade said loudly, "I don't believe it!"

Hilda and I turned. He was holding up a grapefruit.

"I hope you like them," Hilda said. "I thought they'd be a nice change. They're the pink ones. They always seem to taste better to me . . . what's the matter?"

I explained.

"You know," Sven said, "not long after we came here we had a run of bad luck. We lived on oatmeal and flour and salt for days. Hilda was muttering that old saw about if we had bacon we'd have bacon and eggs if we had eggs, when an ice fisherman knocked on the door. He said he and his friends were going back sooner than they'd planned, so would we be offended if they gave us their leftover food. It didn't seem right to him to leave it for the animals when there were people who could use it. And he handed us a dozen eggs and almost a pound of bacon. A few days later some of his friends came up and rented both of our cabins—that's all we had then—and stayed ten days. We ate for the rest of the winter." He touched a grapefruit. "Things like this point the way."

After we'd had coffee and Sven had persuaded Ade to keep his beard—such marvelous local color for the tourists, Hilda added—they went along to the Lodge and we heard a truck huff and pant to a standstill at the top of the path.

The driver came down the hill and said, "I'm starting to fill up the lodges and thought you might need some gas and oil."

"Kerosene," I said. "I've been carrying around one lamp for two months."

"I've only got a five-gallon can," Ade said. "Do you sell that little?"

The man pushed his cap back and rubbed the red line on his forehead.

"Sure, but I've got a couple of old drums on the truck. You can have 'em cheap. What say we set 'em near the road where I can get the hose in? I'm not hauling kerosene, but you can light up like a Christmas tree from now till fall with a drum of number one fuel oil. It's cheaper . . . and the other drum'll hold gas for your outboard."

Ade was sliding into his jacket when I mentioned that we didn't have an outboard.

"No motor?" The oil man looked toward the shore. "With a boat like that?"

"Later," Ade said, as they turned away. "One thing at a time."

When Ade brought me the bill he said the quantity prices were so good that he'd bought gas, too, for when he had the light plant going. I looked at the amount. $19.93. I opened the checkbook, idly noting that I had written no checks since the first of the year except for taxes, the mimeo, and the meat. I went further back, looked unbelievingly at the stubs, did some figuring, checked again. I had transferred a wrong figure. Our balance, instead of $319.98 as I had it written, was only $16.08. Horrified, I called Ade, showed him the stubs, touched the bill.

"We can't pay it. And there'll be those chickens, and feed for them . . ."

"Take it easy," he said and searched through some drawers till he found the wallet he no longer had reason to carry. He took two tens and a five from it.

"Put that in the bank and we'll have more left after we pay the bill than we have now."

"Where'd it come from?"

"You gave it to me . . . for a shirt. Remember?"

And I did remember. It had been my gift to him on his last birthday in Chicago, money for a really nice wool shirt to wear up north when we found our vacation spot. He went out and I heard the thunk of his ax while the shirt he hadn't bought became a symbol of all the things we no longer had— shower baths and unstained ceilings, fresh vegetables and Coca-Cola, *Dragnet* and book clubs. I couldn't remember when I had cried before, but when I stopped sniffling over the deposit slip and the check to the oil company I knew that what really had upset me was the fact that I wasn't doing much to help our now almost empty exchequer, or even trying to. The sale of a few books I no longer needed, an idea or two, a little correspondence for Ade, an ill-timed attempt to do a magazine story that would have been mostly pictures. It simply wasn't enough.

I was still acting like a vacationer. It was suddenly clear to me that "spare time" had gone along with "days off." This was a venture of the most cooperative type. It was high time I stopped writing long letters about the beauty of our surroundings and used those hours to do something that would bring in my share of the necessary cash . . . if I wanted to stay here. And I did want to stay.

Instead of letters I'd write something I could sell. But could I? True, I had once written a short-short story for a newspaper syndicate and been paid five dollars for it, and there had been some mention of my being capable of doing the story for the Magazine, but this was hardly indicative of literary genius about to burst on a palpitating world. I gathered up recent copies of a writers' magazine I had subscribed to ever since the miraculous incident of the newspaper sale and went over the market lists. I couldn't possibly do anything listed there. Well, I'd keep watching the new issues—the magazine still had more than a year to come. I'd keep thinking and try my hand if I got an idea. There didn't seem to be anything else I could do.

Ade and I held a conference that evening. We considered selling the log cabin and winterizing the summer house but the money we would get for the little cabin would do little beyond pay for the changes necessary to make the other livable all year.

"Anyway," Ade wondered, "what *is* money?"

Next we considered selling the summer house and living year-round in the log cabin.

"We're finishing a winter in it," I said, "and it's squalid and dirty and dark and depressing. Even though it doesn't have to be that way. We *can* live in it as it is, even if we run short of wood for heat and oil for lights—even if we haven't enough to eat. But things in general could get very rough and I think it would do a lot to keep our courage going if we could brighten it a little. If we can't do that, getting into the summer house for a while would have the same effect." I hesitated, confused. "If we hadn't bought the summer house . . . I guess we shouldn't have . . ."

"No," Ade said positively. "If we'd kept the money to live on, we'd be using it now. It'd be gone before we found out how carefully we should have spent it. We'd end up right where we are, only without the summer house. Now that the chips are down, I'd rather not sell either one if we can manage any other way. I mean not till we've clawed out some kind of income—and I don't care how little it is if we can keep alive. If we start selling off at our first really bad spot, what happens when we hit another one?"

When I agreed by silence he asked, "We have what? About twenty dollars?"

"About. And some oil and gas, and lots of wood, and enough grub for quite a while. It'll be monotonous but if we're hungry enough we'll eat it."

"Well, we brought enough undercoat from Chicago to cover the rest of the walls and ceilings here, and there's some more maple varnish. If we thin it, it'll cover most of the walls. That'll make things brighter in here if not luxurious. We can

both feel we're doing something—I mean we can both paint.
I'll have to work on these ceilings first, though."

"Fine. How about a garden? Seeds don't cost much."

"Yes, but the only place we could plant 'em is in that subsoil
the bulldozer opened up last year. We'd need fertilizer and
then we'd not get much of a crop."

"Hey . . . we'll have chickens . . ."

"So we'll have fertilizer next summer. And a garden. All
this, of course, providing something turns up between now
and then."

So we moved necessities to the summer house, where we
could breakfast on the porch with a pin cherry tree young as
spring blooming just outside the screen. Corn cakes and
brown-sugar syrup are filling and in a setting this lovely it
didn't matter too much that we'd eaten them every morning
for weeks.

Ade found some old window shutters leaning against the
far wall of the icehouse and decided to fit them together over
a stone base that had supported the Larimers' dock before the
ice had torn it apart at some past break-up time. I went ahead
clearing and cleaning the neglected garden, getting more done
in less time, now that I didn't have to run back and forth
between the cabins several times a day.

I was nursing a bleeding finger—some dead fern axes are
so hard and brittle that their slanting breaks are like knife
points—when I heard a woodpecker drumming in the woods
between the as yet sproutless garden and the gate. I couldn't
see the bird but I heard the drumming again, and then an
answer from some distance away. A pair. I wondered what

kind. Then I heard the rapid, high-pitched *kak-kak-kak-kak* of the pileated and the male flapped to a landing at the base of a balsam fir. The sun fell through the trees full on him as, clinging to the bark with hooked claws, he hopped upward in zigzag jerks, turning his head from side to side as he tapped the trunk with his beak.

He was the largest of his kind I have ever seen, almost two feet long, and more than two-thirds of this was head and body. His scarlet crest flamed and his red whiskers stood out brightly on the lower sides of his face. There were small white stripes above his tawny eyes, which were set in a black mask, and white and black striping curved gracefully from his face down along the sides of his neck. His back, tail, and wings were midnight black but, as he leaned away from the tree trunk, braced by his short, wiry tail feathers, I saw flashes of white on his sides and breast. Then he made another sound, a sort of whickering, and the female flew to land beside him, showing a magnificent underpattern of white with black. She was not as large as he was, lacked his red whiskers, and had some black blended into the front of her crest.

When they had finished inspecting the balsam, the male drummed again, his head vibrating like a tuning fork, and they both flew to a very large cedar at the edge of the wooded portion of the yard. They hopped around it, tapping, and finally the female began to chip at the bark. Several minutes later her mate began to assist her and I realized they were not boring a round hole to get at ants in the tree but were starting a nesthole.

The doorway was a rectangular oval, made by removing

chips much like small ones cut with an ax. When the hole was finished some days later, a tunnel led through the living wood of the tree to the lifeless heartwood, where the main cavity was excavated, I saw carpenter ants, small brown ones about a half inch long, crawling around inside. The woodpeckers had a convenient food supply and, although the cavity might weaken the tree's resistance to a big wind, the birds would probably give the tree extra years by eating the ants.

I was surprised that the hole was only at my eye level above the ground and very near the path, but decided that if I removed the bushel of chips from beneath the nest site, few people who might walk by would notice that the hole had been freshly cut. They would be more likely to look toward the house because this point was high and gave the first good view of it as you came from the road.

The house lay below the cleared approach with only the small trees beyond it that the Larimers had left for scenic value and some protection from traffic on the lake. In the distance you could see the far shore, sometimes clear and green, sometimes tenuous and misty. The large trees between this house and the log cabin started to the right as you looked down at the building, but the giant spruce at the northwest corner of the porch dominated everything else. It towered almost ten times the height of the fifteen-foot roof peak, the largest tree on all the unhabited part of the lake shore.

One day we saw Big Woodie chipping into the east side of its base. After he had gone, we investigated. When we pulled away flaps of loose bark we found many insect borings in the living wood and saw that wind-induced swaying had split the

four-foot-thick bole. Besides this, the tree leaned away from the prevailing winds, directly over the roof above our bedroom. Our giant had to come down.

While we were trying to contact Jacques or someone like him, because felling such a tree is a job for an experienced lumberjack, Woodie came daily to feed on the insects and increase his notching at the tree's base.

When the next big wind came and the spruce began to crack, we left the house for safety. The tree fought like an animate thing, bending, tearing, straightening again at the slightest lull in the wind, but it was a losing battle. At last it bent lower and lower above the roof and the heavy cracking in its trunk grew steady. The tree raised a little, rolled suddenly on its base, and fell . . . not to the southeast across the roof, but due east in front of the house, under the influence of Big Woodie's notching.

Ade and I kept away from the cedar while the nestling woodpeckers were there. Later in the summer I stepped onto the porch to see the mother, accompanied by three almost grown daughters, investigating the tall, jagged stump of the wind-thrown spruce from which came soft crunching sounds. The larvae of wood-boring beetles, undisturbed by the destruction of their tree, were eating through the wood and had attracted the birds. A week after, Ade led me to an opening in the maple brush, through which we could see two male pileateds chipping at another insect-infected stump. Suddenly one opened his beak in the manner of a very young bird and the other stuffed a beakful of grubs into his mouth. Big Woodie was caring for his son as his mate was looking after their daughters.

Now, when we see the bright flash of a pileated's crest as he flies through a ray of deep-woods sunlight, we think of Big Woodie and the spruce. If he had not found his food in the tree, we should not have known it was dangerous. If, when we heard the tree cracking in the wind storm, we had not known which tree it was, we should have been unable to do anything to avoid the possibility of its falling on us. And, if Big Woodie had not notched the tree where he fed, probably because it was easiest to reach the insects from that side of the trunk, it would have fallen on the house. Without him, we should have been inside. At best this would have been terrifying and destructive; at worst, fatal.

How often the lives of humans are benefited incidentally by the unknown doings of unseen creatures we can never know.

Meanwhile, we did our chores and cleared trash, wrangling the underlying problem over and over in our minds and talking about it now and then, but it always came out at the same place. We had shelter and wood for at least two more years, and light for the same period, if we used only essential lamps and took advantage of the summer's long daylight hours. We had clothes for even longer and, since Ade had proved he could walk for the mail without injuring his health, we could push automobiles into the visionary future. But what could we do when we ran out of food? We had enough for most of the summer, even though it was not too well balanced, but we simply could not buy more without money. Just what would we do when we had nothing to eat?

We didn't know, but a friend in Chicago was sending Ade

small but consistent orders for woodwork and every time we heard from her, it encouraged us to hang on. We said, "Something will turn up" so often that it became our private joke and we more than half believed it.

Since then people have asked us why we didn't buy on credit, or fish and hunt. As to credit, we had never run up bills when we didn't know how they were to be paid, and we didn't intend to start. As to fishing and hunting, neither of us had ever wanted to do either and such a means of livelihood simply didn't occur to us. This must have seemed very impractical to the old-timers, but neither they nor we realized at the time that feeding instead of eating the animals would turn out to be one of the most practical things we ever did.

One afternoon I picked up the water pail and walked along the path toward the brook. Automatically I avoided stepping on the ground pine and bunchberries that had slipped between the bordering stones, but I was so preoccupied with our problems that I had almost reached the bridge before I saw the bear—big and black and shaggy—standing on it. He was leaning sideways against one of the railings, which bent outward as though it might collapse any second under his weight, and watching me in a nonchalant and condescending way. My first impulse was to run, but I seemed rooted and by the time I could move it was plain from the bear's indifferent stance that he knew all about people and had no intention of making my acquaintance if I didn't force myself on him. And surely I had nothing like that in mind. Slowly I controlled the fear that had touched me. As though he knew I was about to go back the way I had come, or didn't care whether I did or not, he turned, hung his head over the rail, and looked with grave concentration into the splashing waters of the brook. He belonged. The little bridge was in his country. Men had built it and might use it, but he had first call on it and could make that stick any time. I turned back to the house with my empty pail. All this was a lot less convenient than turning on a faucet, but it certainly was more interesting.

I stopped short outside the kitchen screen door. A sunburned, middle-aged woman in shirt and jeans was standing by the stove, looking at the embroidery on my kitchen towels. I stepped in and she spoke before I could open my startled mouth.

"Silly to use towels like this up here," she said. "I work at the Lodge. Sven sent your mail. I was coming this way, anyway."

"Thanks." I put the pail on the table and slid the envelope into my shirt pocket. Firmly stifling a desire to tell her I didn't have any plain towels at the moment, I said, "I've been watching a bear down on the bridge."

She went to the window and looked out. "There's nothing there."

"There was. He's gone, I suppose."

She looked at me pityingly. "All this talk about bears is for the tourists. You probably saw a big dog. Well, I must get back."

I watched her all the way to the gate, wishing that the bear might march onto the path in front of her. But he didn't, and I opened the letter. It was from my aunt and two uncles, my last living relatives, and it said: "We want to have a small part in this new life of yours and intended to send this for Easter, but we've all had a touch of the flu. You won't mind getting it late, will you?"

Enclosed were three checks, each for a hundred dollars.

I sat down in the living room and thought about these three people, a part of my earliest memories, whose Victorian house was as much home to me as the one in whose master bedroom I had been born. They could not know how much their gift meant to us and I had no words to make them understand. But there was no need for such words. I had not seen them for years. They were far away in miles, even farther in way of life. Even so, this did not matter, for they knew, as I did, the really important thing—that neither time nor distance can separate those who are linked by the unbreakable bond of love.

I picked up the pail and started to the bridge again, dazed by our good fortune, but with my mind free now to sense what was around me. In sunny spots the white stars of the bunchberry were already opening and the buds of the blue-bead lilies swelled at the top of their tall stems. Wild strawberry blooms hid under sprouting ferns and grasses like bits of leftover snow. Relaxed brown toads blinked in damp shade and brightly spotted green frogs hopped away from me. A chipmunk—very small—fled the path with a squeak and watched me from the top of a stump that was garlanded with trailing strands of dark green, soon to be covered with paired, pale-pink, twin-flower bells. I stopped on the bridge and leaned against the rail as the bear had done. The frilling water alternately revealed and concealed an empty pop bottle. I picked my steps over the stones that edged the brook, to dip my pail into a pool below a miniature cataract and stretch to pick up the bottle. Idly, I wondered who had put it there. Then I sat on a boulder and leaned back against the rough trunk of an old birch, and everywhere was the singing of water and the sighing of wind and the scent of balsam in the sun.

4

Three days later when I was stacking canned vegetables in one of the summer-house pie chests and Ade had gone to the log cabin for more, Hilda came down the path, carrying a large box from which rose shrill cheeping. Our chickens, just eighteen days earlier than we had expected them.

"The Greenfields *never* came this early before," Hilda said, placing the box on the kitchen table. "They did bring you plenty of starter feed, but the trouble is these chicks are so young they'll have to be kept warm. In two or three weeks they'll be strong enough and the nights'll warm up so they can make it without heat. But the G's have a brooder, of course!"

"Heavens! It'd take two weeks for us to order one and get it up here," I said. "We'll have to keep them in the kitchen and use the stove for night heat. We couldn't do anything else, anyway, because Ade hasn't a place fixed for them yet."

"That's going to be a lot of trouble," Hilda said, and smoothed a tickling hair into place.

"Trouble or not, that's it. D'you suppose we can keep some over for eggs?"

"In all the cold? Well . . . you can try. We used to have them but only in warm weather. In fact, we had them first and the G's bought our old brooder. Everyone told us we couldn't raise them because of weasels and foxes and so on, but we only lost three by accident in five summers. That was the time the bear climbed over the fence and fell on the poor things. He mashed them flat as pancakes."

Ade arrived, admired the livestock—and very cute they were, as black and noisy as baby crows—wrote a check for the Greenfields, went up to the car with Hilda to get the feed, and returned to help me settle our guests, twelve each in two small washtubs, wire-covered for safety and corrugated-paper-lined for warmth.

The chickens thrived, but I didn't. When the outside night temperature drops to near freezing, and sometimes below, you can't just build a fire in a little cook stove and expect the room to stay warm until morning. Especially this kitchen, which had been designed for summer coolness with walls made of single boards. I had to set the alarm and get up every two hours to keep just enough fire but not so much that the chicks would suffer from big temperature changes. I insisted that a little thing like broken sleep meant nothing to me, but after three nights I was ready to let Ade take over the last early-morning stove firing.

We were sitting in the kitchen at seven o'clock, drinking coffee and trying to wake up, when someone tapped gently on the door. I gave a mental groan, looked at my bare feet and wilted robe, at Ade's tangled beard and bleary eyes, and stretched my arm to open the door.

A strange man who simply exuded clear-eyed freshness was standing diffidently outside.

"I represent the United States Weather Bureau," he said, sniffing the air.

I became acutely aware that the kitchen smelled as thought it ought to be taken out and buried and that we looked as though we ought to be tossed into the hole after it. We managed, however, to introduce ourselves.

"I'll come back later," he said politely.

"We can't look any worse than we do now," I said. "Come in and have some coffee—that is, if you can stand it in here. It's chickens."

"Oh." He put more into the sound than I would have thought possible. Once inside he poked a finger through the wire to have it immediately nipped by a small beak. "Say, they're cute, all black like that, and you'll be able to put them outside before long. I should have recognized the—uh—scent. I used to raise them myself, before I moved to Minneapolis."

Ade and I woke up immediately. We were soon well posted on the care and feeding of chicks and eventually learned what had brought the weather bureau to our door. For some years a man had tended a rain gauge nearby but was now leaving for the winter.

"It should have been moved last fall," our visitor explained, "but—uh—there was some question as to whether you would care to winter here and it's best if the gauge is tended year-round. If you're interested . . ."

Enviable tact, I thought, and said, "So we've heard, about our staying, that is."

Ade was very interested so the man went next door to install the instrument in the clearing south of the log cabin, while we made ourselves presentable. Then I aired the kitchen and stirred up corn cakes and brown-sugar syrup for three.

Over breakfast we were told about winds and fronts and the care and feeding of rain gauges. ". . . and tending the gauge carries a small—a very small—monthly emolument," the quiet man finished, stating the amount apologetically.

"Any amount is money up here," Ade said, not quite keeping a note of glee out of his voice, while I multiplied by twelve and saw the federal government paying our local taxes— such taxes then being much less than they are today.

Ade ordered chick wire for the run, to be roofed with wire against interested hawks, and went to work converting a small outbuilding into a chicken house. I finished my yard cleaning, to a reasonable point, that is, and began to see the profusion of violets scattered under the grasses. I love violets, so much that I wore fragrant dark-blue ones when I was married. So I troweled up a market-basketful and made myself a bed of them along the bare east wall of the log cabin. When I went back some days later to see how they were doing, I found the bed richly green from recent watering, with blue and white blossoms lifting everywhere inside an edging of pale-pink granite chips. Ade had remembered my wedding flowers and added the edging to tell me so.

Now we had heavy rains and warm days. Ground vegetation began to rise, and so did mosquitoes and black flies. I can ignore mosquitoes—they don't carry anything harmful up here—so I just let them bite and go their way, but black flies are another matter. These little humpbacked fellows inject an anesthetic and anticoagulant together so that you either discover blood trickling from the place where one has been or, as was usually my case, find a welt, sometimes purple from subcutaneous bleeding, that looks like the mark of a blow and stays for weeks. In self-defense we wore heavy underwear, covered our ankles with folded-over winter socks, and pinned our collars and sleeves and pants legs tight against the flies' entrance. Even so, and with faces and hands well doped, the hovering clouds around our heads made it almost impossible to work outside. Besides, we were so accustomed to cold that the warming days were stifling to us in the heavy clothes.

When I developed a rash from the repellent, I gave up. I was sitting on the porch one afternoon, scratching, when Ade came back from the Lodge with the mail. Sven followed him and they settled on the sofa we had moved from the log house.

"Hi, Sven. Why didn't you tell us we'd be more likely to run for our lives in fly time than in the winter?"

"Thought it would be a nice surprise," he said. "Hilda has the same trouble. She keeps inside as much as she can till the worst is over."

"Which will be . . . ," Ade said on a rising note.

"Not long. A month maybe. They're worse than usual this year . . . more rain. You missed 'em last spring."

"Which I'll be glad to do any time," I said, while Ade scraped at his ankle, producing a sound like grating cabbage.

"I'll bet I got fifty bites, just walking up the road to the Lodge," he said.

Sven cleared his throat. "That's what I want to talk to you about—transportation. Thinking of getting another car?"

"Not even thinking," I said. "No point. That accident really put things like cars out of our reach."

"How about an outboard?"

I looked wistfully over the beckoning blue water. "It's not much fun to have an eighteen-foot boat and not even oars for it."

"I'd settle for a five-horse," Ade said, "if I could. Just enough to push the boat up for mail and take us out now and then. But they run too high. If they were about fifty bucks now . . ."

Sven slapped his hands on his knees. "That's all settled, then," he said. "I'll bring your five-horse motor along in a couple of hours. She's in fine shape except that I can't rent her out because she won't troll any more. But you don't fish."

He got up and strolled away while we stared at his back.

Early that evening I was in a complete dither. We were going to take *our* boat and go on a picnic. Even Ade didn't know that I'd never been in a small boat before. I'd seen row boats on the creek, flat-bottomed skiffs mostly, when I was a child, and I'd done some sailing in the East before 1929, but this was something brand-new.

Every cloud made me sure it was going to pour. When Ade wanted to make up the oil and gas mixture for it I gave him a glass measuring cup to be sure there wouldn't be any guesswork. Every time the motor died under his experimental maneuvering I was sure he didn't know how to run it. With all this, when he came from the dock and said, "We're all set,"

I realized that I had forgotten to pack our lunch. So he sat and looked superior while I went into a flurry with edibles and managed to get sandwiches and salad ready with only the minor mishap of dropping the margarine into the water bucket.

"Let's keep out from shore," I said as Ade pushed us away from the dock. "I wouldn't like to look like those people who go along and peer and point."

"I've seen a lot of houses, and I'm sure there are better things to see around here," he said and started the motor.

The water was smooth and pale until our wake slashed through it and rolled away, V-shaped, behind us. The willows were silver green along the shore and the tops of the birches were misty with their young, unfolding leaves. Far back among the rocks, under the overhanging roots of a storm-gnarled cedar I saw a melting, rounded bit of ice that had stayed on defiantly. We passed a rotted boat haul-up at the edge of a clearing grown up with weeds, and then a cabin, with high-peaked roof and green-painted logs, but looking strangely bare because all the trees had been cut out around it. I thought pleasantly of the little log house, nestling in the palm of the forest's hand, shaded from hot sun and protected from Arctic wind by our trees.

We swung out to round a point that pushed into the lake like a barrier. Beyond it the signs of man were gone and the forested shore stretched ahead, guarded by the pine-crowned hills to the south. This was the land as it had been since the forests covered the scars left by the last recession of the glaciers. This was what the first explorers had seen. Had Leif

Ericson's men really ever come here? This was the route of the *voyageurs*, sliding down the lakes in their fur-laden *bateaux*. This was the hunting ground that had once belonged to the proud Ojibways. Somewhere in time the strains of "Alouette" rang across these waters and the smoke of Indian campfires drifted on the air.

The country grew wilder as we approached the east end of the lake. Ridges of bedrock slashed through the thin, forested soil and showed their edges as dark cliffs. Islands, their shores washed to bare rock by the ceaseless buffeting of restless waters, were all about us.

Wind had risen in the northwest. The water began to roll and jagged black rocks appeared like teeth in the lows between the swells. We headed away from their treacherous bite, back into deeper water, and passed an island, no more than a huge table of rock cleft in the center, with one stunted pine growing in the cleft. Its top was squeezed by the winds so that it looked as if it might have modeled for a Japanese painting. The wind tore through my hair and spray spattered against my face. The water was indigo, covered by a shifting golden filigree, trimmed with lace as whitecaps foamed around us. But the boat was built to take rough water and, when Ade angled it into the big waves, it skimmed effortlessly up and down their slopes.

Ahead of us was a bay shored by a crescent of sand. Ade pointed to the lunch and turned into the quiet water. We waded ashore and pulled the boat up on the sand. More sun came here than in our yard and wild roses, pink and delicate, were already blooming. At the far end of the crescent a froth of yellow lilies moved lightly against a background of rushes.

The woods were very thick around the edge of the sand behind us, small trees and brush that had grown up during the twenty-five years after the last fire to burn over that land. I had read that there had once been a Hudson's Bay Post fronting on this beach, but had no desire to look for what traces might remain in the earth after the fire and the new growth. I looked east at the lake, its shores untouched by man as far as I could see, and wondered how long it would be before someone would bulldoze and shovel, hammer and build, change forever the wild shore.

The brush rustled down the beach from us and a doe led a fawn out of the thicket to drink. Her child was small and spotted and very new, had probably been walking on his wobbly legs only a few days. We scarcely breathed. The doe saw us, tensed, relaxed, drank hastily, then nudged her youngster back into the brush out of our sight. Near the wooded shore at the end of the beach we heard splashing and watched an otter climb onto a fallen log to dive into the water and come up with a fish.

Ade said, "That reminds me . . ."

I opened the lunch.

Then the gulls came, wheeling on wings turned magically gold by the westering sun, crying gently, dipping to snatch floating bread fragments. We had a drink from the clear water that washed over its jewel-colored stones, and pushed off for our cabin.

I watched the water, falling away from us in angled ridges, scattering gilded droplets, fading into our pale track that itself would fade away. Water . . . the only surface on which man has not been able to leave his impression since the first created day. We were leaving no more of an impression on the passing days than on the water, but I was conscious of the satisfaction that comes from the completion of necessary tasks, of the joy that grows from simple things.

The sun was just touching the western hills as we slid into the dock. Every leaf and twig stood out in the clarity of the tawny light. The sky was green in the north and the wind had died. The slowly rolling water was purple and bronze, dark with the coming night, bright with the fading day. It had been a good day—and our tomorrows were waiting. What kind of days they would be depended on us.

7 Transition

The chicken run was built, their small building was fitted with feeding trays, water dispensers, and perches, and the nights were comfortably warm by the end of May. The chickens had grown so fast that they crowded their tubs and I thought they would like being put into their run. Instead, they uttered terrified *wheeps* and cowered together against the building wall, staring upward with as much of an expression of horror as a chicken can manage. I looked for some hovering bird, but there was nothing.

Ade heaped them helter-skelter into one of the tubs and poured them out inside the building, propping open a low door into the run.

"Simple," he said in answer to my puzzled frown. "They've never been outside before. That great big sky is pretty scary when you're only a little chicken."

One by one they made their way out and, in a few days, were almost too brave because not even a bear wandering by scared them inside. They announced all arrivals with shrill squawks, though, so we were able to keep an eye out for anything that might harm them. This squawking was also handy in letting us know when people were coming down the path.

Our first visitors were the summer-home people who had brought the chickens. They approved of their quarters and invited us to join summer card games. Neither one of us cares for cards and we had no money to gamble with, so we thanked them and refused. This, I learned later, was not considered neighborly.

Beginning with the Memorial Day weekend, visitors to the Lodge began to drop in, the majority of them concerned with seeing the Larimer house. It seemed that the Larimers had kept themselves to themselves and were therefore objects of interest and speculation. It didn't take long before Ade and I heard that we were, too, for the same reason and because we had done the unprecedented thing of moving here.

During the summer mail came to the Lodge every day except Sunday and I went with Ade in the boat a few times with the idea of quashing any notion that we were mysterious strangers. However, my going seemed to guarantee that the mail would be at least an hour late and I found it wearying beyond thought to sit on a bench in the lobby and explain over and over to the vacationers why Ade and I didn't spend our time just having fun.

I'll always remember the lady who said, every time we met, "You *must* take time to fish. I don't see how you can *live* without fishing."

Finally I said that we'd managed to get along quite a few years without it, and heard later that I had criticized the lady because she saved food money by fishing!

I should have been safe from putting my foot in my mouth in my own kitchen. But there came the day when one of the young cockerels lost a fight and I brought him into the kitchen to do a little surgery on his torn comb. I had restored him to the run and was cleaning the bloody kitchen table when a woman I had seen at the Lodge but not met came to the door. I apologized for the mess and said, "I don't suppose you ever tried to operate on a chicken."

She said, "No, I never did," in a stiff tone, explained that she'd only stopped to say hello, and went. I thought this strange so I mentioned it to Hilda some weeks later.

"Oh my goodness!" she said, and went into shouts of laughter. When she had wiped her eyes: "She's a doctor."

I had never thought of myself as one of those people who manage to say the wrong thing as matter of course, but I had such a talent for it here that it was probably all for the best that Ade and I were too busy to get around to meet many people.

One day when Ade was reflooring the part of the icehouse that didn't still have ice in it (we had decided it would be more useful as a work building for him), I had some quiet hours to plan the winter grocery order. I settled with checkbook and last fall's grocery list. The little sums from woodwork were beginning to add up and I could count on a definite small amount from the weather bureau. After I estimated funds for regular bills to come, the balance was, of course, less than I had expected. I was rechecking my estimates when Joe Elliott, who handled our insurance as well as our legal matters, dropped in. He had been at the Lodge and thought he'd see how we were getting along.

This was the perfect time to increase the insurance so that we would have reasonable protection and to get a definite figure, which *might* be better than my estimate.

We settled on a valuation for the house and contents. Then Joe suggested a slightly higher-priced policy that would pay a percentage toward the loss of any of the outbuildings. I looked doubtful and he said, with complete seriousness, "It could be important. Suppose you had a grass fire and your toilet burned down."

I managed not to jump but nothing that had happened to us so far had so strongly brought home to me the magnitude of the change we were making. I said, "I forgot," and agreed to the policy he suggested. Altogether, the cost was twenty dollars less than my estimate and I felt positively wealthy as I again settled to work on the grocery list.

When Ade came in for dinner, I showed him the final list, considerably pared down from my first one.

"Shouldn't we have a little more canned meat? This looks like we'll have to get most of our meat by mail." Silently I handed him the list of expenses. "Oh. Well . . . I like pancakes."

Keeping my opinion of pancakes to myself, I sealed the list into its mailing envelope.

Two weeks later we had received no reply from the grocer.

"If we don't hear from him today," I told Ade as he left to get the mail, "call him and see what's holding things up."

Ade tossed an envelope into my lap when he returned. I

took out my list and a note, which I read aloud: "Sorry I couldn't write earlier. Have been out of town completing sale of my secondary business in bottle gas. The truck went along with the business. Consequently I cannot make any more deliveries to you, but will be glad to mail anything you want."

I went numb. We had one can of beef stew, one package of spaghetti with mushroom sauce, two cans of dried beef, about thirty cans of vegetables, two cans of milk, enough flour for maybe two loaves of bread, less than a quarter pound of margarine, and a little baking powder, sugar, salt, and pepper. There was absolutely no question of our getting food by mail because of the postage. Anyway, Ade could do without carrying a week's groceries on his back when he walked those three miles from mailbox to cabin every winter Saturday.

After a long silence Ade said, "There's almost no chicken feed, either."

"Could we . . . eat some of them?" I asked uncertainly. I had found out soon after we moved the chicks into their outside quarters that I would have to avoid them as much as possible or I'd not be able to cook them, let alone eat them.

"They're too small yet. If I have to, I'll turn 'em loose. They'll probably not wander far and they'll find plenty of food in the woods . . . but they'll likely be caught by something. And you've been counting on having fresh eggs next winter." He reached up, seemed surprised to find his beard there, then ruffled it until it looked like that of some ancient prophet on a wind-swept hill. "But we have to eat . . ."

I snorted. "A great truth, clearly stated. The problem is how."

We thought. My mind produced unbroken blankness. Then Ade snapped his fingers.

"Hilda and Sven have a store and they buy for the Lodge, so they must deal with a wholesaler. Why can't we?"

"We're not dealers," I said, pessimistic about the whole thing.

"What difference would it make if we buy by the case? Call Hilda."

I did and she said, "*Why* didn't I think of that before? They ship to lots of people up here, and they have everything. You'll save so much! Send Ade down and I'll give him a catalog. Just mail your order and the freight'll bring it up in a couple of weeks."

It is a real experience to have an eight-month supply of food to buy and the catalog of a wholesale grocer to glean. All kinds of things you ordinarily would not think about are listed and, if you have always bought in small quantities from retail stores as I had before we moved, things look so temptingly cheap. But it doesn't take long to learn that twenty-four-can cases of vegetables at $2.05 and meat at $4.86 (those are real prices from those less expensive days) can add up in a hurry. This company also sold half cases, so I managed to get us a variety and quantity of food that the average housewife would never see except in a store. When I finished, my order was larger than the one I had previously written for the local grocer and the cost, including the freight, would be a little less.

Some six days later I looked into the pie chest that still had some food in it.

"What'll you have for dinner . . . green beans, peas, carrots, or tomatoes?"

"Peas," Ade said. "What with 'em?"

"Oatmeal."

He made a subdued sound. "What else?"

"Nothing."

"Ugh! I hope we have milk and sugar to put on the oatmeal?"

"You can have some sugar," I said, as I set about warming the peas and simmering the oatmeal. "I'll need the little bit of flour and the half can of milk that's left. I can stretch something with 'em."

We went through the beans, carrots, and tomatoes, and were back to peas again when Ade came in from the log house, all smiles, and said, "Get a kettle and come on."

Mystified, I did. When we emerged from under the big trees I saw the once bare, bulldozed ground south of the cabin covered with late-blooming dandelions. Horsetails were growing there, too, and young ferns, but the despised weed of the suburbanite made a sheet of gold here, unbelievably cheerful and lovely.

I suddenly wondered what I had been doing with my eyes for the past three months. One of the things I had particularly wanted to see was which plants grew first on the barren ground. The city habit of minding my own business, of ignoring surroundings which had nothing to do with me, was with me still. Here the whole outside was my business and was perhaps more important than all my fussing around with dusters and brooms. In any case, it was important because this was the earth, the wild earth, the source. I let my eyes wander slowly over the golden fleece before me and said, inadequately, "Lovely."

"Sure," Ade said. "Edible, too, though." I looked up and started to smile at a childhood memory of picking dandelion greens in our backyard. "Yep," Ade said, reading my mind. "Greens, and can you make some kind of batter?"

"Salad, too," I said. "As to batter, it won't be fancy. What for?"

"Aunt Mayme used to fry the flowers in batter on the homestead."

"But I've nothing to fry them in."

"That's what *I* thought. Then I found that bacon grease we were saving for the birds. It's in the ice I took out of the icehouse to do some more of the floor, and it's perfectly fresh."

The next day I rationed the oatmeal between us and the chickens and gathered leaves and bunchberries for them. The bunchberries were a big hit, but even their amount was limited.

When I used the last of the flour and some of the beans and peas in a casserole that tasted like nothing on earth, Ade, after manfully swallowing some of it, said, "This reminds me of the Navy."

"I thought they fed you well."

"They did, but once our stores were low and we had to ride out a typhoon. We had weak coffee and weevil-bread for days. They sifted the bugs out of the flour but they couldn't sift out the taste."

I sat, looking with disgust at the casserole, as he went out to give the last of the oatmeal to the now pitifully hungry chickens. I was thinking that we at least had *something* to eat and ought to be thankful for it, when I heard the chickens crying for more as Ade came back into the kitchen.

"I'm going to call Hilda," I said. "I can go without food for a while and so can you—we learned that back in the thirties —but those guys out there are completely helpless. Hilda'll have some oats or corn meal or something." I hate borrowing and was very cross. "Who's making all that racket?" I snapped as a car horn blew.

"If you'd tried looking toward the road instead of at whatever that stuff is we've just tried to eat," Ade said, "you'd have seen the freight truck go by."

I put the contents of the casserole out in the woods where some wanderer would no doubt find it delicious, then went next door to see boxes, crates, and bags piling up in front of the log cabin.

I dusted shelves and cupboards and, when the unloading was done, picked up a crate, saying, "I'll help you haul 'em in."

"Not yet you won't." Ade glanced at the freight bill. "This consignment weighs two thousand eleven pounds, and I'll have to put braces under the kitchen floor or we won't have any kitchen."

.   .   .

2

With the coming of August thunder showers crashed and flashed and poured after sunset or in the depths of night, but most of the days were warm and bright, with daisies and everlasting and yarrow scattered in the open spaces like scraps of lace set out to whiten in the sun. I went every day to watch the changes on the bulldozed ground and saw raspberries establishing themselves with zest and dark-green moss starting up on the earth like the thinnest and softest velvet, covering the damp area above the spring that had once made our basement brook. The dandelions put out new blooms and attracted chipmunks—plump, reddish ones with clear black-and-white stripes on their sides, and smaller ones with thin stripes that reached from nose to tail, and tails that stood straight up when they ran. They loved the dandelion seeds and pulled down the long stems to bite off and discard the white "wings" and carry home the food in their cheek pouches. They ran up the tallest trees, too, agile as squirrels although they did not make the squirrels' death-defying leaps from branch to branch. I could always count on the antics of the squirrels and chippies to brighten my dull moments.

Ade had finished enclosing the open lake side of the icehouse and was preparing winter quarters for the chickens. On rainy days he planned the location of the electric outlets, then started to wire the log cabin.

A month earlier he had sent some of his notepaper to a gift shop in the Village for trial. It was so well received that we decided to place a small ad in one of the nature magazines, since the paper had deer, and bears, and feeding birds, and a lot of forest atmosphere. I had never subscribed to any of these magazines so I went with Ade at mail time one day to look at copies Hilda kept in the lounge for the guests. I selected *Audubon Magazine* and turned to the contents. I had not skimmed half a dozen pages when I knew that I had not seen my forest for its trees. I had material to write about, floods of it, all around me. I borrowed the magazine.

After I took care of Ade's notepaper advertisement, I thought that a tame weasel and hand-fed fishers might be unusual enough to interest the editor, John K. Terres, so I wrote to ask him.

Two weeks later he replied that a tame weasel and hand-fed fishers did indeed sound interesting, but was I sure these were fishers? Fishers had such a reputation for shyness, ferocity, and so on. I understood his doubts, but with luck would be able to prove my claim to visiting fishers. Ade had taken some pictures through the window with an old box camera, loaded with film we had bought in Chicago, but we hadn't felt we should spend the money to have the film developed. I mailed it to the Village in a hurry and soon had several snapshots fuzzy but identifiable. I sent them to Mr. Terres, who replied enthusiastically. So, knowing more about weasels and seeing the fishers as a second subject, I wrote something of the right word-length and mailed it. It came back with clear and helpful suggestions for improvement, and a reminder that I had not identified the species of weasel—long-tailed or short-tailed?

Such meager references as I had said that both *might* be found here; that sizes varied in different locations, and the size-range of the largest short-tailed weasel overlapped that of the smallest long-tailed; and that the length of the black tip on their tails was variable, too. I needed to get to a library, and that was impossible. There wasn't even one in the Village at that time. I wrote, explaining to the editor why I could not identify my weasels. By return mail he recommended an up-to-date field guide to mammals, told me the price and where to order. I looked at our tiny bank balance and knew I couldn't gamble even the small price of the book.

I don't know what I replied to Mr. Terres (I didn't have enough paper to make carbon copies of any but the most essential letters) but the next week's mail brought a copy of the book, with a letter that said it would be well worth the investment if it would make it possible for me to identify my weasel.

I was touched and encouraged by the kindness of this busy man in New York, and I didn't waste any time. I looked at the pictures in the book, saw that the long-tailed weasel had a white belly in summer but that the short-tailed had not only a white belly but also white feet. I remembered Walter's white feet after he'd changed into his summer coat. I rewrote the article.

In mid-September, when the summerhouse grew chilly at night even with the fire and we were getting ready to move to the log cabin for the winter, I received my letter of acceptance for the article, "for which we will pay you fifty dollars."

Ade crowed with delight but it took me a long time to believe that the letter was real—until the check came, in fact. Then I remembered the little girl who wrote a paper in which she said that some day she was going to live in the woods and write about what she saw. The little girl hadn't meant it, of course, or perhaps she did without knowing it. If so, it was not surprising that the first signs of a hidden dream coming true so·many years later did not seem real. Anyway, here I was with Ade, deep in the woods, with my first earnings from nature writing in my hand.

3

We were barely settled in the log cabin when a freak storm surprised us with nearly a foot of early snow, heavy flakes that bent the branches of spruce and balsam until their silhouettes were narrow as those of Lombardy poplars. The copper and brass and bronze of the autumn leaves shone incongruously through the white, and multiflowered purple asters and sprays of goldenrod bloomed as though miraculously called from the snow.

I happened to look into the woods from the west window that afternoon and caught a flash of scarlet. Then sunlight glinted on a gun barrel and a hunter hove into view, simply resplendent in an outfit straight from the stock of one of the best sporting-goods houses. Hunting what? Then I recalled that the grouse season had opened a few days earlier. We didn't have any grouse as far as I knew, and there were no grouse tracks on the snow, so I wondered why the man had come this way. He couldn't have failed to see the house. I was about to call Ade and ask him to go out and tell the intruder that we lived here and would rather he did his hunting in some safer place, when he raised the gun and aimed at the window. It was a .410 shotgun, not the deadliest weapon he might have carried, but one guaranteed to reduce a window to basic particles with one blast.

At first I was frightened and drew back. Then, as he slipped from tree to tree, aiming from every vantage point, I concluded that he was playing cowboys and Indians, or something equally silly for a grown man. I called Ade from the workroom.

"Right now I think he's being Geronimo attacking the fort," I said. "You don't think he might get carried away and start popping, do you?"

"I hope not. I'd hate to have to put in a new window. It'd be midwinter before I could get the glass up here."

Our friend had now skulked to a position under one of our tallest spruces, which stood some thirty feet from the cabin. There he stopped, leaned the shotgun against the tree trunk, barrel-down in the snow, and surveyed the house.

"If he fires that thing, he'll blow his head off," Ade said. "This snow'll pack the barrel like mud." He snapped his fingers. "Oh brother! I've just had the finest fiendish thought of my life . . . and I can carry it out for once!"

He took a heavy pistol out of a drawer. "Keep your eye on

the tree when you hear the shot," he said gleefully and went out without a sound.

The hunter was peering at the window through cupped hands when the pistol roared. He grabbed up his shotgun and froze, holding the gun vertically in front of his face and body as though presenting arms. Then I saw the snow moving at the quivering top of the spruce, where Ade had put the heavy slug. The snow slid gently, shuddered, gathered momentum and more snow, then rushed down to strip the branches and pour over the galvanized hunter like an avalanche. For a moment he stood, a half-buried toy soldier, then he broke track records through the woods and out of sight.

I was collapsed on the daybed when Ade came in, doubled over with laughing.

"There's just one thing," he said between chortles. "I'd like to hear the tale he'll tell of escaping some bush-happy woods-man in a hail of bullets."

The snow melted in three days and, although we thought it too early to begin serious bird feeding, we moved the bench from under the window to stand beneath a cedar tree some twenty feet from the kitchen door. We spread a little cracked corn on it and put a scattering of scratch feed near the clear-ing on the path from the summer house, where birds often came down to pick sand and gravel.

The next afternoon Little Bear arrived.

When we first saw him he was standing on his hind legs, licking the corn from the bench, which is twenty-two inches high. Little Bear had to stretch to rest his arms on its top. His coat was shiny black and so thick that its hairs stood almost straight up. Underneath he was pleasingly plump, no doubt well fed on garbage from the dumps near the resorts. Now that the tourists were few and the resorts closing, he was making the rounds of the woods, looking for food.

He finished the corn, dropped to all fours, and turned toward the cabin. From the front he looked as though he were wearing an over-size Hallowe'en mask, thickly whiskered at its lower edge. The brown on his nose was very dark, and his face had an innocent expression. He stood for a few minutes, head swaying from side to side and nostrils busy, then stepped hesitantly toward the cabin. I bumped the screen against its frame and Little Bear jerked back and hurried around the corner of the building. He loped past the north windows. His legs were stumpy and he looked much like a rocking horse, loosely covered by a bear rug that bounced with every stride. When he came to the drainage ditch at the west side of the clearing, he stopped for a big drink, then ambled through a patch of three-foot balsam firs to reach the path to the summer house.

He paused at the scattering of scratch feed. He tasted and liked it, lay flat on his stomach with hind legs stretched out and forelegs curled around the grain and licked up the food at his leisure. This done, he rolled on one side and cleaned his face and paws thoroughly, finishing with a good scratch behind his ears and an enormous yawn. He settled, nose on paws, and dozed, opening an eye or moving an ear occasionally. When he had rested he rolled onto his back, waved his legs, flipped to his feet, and walked slowly down one of the deer trails, his ridiculous excuse of a tail held out from his body and twitching.

An hour later I heard a strange and hair-raising sound that made me think of a prehistoric creature clattering his scales. It came at short intervals from several locations in the woods and then started near the cabin. I looked out and saw Little Bear clinging to the rough bark of our largest and thickest white pine, which towers above the place where he had found the scratch feed. As he hunched upward—hind feet, fore feet—his claws rattled on the bark. When he had climbed fifty feet to the first branches, he lifted himself easily from one to another until he came to a point where a storm had topped the tree long ago. Here the branches had spread like the fingers of a giant hand at the base of one branch that had turned upward to give the tree a new top. Little Bear moved around these spread branches until he found just the place to lie prone, a fore and hind leg hanging over each side of his chosen branch. And there he slept, with eighty feet between him and danger that might walk the earth below.

In the morning he was gone, and this was good in one way. Small bears will eventually be very large bears. However, I found myself watching for the fat, round, black rear with the twitching tail. There were a few birds and Ade and I decided to put out a little more grain for them, on the path and the bench. If Little Bear came back this would not do him the unkindness of teaching him to nose around buildings.

And return he did in the afternoon, to lick the bench, scamper away when the door bumped, have his drink, clean up the grain on the path, groom himself, and climb his sleeping tree. This went on until the lodges were no longer supplying any garbage and the last of the wild berries had gone with the falling leaves. Then Little Bear spent most of his time resting in his tree, perhaps to conserve for his winter sleep the fat that now made him round as a ball. There was something very touching in the way he made the rounds of the yard and followed his path through the small balsams. On each trip he walked over one little tree that snapped up behind him, giving his rump a sharp slap. He always looked around carefully, then stood, a picture of ursine perplexity.

In order to give some feed to the now numerous migrating birds without having Little Bear discover that we were the source of the grain, we took advantage of his daily short walk. The clatter of his claws on the bark as he came down told me to get ready and, as soon as he was well out of sight, I put grain on the bench and under his tree. One afternoon he changed his pattern and was standing on the lowest branch, arms resting on the one above, chin over arms, looking down at me. I sat down at the base of a nearby tree, grain can uncomfortably behind my back, and looked up at him. Eventually he climbed to his resting place and I backed all the way to the cabin. I've been told bears do not see well, but I wanted to take no chances on having him spot the can.

I loved to watch him, so high in his pine. When the wind was light, he braced himself for sleep and let the tree rock him. When high winds came, he hung on tight to the big limbs, changing position with the wind's direction. By now, as a diversionary measure, I went to the tree at irregular intervals without the grain can, and for a few days he came down

to the lower boughs and we stood, contemplating each other. Finally he resumed his strolls and feeding the birds was easy again.

Then the new owners of a cabin gave us a windfall of animal food, left behind by the former owners. Among other things were two large jars, one of crystallized honey, the other of peanut butter, both of which had collected a large number of unfortunate ants. There was also a two-pound bag of squashed marshmallows, very sticky. Perfect for Little Bear . . . but I simply don't believe in feeding bears. Could I compromise . . . arrange something like our grain-for-the-birds system? Well, I could try.

I took long walks over all the animal trails and through parts of the woods where there were none so that my scent would be common to Little Bear wherever he went. When I was sure he was not around, I left the marshmallows in one place and the honey and peanut butter in a flat pan in another. I didn't have the fun of seeing him eat the goodies, but I still have the pan, retrieved much later, marked by his teeth as he worked on it to get the very last morsel.

The next day he made a hollow in some brush behind a mound of earth and, for a week, whenever Ade or I walked in the woods we saw two round ears above the mound by day and a pair of watchful eyes glowing in our flashlight beam at night. Maybe he wasn't trying to find out where his bonanza had come from, but I'll always believe that he was.

At about this time I read of a woman in Alaska who had a tame Kodiak bear. There was a picture of him standing outside her door—all of eight feet long and half as tall with weight to match—taking a tidbit from her fingers. Of course, she had to replace screen doors and windowpanes now and then when something annoyed the big brownie, but she expected this with so huge a begging visitor. And I played with the idea of having a tame bear of my own, Little Bear grown up, friendly and, if handled carefully, not too dangerous. But the woman in Alaska had no near neighbors and tourists did not pour through her area. Here any taming of Little Bear could only lead to disaster for him and a feeling of guilt and sorrow for me.

Then came a skim of snow and freezing nights. On the last day of October Little Bear made a careful check of all the food sources in the yard. He clawed open rotten stumps he had visited earlier, licked up every particle of grain on and around the bench and under his sleeping tree, sniffed at every burrow, and tried with all his strength to chew into a post which an old woodpecker drilling marked as once having held ants. And how I wished I had another bag of marshmallows for a going-away present, so to speak.

His checking done, he took a big drink from the spring water that still flowed in the drainage ditch and sat on the bank above his drinking place. His hind legs stuck straight out in front of him and his belly was so fat that only his feet showed. It began to rain and still he sat. Then, at his moment of decision, he got up and walked up our path toward the road, looking neither to right nor left, his wet coat parting neatly down the middle of his back and showing a cowlick effect above his tail, which was still busily twitching. And so he was gone for the winter.

He returned in the spring and for three weeks came through the yard daily as he followed his routes to his feeding places. We did not see him after that, but we miss him still.

I hope he is alive somewhere, a big bear, strong, and wise not only in the ways of his forest but also in the ways of men who may come there. If I ever see him again, I'm sure I'll know him, because even in the rangy dignity of his maturity he'll still be twitching that funny little tail.

4

Meanwhile the chickens had been going as chickens do, one by one. I'd grown too concerned about them during the temporary food shortage to enjoy eating them, and Ade wasn't enthusiastic either, but we could not keep them all and they helped out. We both knew that until we had something more substantial behind us than the sale of one short article and a small amount of notepaper we'd have to make use of every helpful bit. We'd have to do this for a long time, even when—and if—I sold many more articles and Ade's notepaper sales were greatly increased. On the brighter side, he was starting to get orders by mail from the small ad I had placed and I wrote the story of Mrs. Mouse's miracle, which sold at once. And when Ade brought in the very first fresh eggs from our hens they encouraged us even more, although I don't see now why we felt that the eggs were *our* accomplishment.

The weather had been relatively mild since the early snow-storm and Ade's chain saw and ax were busy turning the cord-wood by the road into split lengths for winter cooking and heating. I climbed onto a makeshift scaffold and covered the workroom ceiling with white undercoat. Painting a slanting ceiling whose panels are separated by beams that must be avoided was very hard on the neck, and the job wasn't made easier by the Celotex surface, which slurped up brushfuls of paint like a sponge. It took me ten days, but the result was fresh, clean, and cheering. Once I was again used to looking forward instead of overhead, I set about moving cases of gro-ceries which had been stacked where they trapped feet and reached out to whack shins. By the time I had finished lining the offenders at the base of the living-room wall behind the curtain where we hung our clothes, I was creaking all over, and flopped on the daybed to read some neglected mail.

A Chicago friend wanted to know when we were coming back to civilization. I looked out of the window and up through the bare lacework of a birch top to the blue, blue sky. I smelled the faint fragrance of balsam smoke from the stove. I listened to the querulous piping of some nuthatches. I thought of the woodpiles and my white ceiling and the stored groceries—of the fall work behind and the winter chores ahead. Of the dim, tantalizing glimpses of possible indepen-dent careers. Civilization? We were as civilized in our forest setting as my friend was in her concrete beehive, but it would be useless to try to tell her so. I'd just write that at present we were not planning on returning.

Ade's voice broke into my thoughts. "Come see the chicken-house."

He had revamped an old shed Carl had used for storage of dynamite. The roof was weather-proofed with sheet metal and scraps of the old blue roofing, the walls were warmly covered with two layers of building paper, and the inside was newly whitewashed. The floor was cushioned with dry grass and a water can was wired firmly to the walls in one corner, ". . . so they can't upset it," Ade explained. "The feed tray on the inside of the door lifts out for cleaning and the little window above the tray is double, so it won't frost over. They'll get more light and can see out. This lantern in the corner supplies heat and that section of stove pipe with the wide lower end carries off the fumes from the oil. There's a screened ventilator up here . . ."—he pointed above the door—". . . and another one at the top of the roof. This wire screening wraps around the lantern and fastens to these hooks on the wall so they can't set their feathers afire from the hot chimney. And here's an extra removable screen door for warm days. And a perch and a laying box."

It was neat and ingenious, a veritable modern flat for chickens, and I said so. "But it's so small. How many are you keeping?"

"Three. There's no way to heat a place big enough for more, and we couldn't let them freeze and suffer. Anyway, hens don't lay when they're too cold."

"We won't have many eggs, but even a few will be a treat. How many do you suppose . . ."

"Well, not more than two in a day. The third one's a rooster."

"Thinking of raising some in the spring?" I asked, knowing perfectly well that neither one of us could ever eat chickens we'd nursed along from their first cheep.

"Not exactly . . . he's kind of a pet. You'll like him. I'll go get 'em now."

He returned with the rooster sitting comfortably on his bent arm and the two hens trying to poke their heads through the chick wire that covered the basket they rode in.

"Here—take the Crown Prince," he said, handing me the rooster, who settled on my arm as though we were old friends and began to investigate a shirt button with his beak. Ade reached under the wire mesh and, ignoring squawks that said plainly the hens knew their end had come, lifted them out, holding one in each hand by the base of the wings. They hung quietly, wings up, feet down, and looked around with interest.

They were beautiful chickens, with black feet and beaks, opalescent black feathers, scarlet combs, scarlet and white touches on their faces, and inquiring yellow eyes. The rooster's comb was enormous, cresting his head with tall points, and the larger hen's, although not as elaborately pointed, was so large it draped to one side.

"Her comb's so graceful she looks like she's wearing a flower," I said.

"I—uh—call her Tulip," Ade said, looking sheepish.

"Very appropriate." I looked at the other hen. "And this one?"

"I haven't named her."

She was small and as underslung as a duck. Her tail feathers were sparse and uneven, both in distribution and in length. Her neck was mostly bare so that she faintly resembled a turkey vulture. Her expression was peevish and she moved her head from side to side as though hunting the source of a very offensive odor.

I burst out laughing. "She disapproves of things on principle. I knew a woman once who looked on the world just like that. What was her name . . . Bedelia!"

"Bedelia." Ade nodded. "Good enough. Bedelia, I might say, is a very special hen. She laid the first egg we had and she's laid an egg every day since, and in spite of her size and shape, her eggs are the biggest. She has another talent, too. I'll let you find out about that in due course."

He put the livestock in their house and fitted in the screen door, the feeding tray attached to its inner side. The Crown Prince drank some water and hopped onto the perch. Tulip began to eat. Bedelia poked her beak into every corner, tried to eat the wire around the stove, flapped her wings, and *crowed.*

"The rooster does better, of course," Ade said, "but I've a feeling Bedelia is unique, the only hen who crows not only in the morning and when she feels like it, but every time she lays an egg."

The sun was low in the afternoon when Hilda and Sven came in unexpectedly.

"We're going to Minneapolis again," Hilda said. "We hadn't intended to but . . ."

"But we couldn't stand you all winter," Sven finished seriously.

"Oh Sven! This time my sister and her husband are going

to take a trip and don't want to leave their house empty—so much bother turning things off—as if we didn't know. Sometimes I think that's all we do up here." She turned to Sven. "I forgot the leftovers. They're in the car." He shook his head and went out. "When they come back," she went on, "we're going to take off. We've never seen the Grand Canyon or the Pacific Ocean or anything. We've stayed so close here, not that we didn't have to, but I'm beginning to think it's a mistake to let one beautiful part of the country blind you to all the rest . . . so we're on our way." She stopped abruptly, probably to catch her breath.

Ade was making wishful noises and I was thinking that there were a lot of places I'd like to see, too, come the day when we'd have the time and money to roam. Then Sven came in with a box, saying: "I left some suet outside."

"On the counter, Sven," Hilda said, "and gently. Don't forget the eggs." She turned to me, smiling. "There's not much but it'll make a meal. And you'll have to use the peas tonight. They're partly thawed."

When they had gone, I turned to the box: two small tomatoes, a package of frozen peas, a quarter of a package of dehydrated potatoes sold for hash-browns, and six eggs.

"Dinner is almost served," I said and started on the kind of improvised cooking one learns to do when supplies are limited.

I poured the potatoes into a saucepan and added a cup and a half of water. When they had simmered to maximum bulk and tenderness, I drained them and put them in a baking dish. I mixed an ounce and a half of dry milk solids, a tablespoon of

flour, some salt and pepper, and sprinkled this onto the potatoes, stirring to get the dry ingredients thoroughly distributed. Then I poured in an ounce of canned milk and
enough water to almost cover the potatoes, dotted on a tablespoon of margarine, and set them in the oven to turn into
simulated escalloped potatoes.

When they were well on the way to being done, I added an
ounce of canned milk and a dash of salt and pepper to the
broken eggs and beat them thoroughly, while a tablespoon of
margarine was melting in a slowly warming large skillet.
After I rotated the skillet until the bottom was evenly covered
by the melted margarine, I poured in the eggs and let them
cook gently until set on the bottom. Meanwhile, I had cut the
tomatoes into quarter-inch wedges, which I now distributed in
the cooking eggs. I moved the skillet to a slightly warmer spot
on the stove and covered it.

While the eggs puffed and set, I prepared the frozen peas
according to the instructions.

When I served, we each had a tomato omelet that covered
half of a large plate, a very large helping of tasty potatoes,
and an over-size dish of peas—all either of us could eat at any
meal, barring our having done hard labor all day.

As I write this, I am reminded of an article I read recently in a metropolitan newspaper, written by a sociologist
who was greatly concerned over the difficulty a woman of her
acquaintance, who was temporarily on welfare, was having in
preparing an adequate luncheon for her three children, aged
seven, six, and five. She had only thirty-five cents for each
child's lunch, a total of $1.05 for all three. I got pencil and

paper and figured the cost of our meal from Hilda's leftovers at our 1968 prices—and food prices are not low here because of the long distance things must be shipped. It came out like this:

2	tablespoons or two thirds	
	ounce of margarine	2.1¢
2	tomatoes	20.0¢
1	package frozen peas	20.0¢
¼	package hash-brown potatoes	10.8¢
6	large eggs	21.0¢
2	ounces canned milk	2.5¢
1½	ounces dry-milk solids	4.5¢
1	tablespoon flour; salt, pepper	2.0¢ (estimated)
	Total	82.9¢

So 83¢ provides a meal, and a nourishing one, that ought to more than fill up three youngsters, and leaves 22¢ out of the original $1.05. The mother might want to give her children a treat so, if her staples were not near vanishing point and she could manage to have this much left over another day, she could buy one of those thirty-nine-cent half-pound bars of milk chocolate for the kids and still have a five-cent start on the next can of milk.

And chocolate is much more than candy. Men who go alone into the empty places of the winter North carry it and eat it for emergency energy, as Jacques did on his hard trek from his trapping camp. In our food-problem days—and later on we had plenty of them, and of cold and hunger during our struggle to establish ourselves—we would have bought that chocolate bar.

This kind of money management and meal-getting isn't a matter of careful shopping because fresh tomatoes and prepared potatoes are almost in the luxury class these days. It is a matter of imagination, I think, because I was so very inexperienced in such things before I came here that I had nothing but my imagination to draw on. I learned to make do because I had to. I keep it up because it makes not only good sense but different meals.

The days slid quietly into November, cold but not very, windless and dry. Ade finished stacking the wood and between the preparing and filling of sporadic mail orders for notepaper, started to undercoat the kitchen ceiling. I got the check for Mrs. Mouse's story and was stirred to spend hours outside, gathering sights and sounds and scents for future writing. There was a little snow, just enough to turn the woods into a three-dimensional tapestry in gray and white and black, and the temperature dropped to begin freezing the remaining moisture out of the air. The Crown Prince announced the mornings as he was expected to, with Bedelia helping, and every day a series of crows and cackles told us our two fresh eggs were ready.

Then overnight, the temperature shot up into the thirties, the snow melted, and the air was heavy with fog. Ade and I stood in the doorway, waiting for smoke, driven into the kitchen by a down draft in the chimney, to clear.

"What would we have done without Hilda and Sven?" I wondered. "So much depended on their kindness—the foundation, our groceries, the motor, the chickens, thoughtful little things like the begonias in there. Even the way they reacted when we came back from town and told them we'd decided to stay. Delighted and matter-of-fact. They couldn't have done more to give us confidence. And I always thought we came up here to be on our own."

"That's what I thought till we'd been here a while. Individually, we were more independent in Chicago. We even earned separate livings and had separate circles of acquaintances. Up here every move we make is tied up with some move the other makes, and often with what someone outside is doing. We're still doing different things to earn money, but they're shared. And you need me to cut stove wood and I need you to tie up mashed fingers. I'd say we're less independent, aside from no longer being an expendable part of some company, but we're free to be *de*pendent in any way we want to. I like it better this way."

We went inside. Ade got some crackers out of a box and munched, saying, "I'm hungry. When d'you suppose today's eggs will arrive? I could eat one fried right now."

I felt a sudden hollowness in my middle. "Did you hear the Crown Prince crow this morning?"

Ade put down the cracker he had part way to his mouth. "No."

We stared at each other, then he bolted outside. I heard the door to the little house open, then a sound somewhere between a wail and a groan. I was at the door when he came back, his face black with soot. "Our chickens . . . our poor chickens. They're suffocated."

I ran past him and dropped to my knees beside the three quiet black bodies he had pulled into the fresh air. Something, perhaps the atmospheric change, had affected the lantern and it was pouring out thick, greasy smoke. I touched Bedelia's comb. She moved.

"Bedelia's alive, anyway," I said. "Let's carry them inside and see what we can do."

Tulip was moving feebly as well as her "sister" by the time we had them on the drawing table in front of the workroom window, but the Crown Prince was ominously still. I didn't look at Ade. The Crown Prince was his special pet and . . . if it would work for people it might work for a chicken! I reached my fingers into the feathers along the rooster's sides and pressed, released . . . pressed, released . . . and heard the lungs sucking air every time. A couple of minutes passed and Ade reached out and moved one of his legs.

"He isn't getting stiff, yet. Maybe . . ."

I wished I hadn't started trying to revive the bird. It wasn't going to work and Ade would feel worse than ever . . .

The Crown Prince opened one yellow eye and sneezed.

Ade began to talk happily to the chickens, I've no idea what about. I got a damp cloth and wiped their combs and wattles and then handed it to Ade, who began to rub at his face, spreading the soot in swathes.

The Crown Prince staggered to his feet, settled his feathers, and flew into Ade's lap. Bedelia looked over the table edge, peered critically toward the ceiling, and turned to the shelf holding my potted plant. After due consideration, she began to select begonia leaves for breakfast. Tulip stood quietly, then hopped to the floor, looked up at us apologetically, and withdrew to lay her morning egg under the table.

5

By the time we were sure the chickens were not going to relapse and die, the wind had swung to the north again and the temperature was dropping. Ade said he wanted to check the lantern thoroughly in case its flare-up had been caused by something other than the atmospheric change, and he thought the chickens would be warm enough in their house for the time he'd be working on their "heater." I thought a chill on top of the monoxide or whatever it was they had breathed might start some respiratory problem that could be fatal. We agreed to take no chances and settled them beside the drawing table in a big box, loosely covered with chick wire. Ade took the lantern to the remodeled icehouse, and I sat down at the desk and uncovered the typewriter. I had hardly squared the paper in the machine when there was a chorus of squawks from the chickens, accompanied by loud bumps.

As I went into the workroom, Bedelia circled past my head and lit on top of the mimeograph drum, her claws digging into Ade's stencil. Tulip and the Prince were quiet and watched her with attention. I tightened the wire over the box and moved toward Bedelia. She shrieked and took off, to land on the living-room floor, and try to make herself invisible under the desk. I got her back into the box after a struggle and covered her footprints—the sticky mimeo ink had already sunk into the bare boards of the floor—with newspapers. Next I looked at the stencil and decided this might be a good omen, because she had not damaged the delicate handdrawn design that had taken Ade eleven hours to complete. He could patch the blank end she had torn. I found a large carton in the woodshed and covered the mimeo with it. Then I returned to the typewriter, wondering just what it was that I had intended putting on paper.

Before I could remember, there was more squawking and bumping and I looked through the door to see Bedelia sailing across the kitchen, narrowly missing a lamp. Sounds of things falling ensued. By the time I got to the scene, Bedelia was on the counter, pecking contentedly at a loaf of bread. Deciding that she *might* stay put for a few minutes, I sidled through the door and went to the shore for Ade.

"Hi," he said, when I stepped into the icehouse. "Pretty neat, huh?"

I looked around the little building and agreed with him. He had fitted the old basement windows into the walls, and lined all the inside except the ceiling with odds and ends of linoleum, also salvaged from the basement.

"Eventually I'll have this really set up and use some kind of stove," he said. "That'll free some space in the cabin. There's nothing wrong with the lantern, by the way. There's water in the oil and the wick got soaked. I'll change the oil and the wick every evening and dry the used wick over night."

"Well, the sooner you get our feathered friends back in their house, the better. Bedelia is descended from a long line of jailbreakers and saboteurs. You'll have to catch her this time."

"Nothing to it," he said, and for him there wasn't. He just walked into the kitchen and picked her up.

By the time the birds were back in their own domain, the kitchen was cold from the opening and closing of the door and I bent over the woodbox to replenish the stove. The earlier sounds of things falling became clear. In the box were a salt cellar, assorted empty spice containers, and a package of graham crackers. The grahams were broken and scattered among the sticks and chips. I had an idea I might salvage them for pie crust or something, but the wood had resin on it and so did the grahams. Grubs of certain wood-boring beetles inhabited some of the wood, too, and this brought shrews to feast on them. I decided the grahams were a total loss. But no. It was time we started winter bird and animal feeding, and graham crackers ought to be very acceptable. I collected the larger pieces in a coffee can and added the part of the bread Bedelia had mangled. Hilda and Sven had left us pounds of suet. The supply of scratch feed and laying food for the hens was somewhat limited, but we had plenty of cracked corn for both the chickens and wild visitors. All this ought to make a banquet, and the sooner we put it out, the sooner we'd know how it would be received—and who would come to eat.

"How'll we handle the suet?" I asked Ade. "What the Petersons brought will last all winter if somebody doesn't carry it all home."

"I can make some little cages and hang them from tree trunks. Wire mesh with wooden backs for strength and wire tops that hinge so I can refill. The squirrels and birds can eat okay and I can bring the cages in at night if we see fishers." He reached for a pencil and paper and began to sketch.

"Something like this if you can see it. It's awfully dark in here."

I glanced at the window. "No wonder. It's snowing."

The first scattered flakes were big and wet, dropping heavily from soggy clouds and melting on the ground. Then, with a slowly falling temperature and a slowing rising northwest wind, the flakes became smaller and drier, and slid to earth along slanting skids of air. The ground began to whiten and the wind built up tiny ridges. Darkness came an hour early and with it snow like crumbs from a great white cake.

We sat in the living room, half reading, half listening to the humming of winds high in the pines and the tap and rustle of snow against the north window.

"This is the way winter begins," I said. "Not at the winter solstice—that's a point in time—and not when the lake freezes over. That's incidental. As far as I'm concerned, winter is snow that stays—and I'm ready to bet this is it."

Ade nodded. "There's a feeling, too, of being warm and inside. You don't feel exactly like that except when the first staying snow comes."

"You feel safe . . . secure. I suppose we shouldn't, not with our uncertain future, but security's an illusion anyway, except for something in yourself. For me, it's a feeling I can handle whatever is dealt out to me, one day at a time."

"We feel it here because we've the necessities gathered together under one roof. Food, fuel—for cooking and heat and light, clothes, that would include the sleeping bags and snowshoes." He was ticking the items off on his fingers and looked surprised. "That seems to be about it."

"Entertainment—my needles and thread, the books, the

animals. And work. It's under our own roof, too."

Ade looked up at the partially finished ceiling. "There are two kinds of work—to fix this place up and to make enough money to buy stuff to fix it up with." He yawned. "Right now the very thought of it tires me."

"Me too. There's nothing that says we can't go to bed early. If you didn't have to get our mail we could burn the calendar and let the clock run down."

He slipped a matchbook cover into his book as marker. "It's hard to remember how we used to do everything by the clock . . . and really not so long ago. Funny. You don't know you've made big changes like that until after you've made 'em."

In the morning the sky and lake were softly blue. The wind had cleared the trees of snow and packed it all on the ground in a thin, smooth, firm layer. The air had that delicate odor that seems to come from snow itself. There was movement high in the trees but no tracks across the flawless crystalline carpet at my feet. All in all, it was a propitious time to set out our offerings of food.

Ade hurried to make and hang a cage packed with suet and I put a few pieces of graham cracker and some corn on the bench. We had hardly reached the door when the whiskey jacks and blue jays swooped down from the trees and an enterprising red squirrel scattered the birds to dig into the corn. The blue jays screamed at him, and woodpeckers, arriving to pick suet from the cage, added their squeals and cackles. To try to give everyone a chance, Ade made two more suet cages and I tossed pieces of graham cracker to individuals, thinking that this might have been the year before. As long as our winters were undisturbed, we could depend on the wild creatures to behave as consistently and as naturally as possible, considering our intrusion into their world.

Next day the chickadees arrived and they and the whiskey jacks soon ventured to drop to our hands for crackers. This lessened the congestion at the bench and gave us a new and worthwhile experience. It is encouraging and lifting to the spirit to have a bird trust you enough to light on your fingers and take food from your palm.

Then I put small, widely separated piles of corn on the snow surface, hoping these would draw the squirrels away from the bench, but a new squirrel seemed to materialize at every pile. They are surely the most consistently noisy of all our wild creatures. Even when eating alone and peacefully, they chir and chitter to themselves, and when two are within shouting distance of each other they never fail to shout insults and threats. Their vocabulary of squeaks and moans, sputters and growls, chatters and hisses, is both astonishing and funny. They are so small to contain such energy and create such a din, and a group of them, each determined to hold a pile of food against the others, can start a notable donnybrook. They dash about at full speed so constantly that the first time I saw one lying prone on a log, legs spread and eyes half closed, I thought he was sick instead of taking a sunbath.

The snow thawed briefly one afternoon, then froze to a crust, thick enough to surround and hold the seeds that had fallen to the snow surface. When I opened the door next morning I carried three of Ade's suet cages in one hand, a can of cracked corn in the other, and a graham cracker in my teeth. Four squirrels leaped at me as though they had been waiting. One danced between my feet into the kitchen. The other three started a chattering, whirligig chase around my shoulders, going round and round until I wondered whether they might turn into butter as Little Black Sambo's tigers had done. One of them sprang from my shoulder to my face, then fled with the cracker, his two companions close on his heels.

After I had swept the corn from the floor, picked up the suet cages, and daubed my claw-scratched chin with alcohol, I looked for the fourth squirrel, a gay and lively little fellow we called Hippity from his bouncy running gait. He had slipped into the house during the fall and had a maddening way of hiding under tippable things. After I decided he had hopped out while I was otherwise engaged, I set my typewriter and my few reference books ready on the kitchen table, where I had a fair light.

I was doing an article on bats and had the first page well started when Hippity's head appeared from behind the books. I went on typing—"The quick brown fox jumped over the lazy dog" or something like that—while Hippity crept toward the machine, always keeping an eye on me. When he was only a few inches away he sat up and peered earnestly at the rising and falling type bars. I stopped typing. He came closer, stood up, and rested his forepaws on the side of the machine. This seemed all right, so he poked his nose forward and looked down inside. I pressed a key and he received a light tap on the nose. He jerked back, not frightened, only puzzled or confused.

Next he went around to the back of the machine, pawed at the paper, and after due consideration jumped up and over it, to land where it was held tightly against the platen. He looked down and settled with his forepaws on his stomach. This was, it seemed, a fine vantage point for watching type bars. When nothing happened, he reached down and touched one and I touched a few of the keys, very lightly so that none of the bars should hit his delicate hand like a squirrel-size hammer. He was chirring pleasantly and I don't know which one of us was having the better time when Ade came in and laid the mail beside me.

I was startled, and then I realized that I had gone into the other kind of time again, where day follows day and their change has little to do with me. I left the table quietly, leaving Hippity staring down from the platen.

When I returned, after glancing through the letters, he was just jumping onto the keys. The bars came up in bunches and Hippity made delighted noises. He pattered with his feet and bounced up and down, waving his hands, snatching at the bars, and murmuring softly to himself. Finally I coaxed him away and outside with a graham cracker, so that I might get on with the work at hand.

After that, every time the door opened and Hippity was around, in he came, to climb onto the table and, if the typewriter was there, bounce on the keys and try to catch one of those elusive bars. I think he was playing. At any rate, he liked what he was doing.

It is a long time now since Hippity scampered around in the cabin, but sometimes when I sit down to type, I can see him sitting on the platen, can almost hear his happy little voice. It is rather nice to have so cheerful a small ghost to share my working hours.

8 A Beginning

The days went by, clear of sky and just cold enough to keep the crispness in the air. A night added an inch of snow to the thin layer on the ground and the surface turned into a welter of tracks as our wild neighbors came to feed. The lake did not freeze and its water rose and fell restlessly before a breeze so light we could not feel it near the cabin, protected by our windbreak of tangled forest.

Ade completed a new series of designs for his notepaper and printed some for stock, while I began to compile a mailing list from replies to his ad and other sources. We hoped to have it large enough to try direct mail sales next fall. I also saw that we ate when hungry, kept the cabin as livable as possible, and spent as many hours as I could writing.

Ade said he had used odd hours all summer on the log-cabin roof whose seams were now so thoroughly plastered with patching asphalt that you couldn't tell whether it had started out red or black . . . and had I anything urgent in mind? I mentioned that the cold drafts along the floor had had my feet aching most of the time the previous winter, and how was the sealing coming along. He said it wouldn't take long to complete after he finished wiring the cabin. He wanted to do that first because he had the light plant almost ready to go and wanted to clear that up before it got too cold. Altogether, we felt that we had the fractious kind of long-range chores well under control.

We started on our winter-night reading and needlework. Having completed *Copperfield, Dombey and Sons, Oliver Twist,* and *A Tale of Two Cities,* we abandoned Dickens for Doyle and Sherlock Holmes. On Thanksgiving, we finished *A Study in Scarlet* and started *The Hound of the Baskervilles.* My needle flew, and I am still wondering how I can use a floral picture, twenty-eight by thirty-nine inches, crocheted out of number-seventy weaving thread in stitches of my own design.

On the first of December, Ade gave the power plant a two-hour trial run. After he had experimented with various combinations of light bulbs and small appliances, he pronounced it ready for service. I had finished remaking some old drapes that day, cheerfully bright and of heavy enough material to help keep the cold from the windowpanes out of the living room. We were sitting on the daybed, feeling full of food, content, and accomplishment when I heard a snapping sound. It seemed to come from just outside the north living-room window, where some elder and maple brush grew.

"I'll bet it's a deer snapping off twigs," I said. "We can't throw a light out the window. She'll run if we even move the curtain."

The snapping continued and grew more frequent.

"Sounds like more than one," Ade said. "I'll slip out the

door and see if I can look around the corner of the woodshed
without frightening them."

He opened the door, yelled as though attacked by grizzlies,
and ran. I jumped to my feet and, through the open door, saw
the whole woods filled with flickering orange light.

Fire!

I was out of my robe and into pants and shirt and boots in
moments. When I stepped outside I saw flames shooting
up twenty feet above Ade's work building, with sparks rising
almost as high above the flames and showering down—a
beautiful and deadly fountain. I was too stunned to feel anything. I only moved, and fast, knowing as I ran that the night
was windless and the sparks were falling into the lake and
onto the snow around the building, but that the lightest
breeze, even an air current set up by the fire, might send them
into the tree tops—and there was no snow or frost in the trees
yet. They were still as dry and combustible as in the fall. I was
halfway down the path when Ade, silhouetted against a
smoky red glare inside the building, staggered through the
doorway and set something on the ground. He went back in
and I shouted uselessly as I smelled the poisonous fumes from
the burning linoleum. The smoke poured from the door in
suffocating black billows and lifted in a swaying pillar, touched
with murky red and dirty orange. Just before I reached the
building he came out again, put something else on the ground,
then ran round the burning wall toward the lake.

I held my breath and stepped inside. A third of the east
wall was burned to charred sticks and the fire was taking hold
on the inside of the roof. I had some idea of carrying some-

thing to safety until I saw flames on a shelf playing around a three-gallon can of gasoline. I ran through the door just before the can exploded and filled the interior with blue-white destruction.

I called to Ade and got no answer. I knew he couldn't hear me above the crackle and roar but I was frightened when he did not answer and had to force myself to go around the building after him. The heat struck through my clothes as the light of the flames showed him to me, sprawled flat on big offshore boulders exposed by the lake's low water. There was a shining layer on the rocks. Ice. I got out of my boots so that my wool socks would grip the slickness. If both of us fell and were hurt . . . By the time I reached Ade, he was sitting up, struggling to get his breath back, and trying to straighten the water pail he had fallen on.

"I'm okay," he said, then added: "You'll get your feet wet."

I ignored this. "Where's the other pail?"

He looked vaguely around. "I dropped it. There . . . behind you."

I filled it. "Here. I'll dip water and you pour it on."

Ade ran back and forth, throwing the water high on the flaming roof, exchanging his empty bucket for my full one. It seemed hopeless. The flames still roared and snapped and now had eaten halfway to the ridgepole, but we kept on. Then I felt a drifting of air. Sick at heart, I looked toward the trees, but the sparks were not touching them. They were blowing out over the lake, falling around and on me. The heat stung my face. The smoke choked and blinded me. Then I caught the smell of burning wool from my shirt. It almost smelled

good, for shirts can be mended or worn full of holes, but two hundred years would only start to replace our forest if it burned.

A long time later I became aware of some change and realized that the flames were not so high and their roaring had subsided so that I could hear the hiss as Ade threw the water onto the hot roof or up against the smouldering ceiling. As the water trickled down the walls, the fire was slowly dying. Suddenly it seemed even more important to put it out, to save the remains of the little building.

Time after time it seemed that we had succeeded, and then something exploded—a can of turpentine or oil—and we gathered our strength to put out the new blaze, started where the flash touched already dried, hot wood. But at last the red light was gone and there was only the stench of charred wood and linoleum.

The breeze had died and the smoke had settled into a kind of smog. I could see little as I wearily clambered over the rocks to join Ade on the shore.

"I found these on the rocks," he said, handing me my boots. "I'll go get a light and look around."

"Thanks," I said, and decided not to put the boots over my soaked socks. "And you'll do nothing of the kind. We're going back to the cabin. We're chilled and wet but we're too tired to feel it."

"Maybe you're right." He crossed the rocks to fill both pails, and we left them in front of the building, covered with a piece of roofing he had pulled from the eaves to reach the flaming boards beneath. Some small creature might brave the stench, come to investigate, fall into an uncovered pail, and drown.

"I'll come down later to see if things are all right," he said, as we more or less pulled each other up the steep path. "This thing may be out, and it may not be."

He was limping badly, but this didn't seem to be the time to argue about who would check up later. The cabin was still warm, although the fires were out. I looked at the clock as I poked the ashes in the stove.

"It's after twelve! When did we go down there?"

"Around eight." Ade poured luke warm water from the kettle on the stove and began to scrub the soot off his face. "I don't see how it got started. I shut off the power plant two hours before that."

"A spark from the exhaust, maybe. Fell on something dry and caught. It just took it awhile to get going. We'll probably never know . . . what's the matter with your hand?"

"I did something to it when I fell. It's pretty swollen, isn't it?"

"It's burned, too. If it doesn't look better in a day or two, you'll have to get to town some way and see the doctor. That's your drawing hand. And there's an awful bump above your right eye."

He looked in the mirror. "Maybe I'll have a black eye. Then I can tell people you hit me." He reached for his jacket. "I'll just run back down . . ."

"You will not! You're not only banged up, you're so exhausted you're shaking. You'll drink this tea and have the remains of the brandy the Larimers left. Then you'll go to bed. I'm tired but I'm not hurt, and I'm so strung up I couldn't sleep anyway. I'll do the checking. If anything's wrong that I can't handle, I'll wake you up."

I knew how utterly done in he was when he didn't even make a pretense of arguing. He was sound asleep in fifteen minutes.

At one thirty I put aside a book I was trying to read and went to the shore. A spark glowed in one of the foundation logs, pulsing and trying to grow in spite of the drenching the wood had had. I went back to the cabin, found a big chisel in Ade's work bench drawer, returned to chip and tear at the spark until it was gone. Then I drenched the wood, refilled the water bucket, returned to the cabin.

Every hour I checked, but there were no more sparks and after my six-thirty inspection I thought I might safely go to bed myself. But first I wanted to see what Ade had carried from the building. I swept my light around and saw the outboard motor and the cans of undercoat and varnish.

I hadn't expected those things in particular. Just what I *had* expected wasn't clear but it was important that I untangle my thoughts. I had reached that stage of fatigue when eyes are too wide open, sleep seems long forgotten, and ideas float, lightly and with great clarity. I selected a rock high enough to let my feet hang over without touching the water and sat down on the icy surface.

The blue-black sky was jeweled in white and pink and aqua, and distant dying suns were faintly golden. The glittering translucence hinted at those immense reaches of time and space that are obscured and minimized by black-velvet darkness. It was a fit time for thinking.

I let my eyes wander over the burned building. From the

west where I sat it had only cracked windowpanes to show as damage. Odd that we'd not thought of a fire department . . . but really not so odd. There wasn't any fire department and we had forgotten how to depend on such things. We'd gone after the fire ourselves without even thinking about what to do. This was a kind of independence I had not considered before. It had its disadvantages, but its rewards offset them. It was very satisfying to have put out our own fire.

Why had we worked so hard to save the building? Some old logs, some boards. Not worth much, contents and all. And once the wind had blown the fire away from the woods, it was the building we had worked to save. It would have been easier to confine the fire and let it burn, but I couldn't have stood idly by and plainly Ade couldn't, either.

True, he had improved it, planned to use it, but even with his lack of experience he could have put together some kind of replacement from old materials around the place and new lumber and windows the insurance would cover. But then man has worked from his earliest beginnings to keep fire as his servant and not his master. Maybe there is something atavistic in fighting a fire out of control.

Or maybe we were saving something in the building . . . but there was nothing that could not be replaced some day. I thought again of the outboard and the paint Ade had carried out. Those were of first importance to him, and they were also important to our life here. Otherwise, the only things of much value in the building were our radios, a TV set, and the power plant. The power plant. He'd talked a lot of wiring the cabin so he must have missed the electrical gadgets more than I had thought. As far as I was concerned, they didn't matter, as nothing we had left behind mattered any more. It was even a little hard to recall what it was like to flip a switch instead of strike a match.

The distant jewels were stolen one by one from the lightening sky and, as though heralding the dawn, a mournful song lifted from the hills across the lake. I had not heard a wolf howl before, but this lingering and eerie sound could be nothing else—and I didn't even feel strange to be hearing it. It was part of a new world, a new life. The old one was no less real, but now it seemed alien.

Ade came across the rocks and sat beside me. "I woke up and you were gone so long I thought something might have happened."

"Just thinking," I said. "Why did we fight so hard to put out that fire once we felt the woods wouldn't catch? Did you want the power plant?"

"I don't really know, about the fire, that is. But I did want to keep the plant."

"Why? We don't really need electric lights."

"Of course not, but I thought you missed the lights and the radio—lots of things."

"No." I looked blankly at him. "I thought you did!"

He was returning my blank look when the wolf howled again, lonely and wild and free, and dim yellow light began to glow in the east.

"Something's ended," Ade said.

"Yes. And something's beginning."

We got stiffly to our feet. I looked at the half-burned building and laughed. Ade raised his eyebrows.

"I was thinking of that day when you went to town and I

stayed in the cabin. It was so still—and then there was that storm, and the bear. And of how peaceful it was last evening —for a while. I've a feeling we'll always have bears in the basement."

"So we'll tame 'em," Ade said.

Once again we more or less pulled each other up the path toward the cabin, which, not through zephyrs and sunshine, but through storm and fire, had become home.

Helen Hoover (1910–1984) is the author of several books, including *The Years of the Forest*, *The Gift of the Deer*, and *The Long-Shadowed Forest*, all of which have been reissued by the University of Minnesota Press. Before moving to the remote wilderness of northern Minnesota from Chicago in 1954, she was an accomplished chemist.